Michael Owen

Back to Basics

Studies on the Basis of Union of the Uniting Church

Uniting Church Press
Melbourne

BX
9890
.U345
O94
1996

Published by
THE JOINT BOARD OF CHRISTIAN EDUCATION
65 Oxford Street, Collingwood 3066, Australia

BACK TO BASICS

National Library of Australia
Cataloguing-in-Publication entry.

Owen, Michael, 1931- .
Back to basics: studies on the Basis of Union of the Uniting Church

ISBN: 1 86407 158 3.

1. Uniting Church in Australia. 2. Christian union - Australia I. Joint Board of Christian Education. II. Title.

287.93

First printed 1996.

Design by Kelvin
Typeset by JBCE in Janson Text and ITC Officina
Printed by Shortrun Books
JB96/3772

Contents

*The author and publishers
gratefully acknowledge the generous
financial assistance from
Perth Trinity Uniting Church
towards the publication of this book.*

The Preparation of the *Basis of Union*[1]

Introduction

Some time ago, I should not have contemplated writing a paper like this. For I am going to report and reflect both on the preparation of the Uniting Church's *Basis of Union* and on the way in which I was myself able to participate in it. Up to now, I have felt it best to treat the *Basis* as the product of a corporate process.[2] Several things have recently happened to suggest that we are at the stage of needing to lay a foundation for the historical understanding of that process by identifying individual factors and contributions within it.[3] These things include:

(a) Repeated requests from the Revd Robert McArthur of Pymble that I should forward copies from my private file on church union to the Mitchell Library. I finally complied in January 1984 with copies of the more presentable material. If my sources are now open to other researchers, there seems no reason to withhold my own recollections associated with them and reflections based upon them.

(b) I was asked to supervise a dissertation-project that was being prepared by an American minister on the formation of the Uniting Church in Western Australia for a doctor of ministry programme. He received the criticism on the first draft that he seemed unaware of the part played in the union movement by me and others in Western Australia. That made me feel that I had perhaps stayed too much in my role as his "advisor" and let him down by my own reticence. The appropriate way of making more of my own experience available in the future will be by publication open to the criticism of others.

(c) In his review of *Witness of Faith*,[4] Ian Breward[5] expressed regret that, in the introduction to the *Basis of Union*, I had not set the *Basis* in its historical context. There had been various reasons for my not doing so,[6] but one was a fear of not doing it in a

5

balanced way. I now consider that we need to put forward insights from various sides and levels of the process and to allow them to come together

(d) The clear distinction I made in *Witness of Faith* between the Savoy *Declaration of Faith* and the Savoy declaration *Of the Institution of Churches, and the Order appointed in them by Jesus Christ*[7] has been questioned by one or more representatives of the Congregational Churches on the Joint Commission on Church Union.[8] It is obviously possible for us to have differing perceptions and recollections of what happened in the preparation of the *Basis of Union*. We need to discuss the process openly now, while it is still, in part, a matter of living memory.

So I first wrote this paper and then later edited it for publication. It may be useful, if it is read as one, personal account of a period in which so many were coming together by so many paths from so many starting-points, while others again were finally separating themselves off.

Ian Breward writes of the process leading to the Uniting Church and its *Basis of Union* that

> There was a much more ecumenical and theological context to this set of negotiations than those occurring earlier in the century. The quality of the reports produced compared favourably with any of the overseas schemes - an indication of the maturity and vision of the Australian negotiating churches.[9]

One aim of this present study is to illumine something of the ecumenical and theological context with which the churches and those negotiating on their behalf were interacting. Both in the initial paper and, in more detail, in this later form, I have tried to identify what I and others were reading, hearing and thinking at various stages of that process in which I was able to share in some way or another. I have largely tried to exclude afterthought and hindsight, but they will, of course, also be present.

1 The original form of this paper was written for a seminar for ministers held at St Aidan's, Claremont, within the continuing education programme of the Perth Theological Hall on 5 and 6 February 1985. It has since been revised, expanded and provided with notes.

2 Andrew Dutney reflects this attitude, too: "We have already suggested the important contribution to the work of the Joint Commission made by Davis McCaughey, Colin Williams and George Yule. By the nature of the case it is impossible to be very specific about their input. Even where it is quite clear that they were responsible for particular concepts or constructions in the Commission's report, it is inappropriate to make too much of the fact. A hallmark of ecumenical work is its anonymity, and the willingness of ecumenical theologians to refrain from putting their name[s] to products of their own genius. Individual ideas and inspirations must pass through the filter of consultation to gain ecumenical status" (Andrew Dutney, *Manifesto for Renewal: the Shaping of a New Church*, Melbourne, Uniting Church Press, 1986, pp.89f).

3 Directly after the passage quoted above, Andrew Dutney then recognizes a need to "break the rule" he has just stated.

4 Michael Owen, ed., *Witness of Faith: Historic Documents of the Uniting Church in Australia*, Melbourne, Uniting Church Press, 1984.

5 Ian Breward, "Witness of Faith [...]", in *Uniting,* 20 July 1984, p.10. Ian Breward's review had been duplicated and distributed by the publisher and was printed in the papers of a number of synods, which had the result of forestalling other, local critiques. But there was a review by Chris Ridings in *Western Impact,* July 1984, p.4.

6 The decisive factor was the insistence of the Uniting Church Press that it had recently published J. Davis McCaughey's *Commentary on the Basis of Union of the Uniting Church in Australia*, (Melbourne, Uniting Church Press, 1980) and that a full introduction to the *Basis* in *Witness of Faith* would be an unnecessary duplication.

7 *Witness of Faith*, pp.115-117.

8 Davis McCaughey kindly sent me a copy of a response he had sent to Henry Wells on this issue on 7 November 1984, in which he upheld my decision that, in Paragraph 10, the *Basis* is referring only to the *Declaration of Faith*, and not also to the declaration *Of the Institution of Churches*.

9 Ian Breward, *Australia "The most Godless Place under Heaven"?*, Melbourne, Beacon Hill, 1988, pp.64f.

I

While proposals for church union in Australia can be traced back at least to 1901, the year of Federation,[1] it is best for us to take up the story in 1954. Somehow, the Presbyterian Church had allowed post-war proposals for a federal union of the Congregational, Methodist and Presbyterian Churches to bog down. In 1954, its General Assembly of Australia was confronted by communications from the other two churches that virtually constituted an ultimatum: If the Presbyterian Church did not resume negotiations with them they would proceed towards union on their own.[2] The Assembly received these communications "with gratitude"[3] and directed that a vote be taken in all other courts of the church and in all congregations on the question,

> Are you in favour of the Presbyterian Church of Australia resuming negotiations with the Congregational and Methodist Churches with a view to corporate union?[4]

The Assembly also instructed the executive of its Christian Unity Committee that, should the vote be in the affirmative, it was to

> confer with the corresponding Committees of the other two Churches and prepare a possible Basis of Union to be submitted to the next Assembly.[5]

It was natural for Presbyterians to think that the way to go about uniting churches with one another was by getting someone to draft a "basis of union". This term had been used for a number of documents effecting the reunion of churches in Scotland and elsewhere in the nineteenth and twentieth centuries. A review of some of these earlier bases of union would help us to understand what kind of thing the Assembly had in mind, when it asked to see a draft basis of union at its next meeting, and also with what expectations Presbyterians would approach the various drafts prepared in the course of the ensuing negotiations. But even a brief review would take too much space at this point, so we shall hold it over for an excursus at the end of this study.[6] Some may think it unnecessary to devote so much time to what is largely Presbyterian history. But it will actually be important as a contribution to the self-understanding of those of us who came into union from that side, and to the mutual understanding that we still need to foster within the Uniting Church. It requires, of course, to be complemented by studies of reunions within Methodism and of the history of unions of Congregational churches.

To continue to tell the story from the point of view of the Presbyterian Church, the executive of the Christian Unity Committee was, in the event, satisfied that the voting in congregations, kirk sessions, presbyteries and state assemblies "could be accepted as a very clear affirmative".[7] It did then bring a draft basis of union for a United Church of Australia to the meeting of the General Assembly in 1957.[8]

The Draft Basis of Union (1957) comprised 26 numbered sections and an appendix. Important features of it included:

(a) The name proposed for the new church was, "The United Church of Australia" (II).

(b) All members of the three uniting churches would be members of the new church. Thereafter, new members would be admitted, not by Baptism, but

> by profession of faith in Jesus Christ as Lord and Saviour and a covenant to serve him in all duties and relationships (III).

(c) The faith of the United Church was to be defined (IV) by

  (i) an explicitly trinitarian credal statement of about 125 words;

  (ii) the "Word of God contained in the Scriptures of the Old and New Testaments" as the supreme standard of the United Church;

  (iii) the *Apostles'* and *Nicene Creeds* as the subordinate standards;

  (iv) the way in which the United Church would "hold in honour" the *Westminster Confession* and *Savoy*

Declaration and Wesley's *Forty-Four Sermons* and *Notes on the New Testament*;

(v) the church's exercise of its inherent power to frame, adopt and interpret its own subordinate standards and doctrinal statements, always in agreement with the Word of God and the fundamental doctrines of the Christian faith.

(d) Acknowledging the ministries of the uniting churches as ministries of Christ in his Word and Sacraments, the United Church would accept all ministers of the uniting churches as ministers in full status (V).

(e) Other officers in the church would be elders (XI) and lay preachers (XVII).

(f) The organization of the church would consist of the following councils and courts (IX):

(i) the Church Meeting of the local congregation or congregations within a pastoral charge, which would consist of one or more congregations under the charge of one or more ministers,

(ii) the Elders' Session,

(iii) the Local Council for the pastoral charge,

(iv) the Synod,

(v) the Conference,

(vi) the General Assembly.

Synod, conference and general assembly correspond in scope to presbytery, synod and assembly in the Uniting Church today. The local council clearly foreshadows the parish council that is not to be found in the Uniting Church's *Basis of Union*, but is provided for in its constitution and regulations. The local council in the Draft Basis of 1957 still looks very like a Methodist quarterly meeting. Note, too, the provision for local trustees (XII).

(g) Pastoral charges would be able to call ministers, but

final confirmation would rest with the Conference (V.4). The first minister named for each pastoral charge would be the superintendent minister (V.8). The Synod would induct ministers to pastoral charges (V.3). New ministers would be ordained by the Conference (VI.3).

(h) As sacraments of the church (VIII.), the United Church would accept that

> the two Scriptural Sacraments of Baptism and the Holy Communion were given by Christ and as means of grace through which God works in believers. While the operations of divine grace cannot be limited, these Sacraments are effective signs of the Gospel and spiritual seals of the promise of God.

This Draft Basis of Union had been drawn up at a meeting of the conveners of the relevant federal committees of the three churches considering union; and it was then submitted to their committees, for submission, in turn, to the national courts of the three churches.[9] But the Presbyterian Christian Unity Committee had to report to the Assembly that

> there is a clear difference of opinion between the Federal Executive and a majority of the Victorian State Committee on the value of the Draft Basis and on the procedure to be followed, and this, no doubt, will be expressed at the meeting of the General Assembly.[10]

That difference of opinion was indeed expressed at that Assembly in 1957, but not fully resolved. It and the feelings aroused by it continued to show themselves at later stages of the movement into union and may have been major factors in bringing about the strength of opposition to the final *Basis of Union* in the N.S.W. Presbyterian Church.

The 1957 Assembly merely received the Draft or Proposed Basis of Union. It approved the formation of a joint commission to consist of not more than seven representatives from each of the three negotiating churches. The Joint Commission on Church Union was to have the power to examine and amend any suggested basis of union and to present, if possible, a proposed basis of union to the federal committees on Christian Unity of the three denominations for submission to the next meeting of the three federal courts, as well as to do a range of other related things.[11]

The Assembly also gave the Joint Commission some advice, which the Commission accepted and quoted back in the Preface to its First Report. The Assembly resolved:

> That the Assembly [...]
>
> express the opinion that the work of the Commission would be facilitated if it sought to agree first on the following matters -
>
> (a) The Church's rule of faith;
>
> (b) authority and discipline in the life of the Church;
>
> (c) the ministry of the Church and the order of the Church -
>
> and draw the attention of its representatives to this opinion; and suggest to the Commission that when agreed statements on any or all of these topics become available they should be presented through the Christian Unity Committees to the three Federal Courts.
>
> (d) and that from time to time some account of the state of the Commission's discussions be provided for the information of the Lower Courts of the conferring Churches[12]

It is no doubt right to see in this suggestion from the Assembly the way in which prospective members of the Joint Commission secured agreement from the Presbyterian Church on the approach it should adopt to its task.[13] Union was not to be achieved by "ecclesiastical carpentry", a charge that had been levelled at the Draft Basis of Union of 1957, but by new, common study of central issues of the Church's faith, authority, ministry and order.[14] This had been the stand of the Victorian state Christian Unity committee against the draft prepared by the three federal conveners. While the general theological differences between Victoria and New South Wales were deeply rooted and not to be underestimated, a significant part in the development and formulation of the Victorian stand on this issue was played by the Revd Professor J.D. McCaughey. His participation in the Faith and Order movement linked the Australian church with ecumenical thinking in a way that allowed the *Basis of Union* to be developed in parallel with key ecumenical texts such as

> *One Baptism, One Eucharist and a Mutually Recognized Ministry*, Geneva, World Council of Churches, 1975 (= *Faith and Order Paper*, 73),

and its further development in

> *Baptism, Eucharist and Ministry*, Geneva, World Council of Churches, 1982 (= *Faith and Order Paper*, 111).

From that time on until the 1964 Assembly, Presbyterian consideration of union negotiations and proposals was complicated by tensions between the executive of the Christian Unity committee, based in Sydney,[15] with the Revd Dr W. Cumming Thom as its convener, and the Presbyterian representation to the Joint Commission on Church Union, which was inspired and convened by Davis McCaughey and contained a majority of Victorians.

NOTES

1   See Frank Engel, *Australian Christians in Conflict and Unity*, Melbourne, Joint Board of Christian Education, 1984, pp.164ff.

2   "[Communication] II. Re Union Negotiations - Congregational Church", in *Minutes of the Proceedings of the General Assembly of the Presbyterian Church of Australia held in Sydney, September, 1954, Session Twenty-Sixth*, p.170; - "[Communication] III - Re Union Negotiations - Methodist and Congregational Churches", *ibid.*, pp.171-172. (From now on the minutes of the proceedings of successive general assemblies of the Presbyterian Church of Australia will be referred to by the symbol *BB* for *Blue Book*, together with the year of the respective assembly.)

3   *BB 1954*, min.82.2.

4   *BB 1954*, min.82.3. - 'Corporate union' means a scheme under which the various churches would unite to form one new body. One alternative was 'federal union', under which the churches would form a confederation for certain agreed purposes, but each church would still retain its own identity.

5   *BB 1954*, min.82.6.

6   See below pp.105ff.

7   Report of the Christian Unity Committee, *BB 1957*, p.92.

8   Contained in the report of the Christian Unity Committee, *BB 1957*, pp.92-100. The end of the Draft Basis is not clearly divided from the continuation of the report. Appendix A, on the inauguration of union, clearly ends on the fourth last line of p.100, for the next paragraph begins to describe the drawing up of "this first Draft Basis" and so no longer forms part of the document.

9   Report of the Christian Unity Committee, *BB 1957*, pp.100f. - The use of the term 'federal' here is quite distinct from that explained in note 4 above. The word here carries its normal meaning in the Australian political context and refers to the national, as distinct from the "state", level.

10   Report of the Christian Unity Committee, *BB 1957*, p.100.

11   *BB 1957*, min.60.3-4.

12   *BB 1957*, min.60.5. - The lay-out of this resolution in the minutes of the Assembly is here reproduced. But the text under (c) commencing "and draw the attention [...]" obviously refers to all that precedes and should not have been indented as if it referred to (c) alone.

13   The minute of the proceedings at this point states that, "By leave Clause 5 was moved and seconded and approved as follows [...]"(*BB 1957*, min.59). This indicates that notice had not been given that the clause would be moved in this form, which indicates, in turn, that it had been formulated only shortly before the debate.

14   On this approach see, too, Andrew Dutney, *Manifesto for Renewal*, pp.13-16.

15   The Christian Unity report to the 1959 Assembly refers to "the Executive, which is identical with the State Committee of New South Wales" (*BB 1959*, p.90).

II

By the time that the General Assembly of Australia met again in September, 1959, the Joint Commission on Church Union was already able to submit its first report, *The Faith of the Church*.[1] It consisted of an introduction and two parts:

I. The Faith We Have Received,

II. The Faith We Affirm in Common.

It was hoped that Part II, "The Faith We Affirm in Common", might, revised in the light of comment, provide part of the final basis of union. It was itself subdivided into three parts.

Part A of Part II said "Where the Church's Faith is to be Found". It identified faith as faith in Jesus Christ, the Word of God, and listed, as sources of the Faith:

1. the Holy Scriptures,

2. the Creeds of the Ancient Church,

3. the Confessions of the Churches of the Reformation, and

4. the Affirmations of the Evangelical Revival.

Holy Scripture (1.) was related to Jesus Christ as

the unique earthly instrument through which the Church hears the living Word by which her life on earth is tested and renewed.[2]

As creeds of the Ancient Church (2.), there were listed the *Apostles' Creed*, the *Nicene Creed*, the *Chalcedonian Decree* and the hymn known as the *Te Deum*. They were seen to have, to differing degrees, a three-fold function:

(a) as acts of allegiance or affiance to a Person;

(b) as a framework for the instruction of believers; and

(c) as ways of protecting certain essential doctrines of the faith.

Of the Reformation confessions (3.), the Report had, in particular, the *Scots Confession*, the *Westminster Confession* and the *Savoy Declaration of Faith* in mind.[3] It valued in them along with the central place they gave to the person of Jesus Christ,

(a) their constant appeal to Scripture;

(b) their systematic exposition of Christian doctrine; and

(c) their assurance that there resides in the Church a power of teaching and setting forth the faith.

From the Evangelical Revival (4.), the Report took up in particular John Wesley's *Sermons* and *Notes on the New Testament* and it highlighted the evangelical emphasis on

(a) faith as response in trust;

(b) the witness of the Holy Spirit; and

(c) growth in grace.

In this part II.A. of the First Report, we have before us material that has indeed been moulded in the continuing discussion into what we now have in the Paragraphs 5, 9 and 10 of the *Basis of Union*.

The next part, II.B, has not survived as well. It is headed, "Our Confession" and is an attempt at a modern confession of faith, in the form of a recital of saving history. Apart from an opening trinitarian confessional and doxological sentence and a rather longer, matching one to close, it consists of six sections, each beginning, "We confess [...]". Each such section may then contain sub-sections beginning, "We acknowledge [...]".

The form of this confession is to be understood against the background of what is said in Part I of the Report about old confessions of faith in Israel, which

> set forth the mighty acts of God, in the election of Israel,
> her delivery in the Exodus and her settlement in the
> promised land[,][4]

and of studies by such scholars as G.E. Wright and Gerhard von Rad. For, in a footnote supporting the statement quoted above, the Report points to:

16

G. Ernest Wright, *God Who Acts: Biblical Theology as Recital*, London, SCM, 1952 and repr. (= *Studies in Biblical Theology*, 8), pp.70-76,

and says that he there provides a convenient summary of von Rad's work in isolating the old confessions of faith in Israel.[5] The works of von Rad's that Wright refers to have been published in English translation as:

Gerhard von Rad, "The Form-Critical Problem of the Hexateuch", in: G. von Rad, *The Problem of the Hexateuch and Other Essays*, Edinburgh & London, Oliver & Boyd, 1966, pp.1-78,[6]

—, *Genesis: a Commentary*, London, SCM, 1961, pp.13-23,[7]

—, *Studies in Deuteronomy*, London, SCM, 1953 (= *Studies in Biblical Theology*, 9).[8]

Von Rad identified the literary form of the Hexateuch (i.e., of the biblical books Genesis - Joshua) by reference to the traditional form of the confession recited at the festival of the first-fruits, which he termed "the little salvation-history *credo*",

A wandering Aramaean was my father; and he went down into Egypt and sojourned there, few in number; and there he became a nation, great, mighty and populous. And the Egyptians treated us harshly, and afflicted us, and laid upon us hard bondage. Then we cried to the Lord, the God of our fathers, and the Lord heard our voice, and saw our affliction, our toil, and our oppression; and the Lord brought us out of Egypt with a mighty hand and an outstretched arm, with great terror, with signs and wonders; and he brought us into this place and gave us this land, a land flowing with milk and honey (Deuteronomy 26:5b-9; cf. 6:21b-23).

One primary expression of Israel's faith in God was the recital of his saving deeds in its own history. The core of that story was the span of history illumined by the promise that God had made to the

Patriarch(s) and made good by giving the land of Canaan to their descendants. Stories of the Creation had later been added to the beginning of the story; and the tradition of the giving of the Law (which originally belonged to another festival) had been inserted at an appropriate point in the middle. The whole biblical story from Genesis to Joshua had grown up by this process; and it was to be understood as the product of faith and theological reflection, not just of interest in the past. An implication for modern theology was that it should speak of God more in terms of his mighty acts in saving history and less in philosophical abstractions. Part II.B. of the Joint Commission's First Report is an attempt at doing that.

Part II.C. of the report is headed "Our Commitment" and spells out how the Church's commitment of faith is made in faith, in love and in hope.

It was around the time of the appearance of this First Report that I returned to Australia after five years of study and work in Germany. In other words, all that happened in the story I have told up to now happened in my absence from the country and with little awareness on my part. In September 1959, about the time that I was settling into becoming the minister of St Cuthbert's, Lorne, the General Assembly of Australia received the Report[9] and invited comment from State Assemblies and Presbyteries on the

> stability [sic] of the statement "The Faith We Affirm in Common" (being part 2 of the report) for that part of the Basis of Union [...] which shall express the Faith of the Church.[10]

It also commended the report of the Joint Commission to the prayerful study of Christian people and instructed the Christian Unity committee in each State to encourage its use in study groups.[11]

A month or so later, I received a request from the Secretary of the Joint Commission, the Revd John Alexander, to edit the Report into a study book, by abridging Part I and providing Part II with an introduction, and questions and assignments for each section of it. I was able to complete that work by the beginning of February,

1960. In May, the Methodist General Conference and the Congregational Union's Federal Executive met and must have expressed similar commendations to the Assembly's. For the study book then appeared, undated, but presumably still in 1960, under the title, *The Faith we Affirm in Common*[12].

John Alexander had also asked me for my criticism on Part II. I find that I did offer some in the letter in which I announced the completion of the work on the study material. But I also made a fuller criticism through the report of the Presbytery of Geelong's Theological Discussion Committee, which was adopted by the Presbytery and forwarded as its comment on Part II of the first Report. Some of the specific criticisms I raised at the time were:

(a) Does not the faith of the Church appear too much as an independent and self-propagating entity vis-à-vis the Word of God?

(b) Does not the way in which the content of the Biblical witness is outlined in II.A.1. and the way in which God's mighty acts are recited in II.B. make Jesus Christ into one theme or one event alongside others, and so derogate from other, fundamental statements about his being the one Word of God, the Son of God and Saviour of the World?

(c) Is it enough to say that the Holy Spirit pointed forward to the things done by Christ and now takes the things of Christ and declares them to us? Or must we not also acknowledge that we have the gift of the Spirit as a result of Christ's work, through his mediation, and as an extension and application of his work?

(d) The use made of the term 'covenant' is unhelpful in a number of ways. What can only be understood as God's covenant with Noah seems to be given overriding significance, so that the covenants with the Patriarchs and with the people of Israel are subordinated to it and it becomes the covenant that is fulfilled in Christ. This fulfilment in Christ is said to have transformed God's covenant with humans into a "New Covenant of grace".[13] The term 'covenant of grace' is taken from Westminster theology, where it is contrasted with a "covenant

19

of works".[14] The latter is supposed to have existed between God and Adam before the Fall. But, once Adam had fallen, all covenants between God and human beings were expressions of the covenant of grace. It is one thing to use the concept of the eschatalogical new covenant. It is quite another to speak of it as the covenant of grace, as if all of the Old Testament covenants had been not of grace, but of works.

Between aspects of the Report and especially Section II.B., "Our Confession", on the one hand, and criticism of this kind, on the other, lay a difference of opinion over the validity and limits of the movement known as "Biblical Theology" current at that time. "Biblical Theology" emerged in the late 1940's and had, as its flagship, as it were, the grey paper-back series of the S.C.M. Press, *Studies in Biblical Theology* (of which fifty volumes appeared in the years 1950 to 1966 alone!).

This movement made the inestimable contribution of teaching rank and file ministers and lay people that one should not read later forms of thought back into biblical writers; but it tended to give the impression that it was easy to avoid such anachronisms, if only one eschewed the language of later theology and went back to the language of the Bible. It also encouraged people to go on as if theology were simply a matter of recapturing biblical ways of thinking, and not also the task of thinking in twentieth century ways in accordance with what biblical writers had thought and said. It tended to see the Bible's authority perhaps more in the way it expressed things than in what it expressed. As the First Report asserted,

> Words and images of Scripture have the depth and sound of revelation[15]

- or at least so the Biblical Theology movement taught us. In consequence, in its own statement of the faith, the First Report tended to combine biblical themes, concepts and allusions as if they contained their own authority in themselves and as if, in consequence, we did not need to think very critically and carefully about the construction we were making with them.[16] In a similar way, debatable modern concepts such as Tillich's "ground of being" came in unquestioned and unexplained.[17]

Alongside the Biblical Theology movement, there was a second common (and not entirely unrelated) source and point of orientation for *The Faith of the Church* and the kind of criticism outlined above: the theology of Karl Barth and of the Barmen *Theological Declaration* of 1934. We may mention them together, since Barth took a leading part in the drafting of the Barmen *Declaration*.

Karl Barth was born in 1886 and died in 1968. His early associations were with the school of Liberal Modernism that stemmed from Albrecht Ritschl and his pupils, but also with the Religious Socialist movement in his Swiss homeland. The Great War deepened his growing estrangement from Liberal theology and his search for a new direction. This search centred on his own preaching ministry and found expression in volumes of sermons he published together with his friend Eduard Thurneysen, and then also in a commentary on Paul's letter to the Romans. The second edition of this commentary took the post-1918 world by storm. It has been published in English as

> Karl Barth, *The Epistle to the Romans*, tr. Edwyn C. Hoskyns from the 6th ed. [1928], London, OUP, 1933, repr. 1950.

In reaction to Liberal scholarship, which he considered to be offering literary and historical comments on the biblical texts out of a neutral detachment, Barth sought to expound Paul's thought from within, employing concepts and imagery from the Twentieth Century in a demanding and provocative way.

The recognition that Barth was gaining soon led to his being called to be a professor of Theology in Germany. In the first semesters of his academic work, he continued his new style of biblical exposition, in lectures on 1 Corinthians and Philippians, published in English as

> Karl Barth, *The Resurrection of the Dead*, tr. H.J. Stenny, London, Hodder, 1933.
>
> —, *The Epistle to the Philippians*, tr. James W. Leitch, London, SCM, 1962.

While he criticized Barth's work in detail, Rudolf Bultmann agreed with the aim of his exegesis;[18] and pupils of Bultmann's such as Eduard Schweizer[19] and Emil Fuchs[20] have continued to own their debt to Barth as well as to Bultmann, however much things later seemed to polarize between the two. Although the new movement in Old Testament scholarship led by Gerhard von Rad and Martin Noth began independently of Barth, many of those who came to participate in it developed a significant affinity to his theology.[21] Barth is thus to be seen somewhere there in the background behind the Biblical Theology movement of the 1950's.

At the foundation of Barth's own work in dogmatic theology lay his doctrine of the Word of God. For many years, the only volume of his *Church Dogmatics*[22] translated into English was the first part-volume of the prolegomena,

> Karl Barth, *The Doctrine of the Word of God (Prolegomena to Church Dogmatics, being vol.I, Part I)*, tr. G.T. Thomson, Edinburgh, T. & T. Clark, 1936.[23]

He offered there a doctrine of the one Word of God in three intimately related forms, (a) the Word revealed, incarnate in Jesus Christ, (b) the Word written, in the Scriptures, and (c) the Word proclaimed, in the Church's witness to Jesus Christ by preaching and sacraments and by all other aspects of its life and work.[24]

In this approach to the doctrine of the Word of God, as in the whole of his theology, Barth showed a clear tendency to centre everything on Jesus Christ. The Scriptures, for instance, are not discussed as God's Word apart from the incarnation of the Word in the living person of Jesus Christ and his dynamic relation to written and spoken human words that witness to him.

The Nazi takeover in Germany in 1933 faced the German churches with the demand of the "German Christian" movement that the Church should recognize and proclaim what God had done for the renewal of the German people by bringing Adolf Hitler to power. Barth became one of the leaders of the opposing "Confessing Church" movement. This movement sought to uphold and renew the Church's commitment to the Gospel through the classic confessions of Reformation times and through new acts of confession in the present. The "Confession Synod" of the German Evangelical Church at Barmen in 1934 adopted a "theological declaration concerning the present situation of the German Evangelical Church",[25] for which Barth had given a lead in the drafting. The central statement of its first thesis says,

> Jesus Christ, as witness is borne to him for us in the Holy Scripture, is the one Word of God that we have to hear, to trust and to obey in life and in death.

The consequential negative clause states,

> We reject the false teaching, as though the Church would be able and obliged to recognize as the source of its proclamation, apart from and beside this one Word of God, yet other events and powers, figures and truths, as God's revelation.

Here, Barth's doctrine of the three-fold form of the one Word of God resourced the Church in the formulation of a new confession of the faith and rejection of error. He also played a significant part in the renewed attention paid to classical creeds and confessions in the twentieth century. Series of lectures on the *Apostles' Creed* have been published as,

> Karl Barth, *Credo: a Presentation of the Chief Problem of Dogmatics with Reference to the Apostles' Creed: Sixteen Lectures Delivered at the University of Utrecht in February and March, 1935*, London, Hodder, 1936.

> —, *Dogmatics in Outline*, London, SCM, 1949 & repr..

There have also been series of lectures on confessional documents of the Reformation, which have appeared in English as,

> Karl Barth, *The Knowledge of God and the Service of God according to the Teaching of the Reformation, recalling the Scottish Confession of 1560*, London, Hodder, 1938, repr. 1949 (= The Gifford Lectures, 1937-1938).

> —, *The Faith of the Church: a Commentary on the Apostles' Creed according to Calvin's Catechism*, London, Collins (Fontana), 1960.

——, *The Heidelberg Catechism for Today*, Richmond, Va., John Knox, 1964.

The First Report refers to Barth in its discussion of creed and canon and of confessions of faith, and again with reference to the seriousness of proceeding to a new confession of faith.[26] It also refers to the new confession of the faith in the Theological Declaration of the German Evangelical Church in May 1934.[27] Its emphasis on the centrality of Jesus Christ and on his being the one Word of God heard and known through the witness of the Scriptures is clearly drawn from Barth and Barmen. Some of the criticism mentioned above is suggesting that the First Report has not followed such insights through consistently enough.

Another source for the thought of the First Report has been the renewal of interest in the course of the Twentieth Century in the theology of the Reformers and the thought of John Wesley. For there is certainly no suggestion there that a united church would get on very well with the Bible alone. Modern appreciation of the Reformation and its confessions of faith as guides to our understanding of the Scriptures is clearly to be perceived in the Report; and it shows a similar willingness to take Wesley's standard writings seriously.[28] This influence, too, links up with the one just discussed, for, as we have seen, Barth had been one of those to take a lead in expounding Reformation confessions and reflecting on their significance. One element in our criticism of "Our Confession" (Part II.B.) had been a concern that, in any new statement of the faith, we should match the clarity, consistency and rigour of Reformation confessions.

In identifying the influences behind the First Report and informing both it and some criticism of it, we must also mention the ecumenical movement and, in particular, the Faith and Order movement. I have already suggested that the difference we observed in the Presbyterian Church between Victoria and New South Wales was fundamentally one between the pragmatic approach of the latter and insights and convictions out of the Faith and Order Movement that Davis McCaughey, in particular, was beginning to share with the Victorian Christian Unity committee. Part I.B. of the

First Report is headed "A New Awareness of the Church" and identifies as "some factors leading the churches in the twentieth century to a new awareness of the Church":

(a)   a biblical perspective;

(b)   a secularized Western world; and

(c)   a world mission.

With regard to the faith of the Church, we read in that section:

> We have no narrowly Congregational, Methodist, Presbyterian - or pan-Protestant or liberal-Protestant - view of that Faith. It is the Faith in its wholeness, the Faith of the Catholic Church to which we would recall men [...].[29]

The Joint Commission was conscious that the union for which it was to prepare was not just to be an Australian affair or one between three denominations that happened to be growing increasingly similar to each other, but an integral part of the renewal of the world church in unity of faith and mission.[30] The effects of this influence can still be seen, particularly in Paragraphs 1, 2 and 18 of the *Basis of Union*, but actually in every part of the document.

The other major influence on the Joint Commission's thinking and First Report was the Church of South India, formed on 27 September 1947. It, before any other instance of church union, was the model that members of the Commission had in mind.[31] A work of some considerable influence at that time was

> J.E. Lesslie Newbigin, *The Reunion of the Church: a Defence of the South India Scheme*, London, SCM, 1948, 2nd rev.ed. 1960.[32]

A comparison of this work with the reports of the Joint Commission shows close relations between them. On the "method of reunion",[33] Newbigin writes,

> [...] if [...] the Church is divided because of sin, there are required of us both a penitent return to Christ and His atoning work, and also acts of obedience to His will.[34]

[...] what is involved is the reunion of divided bodies which are, in spite of their division, nevertheless truly parts of the Church [...] They are parts of the Church broken from one another by sin but yet held still to Christ by His grace.[35]

The fruit of that return to Christ must include fresh efforts of thought designed to clarify theological issues. But the basis of union will not be a theological statement which sets at rest the doctrinal divisions between the separated Churches. It cannot be too strongly stressed that the basis of union is a reality in the personal realm. It is the finished work of Christ for all men, and the unity with Him in the Spirit which is given to all believers. Within this unity there will always be doctrinal differences.[36]

The method of reunion [...] acknowledges that the uniting Churches are truly parts of the Church. Their members are accepted as members and their ministers as ministers. What is taking place is a reunion of divided parts of the Church [...].[37]

As Newbigin understood the reunion in South India, it had begun with penitent recognition of the sin that had divided the separated churches and believing acknowledgment of the grace that had none the less upheld them as parts of the one Church in union with Christ, its Head. It accepted what Christ had given to, and done in, the divided churches by his grace and meant returning to Christ in penitence, faith and new obedience, in order to find the unity that he alone gives.

We can compare with this section I.C.1 of the First Report, "The Way to Confess our Faith: the grace and judgment under which we stand"[38]. In order to enter afresh into the fullness of the Church's faith, there needs to be a fourfold response on our side to the Church's faith as set forth in scripture, creed, confession, liturgy and hymn of praise:

(a) We must acknowledge the given character of the Church's faith.

(b) We must acknowledge our failure as churches to bear witness to this faith in its fullness.

(c) We must acknowledge that in spite of our sins God has blessed and preserved his Church by his Word

(d) We must undertake together, God helping us, to enter more fully into the Church's faith.

We find here the same pattern as in Newbigin's presentation of the South Indian reunion: acknowledgment of given unity, penitence for the failures through which we have fallen short of that unity in the divided churches, recognition of God's continuing grace to those divided churches, and engagement in new acts of obedience.

While that is spelled out here in relation to the faith of the Church, the Second Report of the Joint Commission, which appeared in March 1963 together with a proposed basis of union, applied the same pattern to the Church's faith and fellowship, life and worship. The Preface to the Proposed Basis of Union (1963) describes the way along which the three uniting churches have been led in terms of the same four steps and it makes the following comment on them:

> [...] the way into union has been characterised by justifying grace. The way into union is by the rhythm of the Gospel: awareness of the message, of the call to repentance, of the goodness of God, and of time for amendment of life.[39]

The application of the doctrine of justification by faith to the Church as a whole and to issues of its reunion, as attempted by Newbigin in *The Reunion of the Church*, has determined the overall approach of the Joint Commission to its task.

We should here also note its agreement with Newbigin in not seeking union on the basis of a statement of faith that attempts to resolve all doctrinal differences. To return to the First Report and its discussion of "The Way to Confess our Faith", acknowledgement of the given character of the Church's faith does not centre on some body of doctrine, but on the Scriptures and on Jesus Christ. The understanding of the justification of the Church by God's grace is carried through consistently in relation to its doctrine, too:

> No denomination is justified by its right doctrine, any more than any individual is justified by works of the law. [...] The Church's witness and worship have been declared righteous by grace through faith.[40]

The commitment to enter more fully into the Church's faith is not made in the confidence that a united church will then be able to give full expression to that faith:

> We do this knowing that even then our grasp will be incomplete. [...]

> We stand at a point in history at which we are being called to enter more fully into the Faith of the Church of the ages; but in doing so we have no illusions that we shall complete the task.[41]

It is important to listen to such avowals, in order to appreciate the relative importance to be assigned to Parts II.A. and II.B. of the First Report. "Where the Church's Faith is to be Found", with its identification of Scriptures, creeds, Reformation confessions and Evangelical affirmations, indicates where the Church must continually orient itself, in order to enter more fully into the Catholic Faith. As we said earlier, it is this part of the First Report that has fed on into the Paragraphs 5, 9 and 10 of our *Basis of Union*. "Our Confession" was a serious attempt at doing justice to the need to confess the faith in our own words today. That proved to be something that we were not yet capable of doing. But even if we had arrived at a confession that we wished to include in our basis of union, it would not have been meant as the final, definitive statement of the faith, replacing earlier attempts. It would just have been our way of expressing to the best of our powers the one faith of the Church Catholic, for which we should have continued to seek orientation on Scriptures and creeds, confessions and Evangelical standards.

NOTES

1   *The Faith of the Church: Report of a Joint Commission on Church Union set up by the Congregational Union of Australia and New Zealand, the Methodist Church of Australasia, the Presbyterian Church of Australia*, Melbourne, Joint Board of Graded Lessons of Australia and New Zealand, [1959] (in future referred to as "*Faith*"). - Since reprinted as: *The Faith of the Church: The First Report of the Joint Commission on Church Union set up by the Congregational Union of Australia and New Zealand, the Methodist Church of Australasia, the Presbyterian Church of Australia*, Melbourne, Joint Board of Christian Education of Australia and New Zealand, 1978. - The text has the same lay-out in these two editions, but the page-numbering of the reprint is always two digits ahead of that of the original.

2   *Faith*, p.34; 1978, p.36.

3   *Faith*, p.36; 1978, p.38. - Cf. the statement in Part I, "We claim that whatever their differences in point of detail, the *Augsburg Confession*, the *Scots Confession*, the *Westminster Confession*, the *Savoy Declaration of Faith*, the *Thirty-nine Articles* and the *Book of Common Prayer* of the Church of England, all stand to bear witness to Jesus Christ, the divine Word definitively set forth in Scripture and to call the whole Church to obedience to that Word" (*Faith*, pp.16f; 1978, pp.18f). Here, the *Scots* and *Westminster Confessions* and *Savoy Declaration*, representing the Reformed tradition, are placed alongside a Lutheran document (Augsburg) and two Anglican ones. Note that, at this stage, the *Savoy Declaration* was identified more closely by the further phrase, "*of Faith*" (see note 8 to the Introduction).

4   *Faith*, p.11; 1978, p.13. The relevant footnote (note 1) says, "See, for instance, Deut. 6:20-24; 26:5-9; Josh. 24:2-13".

5   *Faith*, p.11; 1978, p.13, note 1 refers to Wright's *God Who Acts*, pp.70-76,; cf. also note 2.

6   Gerhard von Rad, *Das formgeschichtliche Problem des Hexateuchs* (1938), repr. in: G. von Rad, *Gesammelte Studien zum Alten Testament*, Munich, Kaiser, 1958 (*ThB*, 8), S.9-86.

7   Gerhard von Rad, *Das erste Buch Mose. Genesis. Übersetzt und erklärt*, Göttingen, Vandenhoeck, ⁶1961 (Das Alte Testament Deutsch, part-voll.2-4). - Wright refers to the first part-volume on Genesis 1-12:9, first published in 1949, and to the first part of the introduction, on "Genesis as part of the Hexateuch".

8   Gerhard von Rad, *Deuteronomium-Studien*, Göttingen, Vandenhoeck, 1947, rev.ed. 1948.

9   *BB 1959*, min.90. 3. - The First Report of the Joint Commission is contained in full within the report of the Christian Unity Committee, BB 1959, pp.90-111.

10 *BB 1959*, min.90. 4.

11 *BB 1959*, min.90. 5.

12 *The Faith we Affirm in Common: being an abridgement of Part I of the Report of the Joint Commission on Church Union known as "the Faith of the Church". And with Part II designed for the purposes of study and discussion*, Melbourne, Joint Board of Graded Lessons of Australia and New Zealand, [1960?].

13 *Faith*, p.38; 1978, p.40.

14 See both the *Westminster Confession* and the *Savoy Declaration*, cap.VII, *Witness of Faith*, pp.129-131.

15 *Faith*, p.17; 1978, p.19.

16 There remains a deeper level at which these issues need to be pursued and at which the importance given to biblical language in the Biblical Theology

movement and in the First Report could be appreciated more positively. To what extent is not the imaginative and symbolic use of language actually the primary use, and not a secondary, "transferred" use, at all? Do we not need to pay far more attention to the power and the logic of imaginative language? On the other hand, too much of the discussion in the late 1950's and early 1960's seemed simplistic and biblicistic and, to that extent, not really biblical at all.

17 *Faith*, p.42; 1978, p.44. - "Ground of being" is a central concept in the foundation of Tillich's theology. See, e.g., Paul Tillich, *Systematic Theology*, voll.1-3, London, Nisbet, 1953-64, vol.1, pp.124,129.

18 Rudolf Bultmann, "Karl Barth, 'Die Auferstehung der Toten'" (1926), in R. Bultmann, *Glauben und Verstehen. Gesammelte Aufsätze*, voll.1-4, Tübingen, Mohr, vol.1, ²1954, S.38-64; - ET "Karl Barth, 'The Resurrection of the Dead'", in R. Bultmann, *Faith and Understanding*, vol.1, London, SCM, 1969, pp.66-94. - Bultmann also reviewed the 2nd ed. of Barth's *Romans* in *Christliche Welt* 36 (1922), coll.320-323,330-334,358-361,369-373.

19 Schweizer told me this himself quite emphatically.

20 Ernst Fuchs, "Der Theologe Karl Barth. Zu seinem 80. Geburtstag", in *Zeitschrift für Theologie und Kirche* 63 (1966), S.188-199.

21 In the article on "Altes Testament" in Georg Strecker, ed., *Theologie im 20. Jahrhundert. Stand und Aufgabe* (Tübingen, Mohr, 1983, S.1-60), Werner H. Schmidt, writing of the search for a new direction in Old Testament study after the Great War, says that, "This striving for a new way of seeing things sought to do justice to the fact that Old Testament study belongs within Theology and was initially, from all appearances, not specially due to the influence of Dialectical Theology. The latter's effects on Old Testament study only became noticeable later" (S.2). The "Dialectical Theology" referred to here is the movement led by Karl Barth, Friedrich Gogarten and others in the 1920's.

22 Barth's main work, the *Church Dogmatics*, was never finished. It consists of 13 part-volumes and has been published in English translation by T. & T. Clark, Edinburgh.

23 This was not a very good translation. Once all the other part-volumes had been translated, a new translation was done by G.W. Bromiley, which appeared as The *Doctrine of the Word of God (Prolegomena to Church Dogmatics, Being Vol.I,1)*, 2nd ed., Edinburgh, T.& T. Clark, 1975.

24 See especially *Church Dogmatics*, I,1, ²1975, pp.88-124.

25 "Theologische Erklärung zur gegenwärtigen Lage der Deutschen Evangelischen Kirche", in Wilhelm Niesel, ed., *Bekenntnisschriften und Kirchenordnungen der nach Gottes Wort reformierten Kirche*, 1938, repr. Zurich, Theologische Buchhandlung, 1985, S.334-337; - in English translation: "Theological Declaration concerning the Present Situation of the German Evangelical Church", in Arthur C. Cochrane, *The Church's Confession under Hitler*, 2nd ed., Pittsburgh, Penn., Pickwick, 1976 (= *Pittsburgh Reprint Series*, 4), pp.238-242; - also "The Theological Declaration of Barmen (1934)", in *The Constitution of the United Presbyterian Church in the United States of America: Part I: Book of Confessions*, 8.01—04; - also "Barmen Theological Declaration: Theological Declaration on the Present Situation of the German Evangelical Church, 1934", in Hans-Georg Link, ed., *Apostolic Faith Today: A Handbook for Study*, Geneva, World Council of Churches, 1978 (= *Faith and Order Paper*, 124), pp.148-150.

26 *Faith*, pp.14,17,18,21,27f; 1978, pp.16,19,20,23,29f.

27 *Faith*, pp.24-26; 1978, pp.26-28.

28 *Faith,* pp.19-22,36-37; 1978, pp.21-24, 38-39. - Colin Williams, *John Wesley's Theology Today,* London, Epworth, 1960, shows the participation of one Australian scholar in the renewed world interest in Wesley.

29 *Faith,* p.23; 1978, p.25.

30 An opposing view is reflected in the report of the Presbyterian Christian Unity Committee to the 1959 Assembly, "The breakdown of discussion between the Church of Scotland (Presbyterian) and the Church of England (Episcopal) only serves to emphasize the comparative simplicity of our task, in which we find a very large field of similarity in doctrine, worship, and government" (BB 1959, p.111). - Contrast with this the statement of the Joint Commission in its communication to the 1962 Assembly, "The Commission has pursued its task along the lines laid down in its first Report, namely, that the question to be asked throughout is not 'How do we stick these Churches together as they are?' but 'What belongs to the proper life of the Church as she seeks to express her unity more fully in the service of the mission to which she is called?' To that latter question there are no simple answers [...]" (BB 1962, p.94). - See, too, Davis McCaughey's judgment, "The natural way to begin negotiations among us would have been by adjustment, fitting separated pieces of the Church together; and there were many who said that the problems of reunion between Congregationalists, Methodists and Presbyterians were not great because the three Churches shared the same reformed tradition, had the same view of the ministry, and a similar outlook on all matters of doctrine. These Churches, it was said, were very much alike. Sociologically regarded, there was some truth in this statement. Historically and theologically, it is, of course, nonsense - as we were to find out" ("Church Union in Australia", *The Ecumenical Review,* 17 [1965], pp.38-53, p.39).

31 In the same article, Davis McCaughey enunciates as the second of four critical decisions taken by the Joint Commission, the decision that "the way into union must be according to the rhythm of the Gospel" (*The Ecumenical Review,* 17 [1965], p.41). Towards the close of this section, he writes, "It is perhaps important to record that it was at this point that the attention of the Joint Commission was first directed towards the Church of South India. Of all the unions known to us that union seemed most clearly to have adopted this method of approach. In particular an article by Bishop Newbigin providentially came to hand at a time when we were most bewildered about our way forward" (*ibid.,* p.44). - The article by Lesslie Newbigin, "Anglicans and Reunion", appeared in *Theology* in June, 1958. - Lesslie Newbigin was present as a guest speaker at the National Conference of Australian Churches in February 1960. See his address, "Basic Issues in Church Union", in David M. Taylor, ed., We Were Brought *Together: Report of the National Conference of Australian Churches held at Melbourne University, February 2-11, 1960,* Sydney, Australian Council for the World Council of Churches, 1960, pp.155-169. See also his Bible studies on 1 Peter and "final word" (*ibid.,* pp.93-123,128-130).

32 Davis McCaughey concludes the the footnote in which he identifies Newbigin's article, "Bishop Newbigin had already, of course, argued the point at greater length in *The Reunion of the Church* (London, 1948), and has strengthened the argument still further in the new Introduction to the second edition of that book (London, 1960)" ("Church Union in Australia", p.44, note 1).

33 The title of Chapter 7, pp.104-123.

34 Newbigin, *The Reunion of the Church,* p.104.

35 Newbigin, *The Reunion of the Church,* p.105.

36 Newbigin, *The Reunion of the Church,* pp.105f.

37 Newbigin, *The Reunion of the Church*, p.108.

38 *Faith*, p.29-31; 1978, p.31-33. - It is also instructive to compare this section of the First Report with what Newbigin has to say on "justification by faith" in the chapter of that title (Chapter 6, pp.84-103).

39 *The Church: its Nature, Function and Ordering, Part One being the Second Report of the Joint Commission on Church Union set up by the Congregational Union of Australia, the Methodist Church of Australasia, and the Presbyterian Church of Australia, Part Two being the Proposed Basis of Union for these Churches*, Melbourne, Aldersgate Press, 1964, pp.75f; - repr. Melbourne, Uniting Church Press, 1984, pp.75f. - These two printings have the same page-numbering and will in future be referred to as '*Church*'. - The was also another edition of the Second Report published in 1964, under the title of *The Church: its Nature, Function and Ordering, and Proposed Basis of Union: the Second Report of the Joint Commission on Church Union presented to the General Assembly of the Presbyterian Church of Australia, September, 1964*, Melbourne, Christian Unity Committee and Board of Christian Education, 1964. This edition used the type-setting for the printing of the report in the 1964 *White Book* and *Blue Book* (*BB 1964*, pp.93-134). It was primarily intended for mass distribution in the Presbyterian Church, had scarcely more than half the number of pages, and was half the price, of the Aldersgate Press edition. In all future references, we give the page(s) for this edition as well, identifying it as the "Christian Unity" (edition).

40 *Faith*, p.30; 1978, p.32.

41 *Faith*, p.31; 1978, p.33.

III

To take the story of my own involvement on a little further, I was asked, at quite short notice, to speak at a combined Anglican, Methodist and Presbyterian school of theology in August 1961 on the continuity of the Church. I was to give the Reformed point of view and to be followed the next day by the Revd Father Barry Marshall giving the Anglican.

In the paper I presented there, I suggested that our confession of One Holy Catholic and Apostolic Church implies not only the identity of that church in space, but also its continuity in time. But the oneness and continuity in which we believe face us with the major theological problem of how the Church can be identical with itself and continuous with itself. I approached the problem of continuity by quoting from Article 16 of the *Scots Confession* of 1560, one of the confessional documents mentioned in the First Report.

> As we beleue in ane God, father sone, & haly Gaist. So do we maist constantlie beleue, that frome the beginning thair hes bene, now is, and to the end of the warld salbe, a Kirk, that is to say, ane companye and multitude of men chosin of God [...].[1]

The existence of the one Kirk, and so its continuing oneness and identity in space and time, is just as much a matter of faith, as our belief in the one God, Father, Son and Holy Spirit. Faith in the continuity of the Church reaches back to acknowledge that same Church in the people of God in the Old Testament; and what the *Scots Confession* says of the existence of the Church in the Old Testament shows us the connexion between faith in God and faith in the Church:

> We maiste constantlie beleue, that God preserued, instructed, multipled, honoured, decored, and from death, called to lyfe, his kirk in all agis: frome Adam tyll the cumying of Christe Jesus in the flesche.[2]

Faith in the continuity of the Church is faith in the continuing faithfulness and activity of God. That activity takes place in real human history, just as it centres on the incarnate Son of God, but all historical continuity as such is ambiguous.

> Do not presume to say to yourselves, "We have Abraham as our father"; for I tell you, God is able from these stones to raise up children to Abraham (Matt 3:9).

The true continuity of the Church comes through the work of God within history, as God elects, creates, redeems, and renews his Church, and raises it from death to life. God does this through Jesus Christ and the Holy Spirit, through the words and sacraments of the Gospel. Yet it is neither they nor a succession in the ministry of them that gives the Church its true continuity, but only the active presence of God in Jesus Christ, in and through our witness of proclamation and celebration.[3] All of this was put forward with numerous biblical quotations and references and did, as I could show, have a good foundation in the Reformed confessions. I also thought that it was highly consistent with the First Report's interest in Old Testament confessions of the mighty acts of God. For instance, the fifth article of the Scots Confession on "the Continuance, Encres and Preseruation of the Kirk", from which I derived the above quotation about God's action in preserving, instructing, multiplying and otherwise dealing with his church, bears in its margin as scriptural reference Ezekiel 16, one of the more imaginative and colourful recitals of the story between God and his people. Indeed, the whole article is itself just such a recital.

But my paper was met with heat and, I believe, anger, not only by Anglican participants, but also by such Methodists as the Queen's College professors Colin Williams and Eric Osborn. It was then a surprise for us all on the following evening to hear Barry Marshall say virtually the same things as I had said. I shall have occasion to refer to this episode again.

1   THE | **Confessioun of fa**≈ | ITH PROFESSIT, AND BELEVIT, BE | *the* Protestantes
    vvithin the Realme *of* Scotland. Pub- | *lisched be thaim in* Parliament. And *be the*
    Estatis | *thairof.* Ratifeit and appreuit, *as hailsum, & sound* | Doctryne groundit
    vpon the infallible treuth | *of* GODDIS vvorde [...] (Edinburgh, Jhone Scott, 1561),
    facsimile ed.,, New York, N.Y., Da Capo Press, 1972 (= *The English Experience*,
    555), [Article 16] "Of the Kirk"; - modernized in *Witness of Faith*, p.70.

2   *Scots Confession*, [art.5] "THE CONTINVANCE, ENCRES AND PRESERVATION OF THE
    KIRK"; - Witness of Faith, p.65.

3   See art.18 of the *Scots Confession*, "OF THE NOTES BY THE QVHILK T*he trevv* Kirk,
    is decerned from the fals. And *quhoo salbe* I*udge of the* Doctryne"; - *Witness of
    Faith*, pp.71f.

IV

The General Assembly of Australia met again in September 1962. I was present as a representative of my presbytery. There was only an interim report from the Joint Commission, which indicated that its Second Report and a Draft Basis of Union had not been completed in time for the Assembly, but should appear in time for the next Methodist General Conference in May 1963.[1] Since the Assembly was thought not to be meeting again until September 1965 and the Joint Commission was holding back its revision of Part II of the First Report for inclusion in its Second, it seemed that the Methodists would have a start of two and a quarter years over the Presbyterians in considering the next stage of the proposals. All the old bitterness between the federal Christian Unity convener, Dr Cumming Thom, and the Victorians on the Joint Commission surfaces again in the report in which he presented, and commented on, the interim report of the Joint Commission.[2]

The report came from the federal Christian Unity Committee's executive in New South Wales and complained of a lack both of communication about, and progress in, the work of the Joint Commission.

> The only communication from the Joint Commission on Church Union since the last Assembly was received on Wednesday, 11 July, 1962, after an urgent request by the convener for a report on the deliberations of the Commission and any available documents.[3]

The convener, Dr Cumming Thom, had had access to the meetings and papers of the Commission in the capacity of an observer or consultant since late 1959 and, from 1962 on, after John Priestley's retirement through ill health, as an alternate member.[4] What he had needed was a formal communication for his committee to consider and to pass on to the Assembly. When the Christian Unity Executive met to consider the report from the Commission, "concern was expressed" at (1) "the absence of any revised statement on the Faith of the Church as requested by the 1959

Assembly" and (2) "the absence of a fuller report and a Draft Basis of Union".[5]

> [...] several members [...] indicated a sense of frustration at the three-year silence; and the apparent intention to allow the Assembly to pass without any knowledge of the contents of the two documents at present in the hands of members of the Commission and dealing with the structure of the Church and the Basis of Union. This was considered a slight to the Supreme Court of the Church.[6]

The Joint Commission had suggested that the Assembly might agree that the Second Report should, upon publication, simply be transmitted to state assemblies and presbyteries for comment,[7] but the Assembly refused to do that.[8] Instead, it began to plan to meet in 1964.[9]

Cumming Thom was now appointed as a member of the Joint Commission in his own right. There was a move from the floor to unseat him as convener of the Presbyterian Christian Unity Committee, in order to remove the obvious tensions between him and the Joint Commission.[10] The motion came from the Revd J.E. Owen. My first memory of my friend Terry Luckett is from that debate. He was at that time still from N.S.W.. He rose to defend Cumming Thom, saying, "I am just a simple Welshman. I cannot match the great Eric Owen in oratory", and of course, went on to do exactly that. He ended: "I hate what you are saying" (meaning Cumming Thom), "but I shall fight to the death for your right to say it". With solid support from New South Wales, Dr Thom retained the covenership for another two years. Yet it did not even appear that he enjoyed great popularity among the representatives from his home state. It may be that their support represented a preference for staying with the devil they knew.

The Church: its Nature, Function and Ordering[11] appeared in March 1963. Part I was the Second Report of the Joint Commission, Part II, a proposed basis of union. The second, and longer, part of Part I was on "The Function of the Church: Its Ministry of Worship, Witness and Service". Distinctive features of it and the Proposed Basis of Union (1963) were:

(a) An emphasis on the ministry of the whole Church: The Church participates in the ministry of Jesus Christ. Within the Church there are varieties of gifts and, by the same Spirit, there are granted to each member gifts that must be used in ministry, if the Body of Christ is to build itself up in love, and carry out its true service and witness in the world.[12]

(b) Explanation of the particular ministries of the ordained from the need to build up the whole Body and all its members for ministry: Within the Church and as a gift to the Church, God in Christ ordains some to minister to the community, in order to foster the ministry of the community as a whole.[13]

(c) Interpretation of ministry in terms of Christ's three-fold office as Prophet, Priest and King: The Church participates in Christ's priestly ministry by its worship, and in his prophetic and kingly ministry by its witness and service.[14]

(d) Interpretation of ordained ministry in the same way: The three-fold character of Christ's ministry is reflected in the three marks of the ordained ministry that have almost universal acknowledgment:

    (i) responsibility for preaching and teaching: prophetic ministry;

    (ii) responsibility for sacraments and liturgy: priestly ministry;

    (iii) responsibility for pastoral care and order: kingly ministry.[15]

(e) Assertion of there being essentially *one* order of the ministry in the Church, "the fullness of which belongs to those ordained to the ministry of Christ's Word and Sacraments".[16]

(f) But also an assertion that, within that one order of ministry, the Church is free to assign different functions to different ministers and to name and order them accordingly.[17]

(g) The proposal that after union the Church should initially have the following three-fold pattern of ministry:

(i) Presbyters, as the regular ministers of Word, sacraments and pastoral care in congregations and in other appointments;[18]

(ii) Bishops, with pastoral oversight over presbyters and congregations, but functioning only within the corporate oversight of the presbyters in Presbytery;[19]

(iii) Deacons, ordained for "limited but genuine participation in the one ministry of the Word and Sacraments and in the oversight of preaching and teaching, liturgical and sacramental life, and pastoral care and discipline".[20]

(h) The proposal that the Church should establish a concordat with the Church of South India, "as an expression of oneness with her in the life and mission of the Church, and as a sign of a desire to manifest more fully the unity of the Church across national, cultural and racial boundaries".[21]

(j) The related proposal that, at the time of union, bishops and presbyters from the Church of South India be requested to share with presbyters from the uniting churches in consecrating the first bishops of the Uniting Church.[22]

The combined proposals for a three-fold ordering of one order of ministry, with bishops, presbyters and deacons, and for a concordat with the Church of South India were an attempt to do various things at the same time. It would have taken the Uniting Church into the middle ground of ecumenical conversations through the new proximity it would have to other major traditions that see a historic three-fold order as the inalienable pattern of the Church's ministry. In particular, it would have challenged the Anglican Church in Australia seriously to consider union with the Uniting Church. On the other hand, the establishment of a reformed episcopate, functioning as "bishops-in-presbytery", would have made it much easier, in any negotiations for a wider union, to resist an uncritical adoption of monarchical episcopacy, or of modern diocesan episcopacy with its heavy burden of administrative responsibilities. The proposed alliance with South India would have demonstrated that the Uniting Church identified with the way in which union and the unification of ministries were carried out there, rather than with what was being proposed for North India and Sri Lanka. In other words, all ministers would be accepted on the basis of their previous ordinations, without any supplemental laying on of hands.

A further distinctive feature of the Proposed Basis of Union (1963) was:

(k)   The name 'Uniting Church' for the church to result from the union.[23]

I was told at the time that 'Uniting' had been suggested by the Revd Dr Harold Wood. He certainly seemed to consider that he was putting this name forward for consideration in the booklet entitled, *The Uniting Church of Australia*, where he wrote,

> No name has been officially proposed as yet. The Joint Commission has not definitely considered this matter. Therefore one can only make suggestions.
>
> "The Uniting Church of Australia" may be considered a suitable name. It implies that the three denominations have come together and also that the movement is continuing and other denominations may be included.[24]

Again I was told, and can readily believe, that the use of 'Uniting Church *in*', rather than '*of* Australia', was a conscious imitation of the decision by the confederation of German Protestant churches after the war to change its name from "The German Evangelical Church" to "The Evangelical Church in Germany". A national church has to own that its place is within the nation and that it is there to serve the nation. But it does not belong to the nation, it belongs to Jesus Christ; and its character is determined, not by national traits or aspirations, but by the call and grace of God.

Other features of the Basis of Union as proposed in 1963 were:

(m)   In a series of seven General Articles, the first, "Concerning Doctrinal Standards", took up significant parts of the First Report in a compressed form and dealt with Scriptures, the two creeds and the *Chalcedonian Decree*, Reformation confessions, including now, too, the *Second Helvetic Confession of Faith*, and "the later confessional statement of John Wesley in his forty-four sermons", all in the one article.[25]

(n) A closing "Confessing Act" represented a revision and abbreviation of "Our Confession", Part IIB of the First Report.[26]

(o) General Article 5, "Concerning the Councils of the Church", provided for

(i) Ecumenical Councils;

(ii) The General Assembly as the national council;

(iii) Synods, as state or regional councils;

(iv) Presbyteries, as diocesan councils;

(v) The Council of the Congregation, which was to function as the Parish Council, consisting of the presbyter and deacons of the congregation, together with chosen communicant members, but also through the Church Meeting, which could decide to carry out certain functions of the Parish Council.[27]

This pattern of councils resembles most closely the Presbyterian system of church polity,[28] although, with other names, corresponding gatherings were also to be found in Methodism.[29] The place given to the Church Meeting is an attempt to include one of the strengths of Congregationalism.

(p) The seventh General Article was headed, "Concerning Revision of Statements of Doctrine". That was quite misleading, because what this article provided was that

> The Uniting Church has the right to interpret the General Articles and to modify and add to them, but always in agreement with Holy Scripture, and consistently with the provisions of the first Article concerning Doctrinal Standards, adherence to which, as interpreted by the Church, is essential to its continuity and corporate life.[30]

So the provisions of the seventh General Article applied, not so much to revision of statements of doctrine, as to revision of the General Articles 2-6, on sacraments, membership, ministry, councils of the Church and orders of worship. All that the Church could do with General Article 1 was to interpret it. The significance of these provisions lies in the fact that there is no corresponding power for the Church to amend part of its basis of union in our present *Basis*. There was, instead, a conscious decision to write a basis of union that ought not to require amendment from time to time.

Seven members of the Joint Commission, four Methodist and three Presbyterian, signed the Second Report with a reservation, in which they expressed the opinion that consideration of the proposals for the creation of a bishop-in-presbytery and for a concordat with the Church of South India should be deferred until after union, and that the appropriate time for considering a bishop-in-presbytery would be "if, and when," the Uniting Church was negotiating for union with an episcopal church.[31]

NOTES

1   *BB 1962*, pp.93f.

2   *BB 1962*, pp.93,94f.

3   *BB 1962*, p.93.

4   *BB 1962*, p.94; - *Church*, p.3.

5   *BB 1962*, pp.94f.

6   *BB 1962*, p.95.

7   *BB 1962*, p.94.

8   See the defeat of G.U. Nathan's amendment, *BB 1962*, min.59.

9   *BB 1962*, min.59, 60.4.

10 *BB 1962*, min.59.

11 *The Church: its Nature, Function and Ordering, Part One being the Second Report of the Joint Commission on Church Union set up by the Congregational Union of Australia, the Methodist Church of Australasia, and the Presbyterian Church of Australia, Part Two being the Proposed Basis of Union for these Churches.* - This report was already referred to in note II, 39 and details of the various editions were given there. Those of the Aldersgate Press, 1964, and the Uniting Church Press, 1984, which have the same page-numbering, are referred to by the short title *'Church'*. The edition published by the Presbyterian Christian Unity Committee and Board of Christian Education, 1964, is referred to as "Christian Unity".

12 *Church*, pp.28f,34,81; - Christian Unity, pp.16,19,43.

13 *Church*, pp.27f,81; - Christian Unity, pp.15,43.

14 *Church*, pp.28,40; - Christian Unity, pp.16,22.

15 *Church*, pp.28,41,49f,81; - Christian Unity, pp.16,23,27f,43f.

16 *Church*, p.82, cf. pp.44,46f; - Christian Unity, p.44, cf.pp.24,26.

17 *Church*, p.82, cf. pp.28; - Christian Unity, p.44, cf. pp.15f.

18 *Church*, pp.41f,82f; - Christian Unity, pp.22f,44.

19 *Church*, pp.45f,47-50,83; - Christian Unity, pp.25,26-28,44f.

20 *Church*, p.84, cf. pp.43f; - Christian Unity, p.45,pp.24f.

21 *Church*, p.77, cf. pp.52-57; - Christian Unity, pp.41, cf. pp.29-31.

22 *Church*, pp.52,83; - Christian Unity, pp.29,45.

23 *Church*, p.77; - Christian Unity, p.41.

24 A. Harold Wood, *The Uniting Church of Australia (Presbyterian-Congregational-Methodist)*, Melbourne, Methodist Publishing House (Aldersgate Press), 1961, p.39.

25 *Church*, pp.77f; - Christian Unity, pp.41f.

26 *Church*, pp.88-90; - Christian Unity, p.48.

27 *Church*, pp.84-87; - Christian Unity, pp.45-47.

28 At that time, the Presbyterian Church of Australia had, as its "hierarchy of courts", (1) the General Assembly of Australia, (2) state general assemblies, (3) presbyteries and (4) kirk sessions, i.e. councils of elders in congregations and parishes. It had general assemblies in the states, instead of synods, because it was a confederation of the state churches. The Church of Scotland's *Second Book of Discipline* is an example of a scheme of councils that included ecumenical ones: "Assemblies are of four sorts. For, either are they of particular churches and congregations, one or more, or of a province, or of a whole nation, or of all and divers nations professing one Jesus Christ" ("The Second Book of Discipline or Heads and Conclusions of the Polity of the Church agreed upon in the General Assembly 1578 [...]", VII.2, in *Basic Documents on Presbyterian Polity with Introductions and Notes*, [Melbourne], Board of Christian Education, Presbyterian Church of Australia, 1961, pp.51- 79, p.61). After what it has to say in detail about congregational, provincial and national assemblies, the *Second Book of Discipline* continues, "There is, besides these, another more general kind of Assembly, which is of all nations and estates of persons within the Church, representing the Universal Church of Christ; which may be called properly the General Assembly, or General Council of the Whole Church of God" (*ibid.*, VII.25, p.65).

29 The Methodist pattern within Australia consisted of (1) the General Conference, (2) annual conferences, (3) district synods, (4) circuit quarterly meetings and (5) congregational leaders meetings.

30 *Church*, pp.87f; - Christian Unity, p.47.

31 *Church*, pp.68f; - Christian Unity, p.37f.

V

Before the Second Report and the Proposed Basis of Union appeared, I had moved to Perth. I was not present at the 1964 General Assembly of Australia, which received those documents and sent them to state assemblies and presbyteries, requesting presbyteries to send them on to kirk sessions and congregations.[1] At the Assembly, a ballot was finally forced for the position of convener of Christian Unity; and the Revd Colin Dyster replaced the Revd Dr Cumming Thom.[2]

My own criticism of, and comment on, the Second Report and Proposed Basis of 1963 were made as I participated in the discussion of them in the Presbytery of Perth and the Western Australian Christian Unity Committee. My chief criticism was in the area of ministry: The approach in the report and proposed basis was, to my mind, not differentiating enough.

The doctrine of the three-fold office of Christ was already under some attack in this century.[3] That attack ought not to lead us to drop it entirely, but it has underlined how much the doctrine is Church theology, interpreting Scripture in a particular pattern. It is primarily a statement about Jesus Christ; and it remains useful for dealing with his authority and work in some connexions. In the *Heidelberg Catechism*, its meaning is certainly extended from Christ, the Anointed One, to the Christian, showing how the believer shares in Christ's anointing and three-fold office.[4] But it cannot be taken for granted that this doctrine will be the best way of identifying "the ministry of Christ himself", from which ministry in the Church is to be derived.

The way in which it was used in the Report and Proposed Basis to give one, all-embracing definition of ministry as participation in Christ's prophetic, priestly and kingly roles certainly seemed to me to have quite unfortunate consequences. The variety of gifts of the Spirit and consequent ministries seen above all in 1 Corinthians 12 and Romans 12 was perhaps mentioned, but not accorded the fundamental place that it must have in any renewal of ministry on the basis of the New Testament. The ministry of the Word, sacraments and pastoral care was thus presented, not as one specific ministry among others, but as the embodiment of the essence of all ministry. It would be unavoidable that ordained, full-time professionals would be seen as the real ministers, in contrast to the spare-time amateurs in the congregation. In the same way, with the insistence on there being only one order of ministry, the deacons would not be allowed a distinctive ministry of their own, but only limited participation in the one order of ministry,

> the fullness of which belongs to those ordained to the ministry of Christ's Word and Sacraments.[5]

The two influences of which I was particularly conscious in making this criticism were (1) modern exegesis of Paul's picture of the many complementary and mutual ministries of the members of the one body, and (2) the pattern of ministry to be found in Reformed theology and church orders.

Works that had been particularly influential in the first of these two areas were:

> Eduard Schweizer, *Church Order in the New Testament*, London, SCM, 1961 (= *Studies in Biblical Theology*, 32).

> Ernst Käsemann, "Ministry and Community in the New Testament", in E. Käsemann, *Essays on New Testament Themes*, London, SCM, 1964 (= *Studies in Biblical Theology*, 41), pp.63-94.[6]

One of the central things that emerged for me from these studies was the way in which Paul stood up for his own Christ-given authority as apostle over against the congregation, yet was also content to lump apostles in with all kinds of other ministries within the congregation as the body of Christ. He did not need to negate the validity or importance of other ministries, in order to elevate his own. Rather, the primary way in which he affirmed his own was by exercising it in the service of the Gospel, and so in the service of the whole pattern of ministries that the Gospel was calling into being and building up within the new community. There is an inherent connexion between Paul's sense of his own calling to be an apostle by the grace of God and the many gifts of grace by which he sees the one Spirit endowing the members of the body with their so many ministries. For the grace by which he, undeserving as he was, was called as an apostle is also the power of God active in his ministry. It is power for service, because it springs from the resurrection of the One who served God and served others in his life and by his death.

If Paul also went on, at times, to insist on his apostolic authority, that was partly to counter the intrusion of others with less ministerial understandings of office and authority and partly to offer an understanding of his own ministry as a model for others with gifts for ministries of their own.

Having to counter the competing claims of other leaders actually put Paul into conflict in himself. For he saw true apostleship as service of the message of Christ crucified, a message and a figure of weakness and folly, shame and dishonour. The last thing that this Gospel or the service of this Gospel was about was standing on one's rights or asserting one's status. But for Paul to allow those who were trying to establish their own superior claims by denigrating his ministry to have the last word would be tantamount to abandoning his Christ-given role. This is what gives rise to the reluctant and paradoxical arguments of the final chapters of 2 Corinthians. A booklet that had a great effect on me and others around this time was

Ernst Käsemann, *Die Legitimität des Apostels. Eine Untersuchung zu II Korinther 10 - 13*, Darmstadt, Wissenschaftliche Buchgesellschaft, 1956 (= *Libelli*, 33).

In the pattern of ministry to be found in Reformed theology and church orders, ministry of the Word, sacraments and pastoral care had its own (non-priestly!) role alongside the separate and distinct ministries of elders and deacons.[7]

It seemed to me that we should develop our overall picture of ministry on the basis of the wide range of ministries exercised by the Church's members and allow for the setting apart by ordination of those called to certain specific ministries that needed authorization and ordering in a more formal way. I have no idea whether my comments at this time contributed to the final criticism and revision of the proposals. With regard to the proposal to have bishops, I was, at best, luke-warm. Since my own conversations and collaboration had, up to that time, been with Anglicans, rather than Methodists or Congregationalists, I believed that the compelling reasons for seeking re-union of the churches required us to seek it with the Anglicans as well as with the others. But I had already been finding great value in the corporate oversight of Presbytery and could not see that that would necessarily be enhanced by involving a bishop in it. Friends who had been serving with the Church of South India were also uttering warnings about the ways in which the bishops were developing there.

NOTES

1   *BB 1964*, min.95.2-6.

2   *BB 1964*, min.95.14(a); 139.

3   See, e.g., Werner Elert, *Der christliche Glaube. Grundlinien der lutherischen Dogmatik*, 2nd rev.ed., Berlin, Furche, 1941, S.405-410; - Wolfhart Pannnenberg, *Jesus: God and Man*, London, SCM, 1968, pp.212-225; - John Frederick Jansen, *Calvin's Doctrine of the Work of Christ*, London, James Clarke, 1956. - It is perhaps not accidental that much of this criticism of a doctrine especially associated with Calvin stems from the Lutheran quarter, which is not to suggest that there is no substance to it.

4   "*Question 32* But why are you called a Christian? - *Answer* Because by faith I am a member of Christ and so share in his anointing, so that I, too, may confess his name, present myself to him as a living sacrifice of thanksgiving, struggle with a free conscience in this life against sin and the Devil, and hereafter in eternity reign with him over all creatures" (in *Witness of Faith*, p.91).

5   *Church*, p.82, cf. pp.44,46f; - Christian Unity, p.44, cf. pp.24,26.

6   Ernst Käsemann, "Amt und Gemeinde im Neuen Testament", in E. Käsemann, *Exegetische Versuche und Besinnungen*, voll.1-2, Göttingen, Vandenhoeck & Ruprecht, 1964, vol.1, 3rd ed., S.109-134.

7   In the form of church government formulated at the Westminster Assembly and approved by the General Assembly of the Church of Scotland on 10 February 1645, the "ordinary and perpetual" officers appointed by Christ for his church were said to be, "pastors, teachers, and other church-governors, and deacons" ("The Form of Presbyterial Church-Government and of Ordination of Ministers; Agreed upon by the Assembly of Divines at Westminster [...]", in *The Confession of Faith [...]*, Edinburgh & London, William Blackwood, 1948, pp.169-187, p.172.) - The pastor exercises the ministry of Word, sacraments and pastoral care in the congregation. The teacher or doctor is also a minister of the Word and has power to administer the sacraments, but exercises a teaching ministry as second minister in a congregation or in a school or university. The other church-governors share with ministers in the government of the Church and, in the Reformed churches, are called elders. The office of deacons is not to preach the word or administer the sacraments, but to "take special care in distributing to the necessities of the poor" (*ibid.*, pp.172-174). - Similarly, in the "Savoy Declaration of the Institution

of Churches and the Order appointed in them by Jesus Christ", "The Officers appointed by Christ to be chosen and set apart by the Church [...] are Pastors, Teachers, Elders and Deacons" (in A.G. Matthews, ed., *The Savoy Declaration of Faith and Order 1658*, London, Independent Press, 1959, pp.121-127, pp.122f).

VI

The General Assembly of Australia met again in September 1967 and considered the comments and criticisms of the Proposed Basis of Union that the Christian Unity Committee had received from state assemblies and presbyteries and collated for the Assembly.[1]

I was present at this meeting. The Assembly carried a long list of requests to the Joint Commission for amendments to the Proposed Basis.[2] They were summarized in sub-clauses numbered from (a) to (q), some of which were again sub-divided into as many as six or seven parts. We cannot deal with them all here in detail; and they would need to be compared and combined with the requests from the Methodist Conference and Congregational Assembly, to give a true picture of the message that the churches gave the Joint Commission. In some cases, detailed proposals were made for redrafting passages in the Proposed Basis. Some features of that document were simply rejected, such as the concordat with the Church of South India, the use of the term 'presbyter' (for which 'minister' was to be substituted), and the proposal for bishops.[3]

One specific request that I regretted and on which I asked a question was for

> [...] the section "Concerning Doctrinal Standards" to be revised
>
> (i) so that all reference to the *Chalcedonian Decree* is removed [...].[4]

In reply, the Secretary of the Joint Commission, the Revd John Alexander said that this was simply in line with the responses from the lower courts of the church. Davis McCaughey told me afterwards that the wording was more sweeping than the replies called for, but that the strength of opposition to the inclusion of Chalcedon from the other two uniting churches meant that there was no point in pursuing the matter. It was, in any case, agreed that the Assembly could only adopt or refuse to adopt the outcome from the responses from assemblies and presbyteries. Amendment in detail would have been far too unwieldy a matter. The Assembly asked for Sections IV, "The Constitution and the Interim

Constitution", and V, "A Confessing Act", to be removed from the Basis of Union. The former was thought to be inappropriate in a basis of union. The latter should be shortened, simplified, and attached to the Basis as an appendix.[5]

Elements that the Assembly wished to see in the final form of the Basis included

> [...] a statement making clear that baptism is to be administred [sic] to both infants and adults [...],[6]

and a clearly defined place for adherents.[7]

At this Assembly, I was initially nominated by the Selection Committee for appointment to the Joint Commission on Church Union. Mr G.U. Nathan attacked the proposed Presbyterian representation to the Commission, arguing that its theological task was completed and that the skills of lay people were needed to work on the constitutional side. He was clearly confusing the role of the Joint Commission on Church Union with that of the new Joint Constitution Commission, but his procedural amendment to refer the nomination back for the inclusion of at least one more layman was carried.[8] I was then reduced to being an alternate member of the Joint Commission on Church Union.[9] Geoff Nathan approached me afterwards full of apologies and said that his whole aim had been to force Davis McCaughey off the Commission! How on earth he imagined that that was to be achieved, especially by the procedure that he had proposed, I cannot think.

I was, notwithstanding, able to attend the next meeting of the Joint Commission as an alternate member in place of the Revd Alan Smart.[10] Among the material that I have sent to Bob MacArthur for the Mitchell Library are notes of my own that I made in preparation for particular sessions of the Commission and other notes that I took as the scribe for Working Group II.

On the first evening of the Commission's meeting, Davis McCaughey introduced a discussion on the nature of statements on doctrine and their place in the Basis of Union. He pointed to the disappointing fact that the discussion in the churches had given little attention to the faith of the Church. Since we must not acquiesce in this relative indifference to the renewal of the Church's grasp on its faith, we had to strengthen the doctrinal section, so as to make our union a call to fresh commitment to the Christian faith. Since the responses from the three churches had taken most of the "excitement, novelty and interest" out of the Basis, by eliminating the concordat with South India and casting doubt on the bishops, the way was free for us to show that the real interest of the proposed union lay in its determination to recover and live by the faith confessed by the church catholic and reformed. Davis raised the question of whether we should not go into union with a "Book of Confessions" like that of the United Presbyterian Church in the USA.[11]

I believe that this address, together with an accompanying paper that he had delivered in Berlin on 2 November and of which he handed out copies ("Union and Confession as a Theological Problem"[12]), gave impetus and direction to the Commission's discussion of the Basis in the light of the comments and requests from the churches. But I see from a letter that I wrote to John O'Neill about a fortnight after the meeting of the Commission, that there was some initial anxiety about the new thrust that he was giving to things:

> Some of the more timid or conservative members were concerned at what looked like an attempt on Davis's part to carry on with new thinking without any attention to the churches' amendments, but it turned out as we worked that his new emphasis on the Faith and on the kerygma and, finally, on Jesus Christ, led us to do full justice to the sort of thing the churches wanted.

Points in the minutes of that session that seem to refer to Davis's address and to foreshadow the turn that the Commission's work then took include:

(a) We need to make it clear that the Gospel - what God has said and done for human beings in Jesus Christ - has priority over scripture, creed and confession.

(b) We need to see scripture as a means of grace, rather than as a rule of faith, and our commitment to it as the text from which we preach.

(c) The problem about creeds and confessions is how to inject them into the thought and life of the Church as sources of mental illumination and spiritual quickening, and not so much as tests of orthodoxy.

(d) After some discussion of the ordination service, the point was made, that "this new approach" (to the service? to the place of doctrinal standards in the Basis?) would give a new point of entry to our doctrine of the Ministry: The Ministry is there to serve the Faith.

It is worth noting this last point, which signals a conscious decision on a new approach to the Ministry, after the churches' rejection of elements of the Proposed Basis of 1963. Here lies the beginning of the path that leads directly to the present Uniting Church Minister of the Word. That same evening the Commission appointed three working groups, of which the second was to look at structuring the section on "The Faith" in the Basis. Davis McCaughey, Eric Osborn and I were included in the membership of that group. The Commission had, however, first to look at the requested amendments from the churches, the Presbyterian ones alongside a collation of those from the other two. That was done in a plenary session the next morning.

There had been one request from the General Assembly of Australia, arising from an amendment by the Revd Malcolm Macleod,[13] that the Commission consider omitting the whole section on Doctrinal Standards from the Proposed Basis of Union of 1963 and inserting instead:

(a) acceptance of the Scriptures as the supreme standard;

(b) recognition of the current standards of the three uniting churches as valid expositions of the Christian faith; and

(c) a commitment for the first Uniting Assembly to set up a commission to prepare a confession of faith within six years.

The Joint Commission rejected this suggestion, with the statement that

> [...] it could not contemplate an approach which would

impose an acceptance by ministers of a pastiche of theological incompatibles.

There then ensued plenary discussion on how best to structure the section of the Basis dealing with the faith, taking into account the suggested amendments.

The working groups met that evening and reported back the next morning. Davis proposed that I should act as scribe for our group. Especially after Davis's address of the night before, I felt both in tune and in sympathy with his current thinking. I also found that Eric Osborn seemed to have changed a little since he had visited Perth a year before to give the first set of a series of lectures in biblical studies at the University of Western Australia. His lectures were published as

> E.F. Osborn, *Word and History: Three Lectures on New Testament Themes*, Perth, U.W.A. Press, 1967, repr. 1971 (= *Lectures in Biblical Studies*, 1).

I had found his lectures most stimulating; and they now provide insight into another part of the background to the *Basis of Union*. I was invited to a meeting Eric had with Methodist students and after that walked with him to wherever he was going next. It was only the second time that I had met him. On the walk, he assured me in complete seriousness that Karl Barth was quite finished: Käsemann had told him to his face that he was the patron-saint of the Pietists. But, as I wrote to John O'Neill about a fortnight after the meeting of the Commission, Eric was now advancing

> a kerygma-cum Johannine Logos-Christology Theology of the Word of God, full of echoes of Barth in his most classical period. We were not allowed to talk about the word and sacraments of the Gospel, because semantically the only word was *the* Word.

The result was that I could easily formulate a group consensus with echoes of Davis and Eric and with which I felt very happy myself. This is attached as Appendix A.

The working groups met again on the next evening. We continued with our work. Group III took up the task, agreed to on the basis of Group II's first report, of combining and compressing the "Preface" and "The Decision to Unite" from the 1963 Proposed Basis and rewriting the section on the concordat to set the act of union in the context of the church catholic and to define the relation of the Uniting Church to ecumenical councils. (In all of that we were adopting amendments requested by the Presbyterian Church.)

The second report of our Working Group II is attached as Appendix B.

Taking A and B, our first and second reports, together and recalling the general consensus at the meeting of the Joint Commission, the following decisions of that time can be emphasized:

(a) The *Basis* was to be simpler, shorter and clearer than the Proposed Basis of Union 1963. It would not have sections and sub-sections with headings, but a flowing text in numbered paragraphs.

(b) A separate paragraph on the one Lord Jesus Christ was to have a controlling position and function in the whole; and other issues such as the Church and the Scriptures were to be stated in relation to him.

(c) A paragraph on the gospel proclaimed was to follow the Christological paragraph to identify that gospel as the manner of Christ's active presence.

(d) The Holy Scriptures should be dealt with in a separate paragraph from the creeds and confessions and related to the *kerygma*, the proclamation.

(e) Membership and ministry should be combined in one paragraph, to bring out the fact that membership is ministry, with a section on ordained ministry following a section on the wide diversity of ministries: "the Ministry of Word and Sacraments as one ministry beside others"; and

(f) The ministry of the Word should be shown to have a dual character

    (i) content to be one charismatic ministry besides others;

(ii) necessary in fact and so with some institutional character, because derived from the historical events of Christ's ministry, death and resurrection and serving to proclaim them.

Some, at least, of these points are worth exploring in some detail:

(a) The decision for a simpler form for the *Basis*, with free-flowing text, numbered paragraphs and no subject-headings.

It is important to remember that the headings in the version of the *Basis* printed with the *Constitution and Regulations* (1986, 1990, 1996) go against a deliberate decision of the Joint Commission's. Some of them, e.g. to Paragraphs 4, 6, 10, 11 and 16, are seriously inadequate and misleading.

(b) The separate paragraph on the one Lord Jesus Christ with a controlling position and function in the whole.

This is, in fact, the most important single decision in the work of the Commission and the one that determines the structure and inner logic of the present *Basis of Union*. Superficially, the union movement was focusing on the Church. Three separate denominations were seeking together to find and express more fully what it means to be the Church, and they were seeking to do that within the context of the one universal church in history and in the present. Union would only be possible on the basis of agreed understandings of church government, forms of ministry, ordination, standards of church teaching, sacraments, and other ecclesiastical matters. The great temptation would be for union to make us all far more church-centred than we already were. In its *Basis of Union*, the Uniting Church now acknowledges that

the faith and unity of the Holy Catholic and Apostolic Church are built upon the one Lord Jesus Christ.

In other words, to find its true unity and identity, the Church has to look away from itself to Jesus Christ, its Lord. He is not just a function of the Church, for the meaning that the Church finds in him cannot be fully expressed in what the Church now is, but has to be announced as promise and hope for the world. But the Church is a function of Jesus Christ, for it has no other point or meaning than living from, and serving, what he means for it and for all people.

One clear model that we were following in adopting this position was that taken by Karl Barth in the opening moves of his *Church Dogmatics*. There, in defining the task of dogmatics, he begins with the Church, which, in dogmatics, engages in self-examination in regard to the content of the talk about God peculiar to itself. But its criterion for this criticism and revision of what it says about God is its being as the Church; and the "being of the Church" is Jesus Christ.[14] In his doctrine of the Church, as in other doctrines, Barth seeks in ways such as this to keep his theology centred on Jesus Christ.

Two or three years after this meeting of the Commission, I tried to work through an aspect of this issue in Barth in the article,

> "Why Church Dogmatics?", in *Reformed Theological Review* 29 (1970), pp.46-55.

There, I set out from Bonhoeffer's early criticism of Barth that, in his doctrine of revelation, the latter was neglecting the Church. It was in this connexion that Bonhoeffer developed his understanding of the Church as a form of revelation, "Christ existing as congregation". In the transition from his incomplete *Christian Dogmatics in Outline* (1927) to *Church Dogmatics*, I,1 (1932), Barth actually went through the changes for which Bonhoeffer had been calling, without even being aware of Bonhoeffer or his criticism!

But Barth at the same time maintained clearer safeguards than one finds in Bonhoeffer against the kind of role reversal in which Christ would become a function or predicate of the Church. I find this viewpoint expressed by Eduard Schweizer in a response to my article,

> It is interesting how K. Barth avoids the identification of the church with "Christus prolongatus" (Bonhoeffer's "Christ existing as congregation" might lead to that pitfall) and always sees Christ as the Lord and Head over against the Church as a corrective statement.[15]

At the same time, it is important not to make too much of this distinction between Barth and Bonhoeffer. It is, at the most, a question of how each sought to do the same thing.

An interesting parallel emerges in connexion with another influence that was generally present at the time of this meeting of the Commission, although I can only establish it in an explicit form slightly after that date. It is found in the thought of Ernst Käsemann. Eric Osborn had been directly involved with him in Germany. I had only ever heard him give one lecture myself, but was familiar with his writings. The same was true of Davis McCaughey; and it is likely to have been true of some other members of the Commission, as well. The clear parallel to the position taken in the *Basis of Union* and by Barth and referred to above is to be found in Käsemann's *Der Ruf der Freiheit*,[16] of which I did not receive a copy until June 1968. I wrote an article review of it over the summer of 1968-69, which was published a little later, but not in full, as

"The Call of Freedom", in *Crux* 72 (1969), pp.16-17,19.

Käsemann's booklet is a polemical response to public attacks by leading conservative evangelicals. In the preface to the unchanged second edition, which is no longer found in the third edition on which the English translation was based, Käsemann suggests that his critics should, before condemning him, at least have asked what it was that had led him and others, after the end of the war and of the German church struggle against National Socialism, to go back to radical historical criticism of the Bible.

> We could have said in answer to that, that the struggle we had behind us had given us uncommonly keen ears vis-à-vis the problems of the Church, the Ministry, tradition, church order, church law, the Sacraments and liturgy in the New Testament, and that we were of necessity always noticing afresh the differences and contrasts in the earliest church. [...] To put it crudely, the doctrine of the Church, which we, in company with others, had set out after 1920 to discover again for Protestantism, was, with all that went with it, not able to assume or maintain the central place

intended for it, as indeed the practical experience of the Church Struggle had already dispelled our illusions precisely on this point. [...] What then is left, but to return, after the manner of the Reformers, to the primacy of Christology, should it still, following the Enlightenment, be hiding itself behind the question of the historical Jesus?[17]

We shall come a little later to the significance of Käsemann's suggestion that giving pride of place to Christology nowadays entails taking up the question of the historical Jesus. This quotation otherwise parallels what we have already seen in Barth and in the *Basis of Union*. Theological interest in the Church cannot simply stay with that topic, but needs to go on to pay direct attention to Jesus Christ, in order to find the basis for dealing critically and positively with the problems that the Church presents. Even if my discovery of this formulation dates from the following year, it illustrates what was in the air as the new directions for the *Basis of Union* were decided on.

But we also need to remember how complex the question of historical influences can be, particularly when it is a question of influences on a corporate process of drafting a theological statement and when the theologians who are supposed to have exerted such influence have developed, changed, and interacted with each other over some decades of time. Käsemann speaks of how he and others had set out after 1920 to rediscover the doctrine of the Church. He did that himself in New Testament studies on the body and the body of Christ (*Leib und Leib Christi*, 1933) and the pilgrim people of God in the letter to the Hebrews (*Das wandernde Gottesvolk*, written in prison, 1937). The latter concept, in particular, has had considerable influence in the ecumenical movement.[18] It would thus even be possible to try to trace an indirect contribution of Käsemann's to the wording,

> The Church [...] is a pilgrim people, always on the way towards a promised goal; here she does not have a continuing city but seeks one to come[,]

in Paragraph 3 of the *Basis*. But English-speaking Reformed

Christianity had always identified more directly than German Lutheranism with Israel in its wanderings[19] and with pilgrims in general; and the idea of the wandering people of God became so common in ecumenical circles that a clear connexion on that point between Käsemann's work and the *Basis of Union* could be impossible to establish.

One of the others we naturally think of as having set out to rediscover the doctrine of the Church is Dietrich Bonhoeffer, with his doctoral dissertation *Sanctorum Communio* (1927). Andrew Dutney identifies the influence of Bonhoeffer in a section of the Second Report of the Joint Commission.[20] In connexion with the new direction for the final form of the *Basis* that we have been discussing, Dutney suggests that it consists in "the introduction of a Bultmannian perspective where Barthian views had earlier been dominant", at the same time accurately noting "an approach consonant with that of Ernst Käsemann", which he sees as even more pronounced.[21]

As I have said above, Bonhoeffer was not uncritical of Barth in the late 1920's, but then saw Barth develop in the very direction he had wished. For a time, there was very close agreement between them. Shortly before his execution, in *Letters and Papers from Prison*, Bonhoeffer criticized Barth and his view of revelation. The initial, and probably greatest continuing, influence of Bonhoeffer in the English-speaking world stems from his latest writings; and it is probably above all their influence that Andrew Dutney establishes in a section of the Second Report. For his part, Barth held to the fundamental position on which he and Bonhoeffer had been agreed, so that, in the preface to the new 1954 edition of Bonhoeffer's dissertation, Ernst Wolf could write,

> Dietrich Bonhoeffer's theological legacy has been being properly discovered step by step for only a few years - if one disregards Karl Barth's *Church Dogmatics*.[22]

Barth himself in 1955 gave the highest possible recognition to two of Bonhoeffer's works, *The Call to Discipleship* and *Sanctorum Communio*.[23] So a general influence of Bonhoeffer through Barth and others has to be allowed for, apart from the direct influence it may be possible to identify at certain points. With regard to Andrew Dutney's suggestion that, in the final form of the *Basis*, a Bultmannian perspective has been introduced in place of the Barthian views that were earlier dominant, it might be more accurate to say that the *Basis* now reflects an emphasis on proclamation common to Bultmann and Barth. It could perhaps be seen as less "Barthian", because containing fewer of the final products of Barth's own theology; but it shares more of his fundamental starting-point and follows his opening gambit in the *Church Dogmatics*. The move back from ecclesiology to Christology is one that Barth and Käsemann make in parallel. In explaining it, Käsemann wrote one more sentence that I omitted from the already long quotation above,

> For some of us there gradually disappeared even the fascination of the Protestant alienation and reduction of [the doctrine of the Church] to anthropology, which modern Catholicism, with the keen nose it has inherited, comprehended long ago and with enthusiasm as a projection of the doctrine of the Church.[24]

In moving on from anthropology to Christology, Käsemann is distancing himself from the way in which Bultmann sees valid faith statements as expressions of human self-understanding. He is manoeuvring in close proximity to Barth and his contention that

> Anthropological and ecclesiological assertions arise only as they are borrowed from Christology. That is to say, no anthropological or ecclesiological assertion is true in itself and as such. Its truth subsists in the assertions of Christology or, rather, in the reality of Jesus Christ alone.[25]

To that extent, the *Basis of Union* aligns itself with Käsemann and Barth against Bultmann, as, too, against possible implications of Bonhoeffer's "Christ existing as congregation". On the other hand, we shall later note how the way in which the *Basis* follows Käsemann in turning to the historical Jesus runs counter both to Bultmann and to Barth.

Resuming our consideration of the main decisions taken at the 1967 meeting of the Joint Commission, we come to:

(c) A paragraph on the gospel proclaimed to follow the Christological paragraph and to identify that gospel as the manner of Christ's active presence.

(d) The Holy Scriptures to be dealt with in a separate paragraph from the creeds and confessions and related to the proclamation of the Gospel.

I believe that the combined significance of the first four points (a) - (d) is that the approach of the Joint Commission to the whole *Basis* was now to emphasize the centrality of Jesus Christ and the doctrine of Christ as the living Word of God, heard and known through Scripture, present and active through proclamation. Insights of the First Report on *The Faith of the Church* had become the criteria for reworking the proposals of the Second Report, *The Church - its Nature, Function and Ordering*.[26]

Davis had suggested that a new approach might give us a new point of entry to the doctrine of the Ministry. That was completely in line with the criticism that I had been making of the Second Report and Proposed Basis of 1963. It was also in tune with Eric Osborn's current thinking. (I remember that he attacked me for suggesting some neat pattern: "Christ, Proclamation and Scriptures, Sacraments", as being happily congruent with Ephesians 4: "One Lord, one Faith, one Baptism". Ephesians 4 and its picture of ministry were out, because Käsemann had shown how clerical they were compared with 1 Corinthians 12.) Other members of our group must also have been happy with the suggestions that:

(e) Membership and ministry be combined in one section, the Ministry of Word and Sacraments as one ministry beside others; and

(f) The ministry of the Word to be shown to have a dual character

(i) as one charismatic ministry besides others; and

(ii) as necessary in fact and so with some institutional character.

There was thus a carefully considered decision by the Joint Commission to use the image of the many ministries exercised by the members of the body of Christ to provide the overall framework within which particular ministries, including the ordained ministry of Word and Sacraments, were to be located and defined. Above all, the reason for this was the recognition that there is an inherent link between this approach to ministry and the Commission's vision of the unity of the Church.

> Unity is integration through mutual service and mutually supporting ministries.[27]

One source of this insight of which I am aware was the study by

> Eduard Schweizer, "The Concept of the Church in the Gospel and Epistles of St John", in A.J.B. Higgins, ed., *New Testament Essays: Studies in Memory of Thomas Walter Manson*, Manchester, UP, 1959, pp.230-245.

Comparing the Pauline symbol of the "Body of Christ" with the Johannine picture of "Christ, the True Vine", Schweizer brings out how the unity of the church and the role of the individual member are tackled differently by these two authors. Paul's picture of the Body contains a strongly unifying element in the mutual service of all the different members. Noone stresses the unity of the church more than John. But that only serves to show how unity has become a problem for him. In the vine, the branches do not need or serve each other. Unity and fraternal love are only demanded, because God wants them and because they are needed, if the Church is to show forth Christ, the true vine.[28]

I can remember Eduard Schweizer speaking of this contrast between Paul and John and the direct link between ministries and unity in Paul. But that cannot have been before his first visit to Perth, early October 1968. He may have been in the Eastern states on an earlier occasion; and we shall have been aware of the above article from an earlier date.

In choosing to begin its consideration of ministry in the Church with the thesis that all members have gifts for ministry and that there is a charismatic aspect to all of these ministries, the Joint

Commission was seeking to overcome polarization between clerical ministries and lay ministries or between institutional and charismatic ministries. Such polarization had been experienced to some extent in the uniting churches, showing itself in strange mixtures of clericalism and anti-clericalism. It also seemed to be reinforced afresh in the document from the Second Vatican Council,

> *Dogmatic Constitution on the Church (De Ecclesia)*, London, Catholic Truth Society, 1965,

also know by its opening phrase as *Lumen Gentium*. While this text demonstrated in so many ways the extent to which renewal in the Roman Catholic Church was proceeding in parallel to, or even in convergence with, renewal in other churches, its tone seemed suddenly to become much more traditional again in the chapter on "The Hierarchical Constitutions and the Episcopate in Particular"; and new insights into the ministries of the laity seemed quickly to be constricted by reassertion of hierarchical leadership. Hence what is said on the ministry of Word and Sacraments in the working group's second report,

> The 2nd Report's[29] stress on the dual nature of this ministry is to be retained, particularly in critical (but tacit) relationship to Vatican II's dichotomy between charismatic and institutional ministries.[30]

The Commission certainly considered that, within the overall differentiation of ministries exercised by members of the Church, the ministry of Word and Sacraments could be seen to have its own distinctive role and character, serving the exercise of other ministries, rather than inhibiting it.

In my letter to John O'Neill after the meeting of the Commission, I wrote,

> I was quite happy with the way things went. We have agreed, largely on the basis of the work of one group in which Davis, Eric Osborn and I participated, to telescope the Preface and the Introduction, to rewrite the Concordat bit in the light of Presbyterian proposals to

make it a definition of the place of the Uniting Church in the Church Catholic, its relationships to ecumenical councils, WCC, churches in Australia and Asia, etc., then to throw in a new, dominating section on the one Lord, to draw the emphasis of the whole away from the Church itself and to emphasize that Christ is the basis of a greater unity than just that of the Church; to follow on with a section on the proclamation as the current form of his active presence, to pull the sacraments up into that section and to build the bit on the Scriptures on in very close connexion with the part on proclamation (so that their authority is seen to be exercised as they are used as a basis for proclaiming the Gospel).

The creeds get a separate section (along with the confessions of the Reformation and those sermons of John Wesley's), mainly in order to show that the Scriptures have a rather unique place. Membership and ministries get shoved into one article, to show that a member is a functioning organ. The Ministry, for which it is becoming increasingly difficult to find a word which everyone likes, will be more clearly rooted in the task of proclamation (instead of being a cheap imitation of Christ, Prophet, Priest and King).

NOTES

1   *BB 1967*, pp.97-100.

2   *BB 1967*, min.48.4.

3   *BB 1967*, min.48.4(b),(j),(l).

4   *BB 1967*, min.48.4(c). - It was conceded that it had been disastrous for the *Chalcedonian Decree* to have been circulated for consideration in the union discussions with the term *theotokos* ("the One who gave birth to God") translated by the title 'Mother of God', as in the Appendix to the Second Report and Proposed Basis, *Church*, p.92. - Chalcedonian Christology is, of course, still represented in the relevant articles of Reformation documents acknowledged in the *Basis of Union*, par.10.

5   *BB 1967*, min.48.4(p),(q).

6   *BB 1967*, min.48.4(e).

7   *BB 1967*, min.48.4(g). - The Uniting Church does have adherents, but it defines them differently from the adherents in the Presbyterian Church, who were "adherent members", i.e. what the Uniting Church calls "baptized members".

8   *BB 1967*, min.87.

9   *BB 1967*, min.140.2.

10 This meeting took place 27-30 November 1967.

11 *The Constitution of the United Presbyterian Church in the United States of America: Part I: Book of Confessions*, Philadelphia, Office of the General Assembly, 1967.

12 J. Davis McCaughey, "Union und Bekenntnis als ein theologisches Problem", in F. Schlingensiepen, ed., *Union und Oekumene*, Berlin, 1968.

13 *BB 1967*, min.47; 48.8.

14 Karl Barth, *Church Dogmatics*, vol.I,1, ²1975, pp.3f.

15 Postcard from Eduard Schweizer, 12 July 1976.

16 Ernst Käsemann, *Der Ruf der Freiheit*, Tübingen, Mohr, 21968; - ET of the 3rd, rev.ed. (1968): Ernst Käsemann, *Jesus Means Freedom: A Polemical Survey of the New Testament*, tr. Frank Clarke, London, SCM, 1969. This translation is marred by a number of serious errors.

17 Käsemann, *Der Ruf der Freiheit*, S.17.

18 "[...] my book on the wandering people of God, the title of which has since created a sensation and is said to have had honour done to it at the Vatican Council itself" (Käsemann, *Der Ruf der Freiheit*, S.14).

19 I recognized this when a German friend remarked on all the hymns in the *Revised Church Hymnary* that express such an identification.

20 Andrew Dutney, *Manifesto for Renewal*, pp.34f, n.12.

21 Dutney, *Manifesto for Renewal*, pp.107f, n.13.

22 Ernst Wolf, ed., in Dietrich Bonhoeffer, *Sanctorum Communio*, 2nd ed., Munich, Kaiser, 1954, S.5. - The ET, Dietrich Bonhoeffer, *Sanctorum Communio: a Dogmatic Enquiry into the Sociology of the Church*, London, Collins, 1963, does not contain Wolf's preface, but one by Eberhard Bethge.

23 Barth, *Church Dogmatics*, IV,2, pp.533f,540-542,641.

24 Käsemann, *Der Ruf der Freiheit*, S.17.

25 Barth, *Church Dogmatics*, II,1, pp.148f.

26 On the other hand, it would be a mistake to think that the *Basis,* in its final form, simply follows the approach of *The Faith of the Church*. When George Yule writes that "the *Basis of Union* of the Uniting Church in Australia insisted that unity must be based on the doctrine of justification by faith; and that Uniting Church is committed to seek the fullness of the faith. To this end, the *Basis of Union* spells out where this fullness of faith must be sought" (G. Yule, "The Westminster Confession in Australia", in Alasdair I.C. Heron, ed., *The Westminster Confession in the Church Today: Papers Prepared for the Church of Scotland Panel on Doctrine*, Edinburgh, St Andrew, 1982, pp.101-103, p.102), he is recalling what was said in *The Faith of the Church*. In the *Basis of Union*, the earlier orientation on the Church's faith has been superseded by one on Jesus Christ, God's living Word. The Basis does say that "the Uniting Church lives and works within the faith and unity of the One Holy Catholic and Apostolic Church" and that it receives the *Apostles'* and *Nicene Creeds* "as authoritative statements of the Catholic Faith". But it does not talk about seeking the fullness of the faith and it does not approach the *Westminster Confession* and similar documents with the question, "Where is the Church's faith to be found?". The *Basis of Union* of 1971 owes a substantial debt to *The Faith of the Church*. But it deserves to be read for itself, and not simply as a later (perhaps not wholly adequate) implementation of an agenda set in 1959.

27 Quoted from the report of the working group reproduced in Appendix B.

28 E. Schweizer, "The Concept of the Church [...]", in A.J.B. Higgins, ed., *New Testament Essays [...]*, Manchester, UP, 1959, pp.230-245. pp.236f; cf.232f,234,235f.

29 This refers to the Second Report of the Joint Commission, *The Church [...]*.

30 Quoted from the report of the working group reproduced in Appendix B.

Appendix A[1]

Joint Commission on Church Union

November 27 - 30, 1967 [...]

Working Group 2 : The Structure

(On the question of the structure to be given to the Basis of Union, with special reference to the way to refer to the 'kerygma',[2] to the Scriptures and to Confession of the Faith.)

The group discussed

(a)   the flow and coherence of the whole Basis

and

(b)   the style and scope of it.

On (b) it was agreed that the. document must state the central agreement in faith (e.g. "Jesus is Lord") as simply and clearly as possible. But it was also seen that some sophistication would be necessary if it were to be precise and adequate as well as intelligible.

On (a) it was agreed:

(i)   to combine and compress the *Preface* and I, *The Decision to Unite*,

(ii)   to rewrite II (at present, *Concordat*) in line with the Presbyterian amendment, in order to set the act of union announced in I in the context of the Church Catholic and to define the relationship between the Uniting Church and ecumenical councils, etc.

(iii)   then, to introduce a section which explicitly goes *back* behind the one Church to the one *Lord*, who is the basis both of its being and its unity, because of the action God has taken in him to draw together all things again in him as Head and to reconcile them to himself. In this way the unity of the Church will be seen to be given in Christ and, in him, to be inseparably tied up with its universal mission.

(iv) next, to speak of the way in which Christ exercises his Lordship through the *proclamation* of him (the preached presence of Jesus Christ). The points were made and accepted that the "word[3] of God" must be shown to be not just a "linguistic event"[4], but Jesus Christ in his personal presence. While, on the other hand, Jesus Christ must be shown to be not just a piously remembered figure, but the living Word of God.[5]

(v) to take up III, 2 (*Sacraments*) in a section on Preaching and the Sacraments (or, the Word and Sacraments of the Gospel),[6] in which it will be stated how through the ongoing witness of preaching and celebrating the Sacraments (in continuity with the original apostolic proclamation) Christ today gathers, constitutes, continues, rules and reforms his Church, bringing men to the obedience of faith. There will be more emphasis on the corporate implication of the Sacraments ("all baptized in one spirit into one body", "because there is one bread, we who are many are one body").[7]

(vi) to treat, then, of the Holy Scriptures, the ancient creeds, the Confessions of the Reformation, and later documents,

(a) attempting to define their relative functions in mediating the Lordship of Christ, the Word of God,

(b) bringing out their character as the response of faith confessed,

(c) re-writing in order to present as clear a picture as possible of the dynamic role these documents play in the Church.

Consideration must be given to the way in which the creeds and confessions are listed. Should it be by foot-note[8]?

(vii) to combine III,3 and III,4 (on *Church Membership* and *the Ministry*) in one section, to bring out the fact that membership is ministry. The sub-section on the *Ordained Ministry* would then follow upon a sub-section pointing to the wide diversity of ministries and present the ministry of Word and Sacraments as one ministry beside others (integrated with them in the common mission of Christ's body) but peculiarly basic thereto because of the way in which the Church is ever again renewed by Christ through the Word and Sacraments of his Gospel.

The Group had no time to discuss the form our present affirmation of the Faith should take.

NOTES

1   The text of the two reports of Working Group 2 at the meeting of the Joint Commission 27 to 30 November 1967 are reproduced here as Appendix A and Appendix B. The format of the originals has been preserved. Corrections that have been made to the text are indicated by notes. These and all other notes did not form part of the original reports.

2   'Kerygma', a neuter Greek noun meaning "what is proclaimed", had been popularized by C.H. Dodd, *The Apostolic Preaching and its Developments*, London, Hodder, 1936, new ed. 1944 and repr.. - "The word [...] *kerygma*, signifies not the action of the preacher, but what he preaches, his 'message' [...]" (*ibid.*, p.7). Dodd rather overstated the distinction between preaching and teaching.

3   In my copy, "word" has been changed to "Word".

4   'Linguistic event' was a term from the work being done on hermeneutics (principles and processes of interpretation) by Gerhard Ebeling, Emil Fuchs and others in Tübingen. Eric Osborn had had some contact with this. (See, e.g., E.F. Osborn, *Word and History: Three Lectures on New Testament Themes*, Perth, U.W.A. Press, 1967, repr. 1971 [= *Lectures in Biblical Studies*, 1], pp.54-60). The phrase, "not just a 'linguistic event'" indicates an awareness that the biblical "Word of God" could, on some theories, be reduced to no more than a development in the expression of meaning by human speech and an intention of understanding it as more than this.

5   Speaking of Jesus Christ as the "the living Word of God" in this context shows the continuing influence of the theology of Karl Barth and the *Theological Declaration of Barmen*.

6   Although some of the material from here is now to be found in par.4 of the *Basis*,

a comparison with par.6 will show how one-sided the heading is that has been placed over that paragraph in some editions, viz. "Sacraments".

7   These quotations are from 1 Corinthians 12:13 and 10:17.

8   In my copy an original "foot-vote" has been corrected to "foot-note".

Appendix B

Working Group 2

While seeking to continue its discussion of the flow and coherence of the whole basis, the Group found that it had first to define the outcome of the afternoon's discussion in the full session of the Commission.

The Group would hand its previous results over to the drafters with the following comments:

(a) The numbering of sections i to vii in the previous report of the Group is for purposes of present reference and is not intended to prejudice the question of lay-out and numbering in the draft.

(b) (iii), on the *one Lord*, should stand as a separate paragraph:-

   (1) because it must be clear that Jesus Christ cannot be reduced to the "kerygma";

   (2) because prior separate-emphasis on the one *Lord* will take the heat out of questions which have been raised about the authority of the Scriptures over the Church or the priority of the Church to the Scriptures. Recognising the one Lord, we shall see that his authority is mediated and reflected within the Church in a variety of ways, none of which can be termed ultimate vis-a-vis the others.

(c) It was accepted that the paragraph on the one Lord would give adequate and appropriate space (symbolized by "three lines") to the *cosmic implications* of Christ's work and his Lordship and would reflect the nuance that the Church's Unity will here be set in the context of its involvement in *Christ's* universal activity.

(d) The next paragraph must begin with the *Gospel proclaimed* as the manner of the active presence of Christ.

   (v) could be combined with (iv) in one paragraph.

The Scriptures should be lifted out of the line of later credal statements, put into (iv) and/or (v) and tied in with the "original apostolic proclamation" (with the possibility noted of indicating the relatively different ways in which the OT and NT Scriptures relate to the earliest form of that proclamation, if this should prove to solve more problems than it is likely to raise). Rather than thrashing out the question of which came first, the "kerygma" or the Church, the Basis should indicate at this point *both* that the written words of the Scriptures serve as the medium by which Christ the living and life-giving Word confronts the Church, its theology and its proclamation *and* that Christ's authority is effective through the Scriptures as the Word is sought in them and proclaimed from them. (The Holy Spirit will certainly need to be mentioned in the context of (iv) and (v).)

(e) The para. (vi) on the creeds, confessions, etc., would follow as outlined.

(f) Careful drafting will be needed to link the paragraph (vii) on *Membership and Ministry* back to what is said about the creation of the Church and awakening of faith in (v).

(vii) Should begin with reference to the fact that what Christ does is to unite men in the fellowship of his life, ministry and sufferings, that he sends them out as he was himself sent. (So a stress on the *apostolic* nature of the Church would be appropriate here.)

The paragraph should then develop a dialectical exposition of John 17 and I Cor 12 (or, perhaps, Ephesians 4) probably without direct reference to them.

(1) membership as participation in the one movement of Christ in ministry to the world; all ministry as created and called forth by the giving of the Word in Christ.

(2) the individuation of the gift of ministry, so that by the one Spirit[1] many distinct gifts, ministries, functions of the divine Word in the life of the Church, are given.

Each member *as member* has his own particular service to perform: Unity is integration through mutual service and mutually supporting ministries.

(g) In the same paragraph (section), the *Ministry of Word and Sacraments* will be placed within the spread of the ministries already outlined. The 2nd Report's stress on the dual nature of this ministry is to be retained, particularly in critical (but tacit) relationship to Vatican II's dichotomy between charismatic and institutional ministries. It is that:

(1) the ministry of the Word can be content to be one charismatic ministry beside others and to forego any pretensions to institutional authority (I Cor 12; II Cor 10-13).

(2) it has factual necessity (and resultant institutional character) because it springs from the concrete historical events of Christ's ministry, death and resurrection and serves to proclaim them.

(h) It is necessary to ensure that the picture of the ministries is not functional to the point of failure to reflect the true nature of ministry. We must see the element of vocation; further, that it is the Holy Spirit who disposes in sovereign freedom over the gifts the Church receives, while it is the Church's place to follow his movement and recognize the ministries he provides.

(j)[2] The section on the *Councils* should be carefully connected to the preceding section on Membership and Ministry, as a description of a pattern of ministry and of the structure of the Church's corporate life.

In this way, the activities and the authority of the Councils will be seen to be ministerial.[3]

(k) Since the tone of the Basis is becoming more confessing, technical stage directions for procedures at the point of union (e.g. on the acceptance of baptized persons as members and communicant[4] members as communicant members, on the creeds and confessions received by the Uniting Church, on the standard of worship, etc.) might well be marked by indentation and smaller type. This will achieve unity of style and greater comprehensibility.

(l) This is not completion of Basis.

? Confessing Act ? of some sort ?[5]

NOTES

1 A page-break occurs at this point. In the following text, there is only one space difference between the indentation of the end of (f)(2) and that of (g). But the lettering and numbering makes the relative status of each quite clear.

2 The sequence moves on from (h) to (j) to avoid an ambiguous (i).

3 'Ministerial' here means, "serving", not "appertaining to Ministers". Activities carried out, and authority exercised, by councils of the Church will be supposed to be serving the activity and authority of Jesus Christ.

4 There is a gap in the duplicated text of the report at this point, into which I have written "communicant". Probably, the typist applied correcting fluid to the stencil, but then forgot to type in the correct word.

5 I have written in these two lines, including the "(l)", by hand. It is likely that I added them in presenting the report at the next plenary session of the Commission. On the logic of what is said in note 2 above, this should have been (m), since 'l' was also used for an Arabic numeral.

VII

I must have talked to Davis McCaughey at some stage about doing some drafting towards the new form of the Basis. He had pointed out that I might not be able to attend a meeting of the Commission again as an alternate and offered to feed in anything that I sent him. In December 1967 and January 1968 we had a long family holiday in Sorrento, Victoria. As in other years, I had an arrangement with the Revd Jack Findlay that I could use his vestry each morning; and I typed up there on his typewriter a draft for some paragraphs of the Basis. It is reproduced here as Appendix C.

After some suggestions on wording for what was to become the first two paragraphs of the *Basis of Union*, the draft attempts the centring of the whole *Basis* on Jesus Christ in the way now achieved in Paragraph 3. We had agreement in the Commission that we should work with the concept of the Word of God, in the manner of Barth and Barmen. That would tie Jesus in with Scripture and proclamation, as the Word within the words, and tie him in with God, as the revelation of the Father. But just to start with a trinitarian statement of Jesus Christ as the eternal Word would give the impression that we had a doctrine or image of God presupposed, which we were reading into Jesus. We had to show, as Barth has in fact done himself, how the Triune God is revealed through Jesus. We had to do that differently from Barth, because Christological discussion had moved on since *Church Dogmatics*, I,1, and the Barmen *Theological Declaration*. Above all, we faced the "new quest of the historical Jesus", which asked how faith that lived from Easter was related to what we knew historically about the ministry and teaching of Jesus of Nazareth.

It was a relatively new thing for us to be facing that question again. From the Great War on, there had been a growing consensus in theological and church circles that it was neither legitimate nor possible to produce a biography of Jesus of Nazareth. The New Testament scriptures were seen to be witnessing to Jesus Christ in terms of the faith of his disciples after Easter; and the right use of the Scriptures was understood to lie in proclamation, confession and theological reflection that lived from Easter faith. Jesus had not just been the founder of a religion or an ethical teacher, but the embodiment of God's presence, action and communication with us. This presence, action and communication of God's centred, not on the life or ministry of Jesus, but on his death and resurrection; and these events were the heart of the Gospel we had to believe and to proclaim.

That was certainly the way we saw things in my student days; and we could claim to have learned it from Barth and from Bultmann alike. But by about 1954, the question of the so-called "Historical Jesus" began to be raised again from within the circle of Bultmann's own pupils. Their concern, which had been stimulated, in part, by the recent demythologizing debate, was that faith could seem to be an arbitrary interpretation placed on the figure and story of Jesus, unless some continuity could be shown to exist between the Easter gospel and what could be ascertained by historical method concerning the human person Jesus of Nazareth. How did historical faith differ from timeless myth? What continuity could there be between the Jesus of history and the Christ of the Gospel, for all the discontinuity of death and resurrection?

The answer attempted in my draft and now given in the *Basis of Union* is that, by raising the crucified Jesus from the dead, God has done a range of things that are intimately related to the content of Jesus' ministry, teaching and death: He has confirmed and completed Jesus' preaching of him as the Father who cares, and so reasserted his right to this world as its Creator. He has resolved the crisis of our human rebellion, which had come to a head over Jesus' interpretation of the commandments and in his consequent crucifixion, and he has done so by asserting his own righteousness in reconciliation and forgiveness. He has inaugurated the life of the new age that Jesus had heralded by his preaching that the Kingdom was at hand.

My own journey to the insight that Easter constituted a link between the earthly Jesus and the Christ of faith had commenced through association with Heinz Eduard Tödt as he was writing his doctoral dissertation, published in English as

H.E. Tödt, *The Son of Man in the Synoptic Tradition*, London, SCM, 1965.[1]

Tödt concurs with Bultmann's identification of three separate groups of Son of Man sayings within the Synoptic tradition, referring respectively to

(a) the Son of Man coming with the clouds of heaven and in association with the angels of God,

(b) Jesus in his earthly ministry with authority to forgive sins, etc., and

(c) the Son of Man who has to suffer many things and be killed, but rise again after three days.[2]

Tödt also agrees that only the first of these groups belongs to the oldest stratum of the tradition. But he goes beyond Bultmann in asserting with confidence that some of this group of sayings stem from the teaching of Jesus himself.[3]

One of the chief reasons for tracing these sayings back to Jesus' own teaching is that the distinction between the coming Son of Man and the earthly figure of Jesus found in sayings like Luke 12:8f and Mark 8:38 // Luke 9:26 could not have been created by Jesus' disciples after his death and resurrection, because they then believed that the coming Son of Man would be none other than Jesus himself.[4]

In Jesus' teaching, the Son of Man is a coming heavenly figure, possessed of a transcendent sovereignty different in kind from the unique authority of Jesus on earth. His coming will represent God's final act of salvation and judgment; and he will, in particular, function as guarantor of the abiding saving significance of the relation that Jesus' followers have to Jesus on earth. On the development that took place from the original sayings of Jesus to the subsequent identification of the Son of Man with Jesus after Easter, Tödt writes,

> By the *soteriological* correlation in the Son of Man sayings the person of Jesus is not immediately linked with the figure of the coming Son of Man; it is not expressed here that the two are identical. The means by which an identification will be effected is a *Christological* judgment. It is highly significant that the Christological knowledge

that sprang up in the earliest period of the primitive community was gained in connexion with Jesus' own words. The Master himself had promised to his own that their attachment to him would be guaranteed and confirmed by the Son of Man. The post-Easter community realized that these words of promise implied a continuity between the one who gave the promise on earth and the one who came to fulfil what had been promised - and in this realization they took the step to Christology. With this knowledge, they went beyond what Jesus had expressed; and yet the judgment they made was not an arbitrary one. For the authority of the one who had uttered the words of promise on earth had been confirmed by the Easter event in a way that led to a new knowledge of his person and gave the impetus for Christological cognition. It was precisely this Christological knowledge that reached back behind the Easter event and referred to Jesus' own words of promise. [...] On the other hand, it also has to be emphasized [...] that it needed the Resurrection event to lead the primitive community beyond its trust in Jesus' soteriologically determined word of promise to that Christological judgment.[5]

As this quotation shows, the renewed interest in the teaching and ministry of the historical Jesus that sprang up in the mid-Fifties did not necessarily imply any departure from the conviction that New Testament faith and Christology lived from Easter. But it looked for real connexions between post-Easter faith and Christology, on the one hand, and the limited amount that we can know, historically speaking, about Jesus in his earthly life and death, on the other. By careful analysis of the Son of Man sayings in the Synoptic Gospels and of other material in the Q stratum of tradition, Tödt was able to show how, for the community of Jesus' followers, God's action in raising Jesus had validated Jesus' message. As a result, the community initially saw its task as being to continue to proclaim that message. It began to develop and formulate a Christology in connexion with the collection and development of the tradition of Jesus' teaching. This was a Christology independent of the Pauline proclamation of Christ crucified and far more continuous than Paul's Gospel with the message of Jesus' himself.[6] For while, for Paul, the Resurrection represented the raising of the Crucified One as Lord, it had taken the community that gathered the material we find in Q back behind the Crucifixion to sayings and promises of Jesus himself.

Another important influence on my own development of a new approach to Christology had come through contact with Günther Bornkamm in Heidelberg and study of his book,

Jesus of Nazareth, London, Hodder, 1960 and repr..[7]

This was the first, and remains as the classic, portrayal of the person and ministry of Jesus with the questions and assumptions of the "New Quest". As the preface makes clear, Bornkamm does not think that faith can be grounded on the results of historical research. But neither does he think that historical enquiry is incompatible with faith. It is precisely through such enquiry that faith may seek to understand what it believes; and, on this search, it finds itself on common ground with anyone who has a serious interest in historical knowledge. This book has therefore been an important resource for those who did not want to reject central insights of modern scholarship into the nature of the Biblical witness, but who no longer considered that such insights prohibited them from seeking connexions between that witness and the historical figure and message of Jesus of Nazareth.

The need to develop my own approach to Christology became urgent with the move to the Theological Hall in Perth at the beginning of 1963. That year, I already had to lecture on Christology for the first time (the class consisting of Des Cousins, Bruce McKane and Gray Birch.) The course included the problem of the historical Jesus and the new quest.

In preparation for taking Christology again in 1966, I worked through Wolfhart Pannenberg's outline of Christology, later published in English as

Jesus: God and Man, London, SCM, 1968,[8]

and I published an article review of it,

"A First Look at Pannenberg's Christology", *Reformed Theological Review* 25 (1966), pp.52-64,

followed by a more systematic critique,

"Christology and History", *RThR* 26 (1967), pp.54-64.

I had known Pannenberg from lectures and seminars in the 1950's, but not been personally acquainted with him. In his use of New Testament material, he linked up, not so directly with H.E. Tödt, but with another pupil of Bornkamm's, Ferdinand Hahn, whose work on Christological titles in the early New Testament tradition,

Ferdinand Hahn, *Christologische Hoheitstitel. Ihre Geschichte im frühen Christentum* (1963), 2nd rev.ed., Göttingen, Vandenhoeck, 1964 (*FRLANT*, 83),[9]

had a marked influence on

Reginald H. Fuller, *The Foundations of New Testament Christology*, London, Lutterworth, 1965.

Hahn by and large followed Tödt's line on the Son of Man title and suggested for other Christological titles as well that there had been an initial eschatological focus, which was only later shifted to a reference to Jesus in his earthly ministry, on the Cross or in his present, risen lordship. His overall thesis was, for me, not as convincing as Tödt's.

In Pannenberg's Christology, I found an attempt to use the revived quest of the historical Jesus to overcome what he calls the "*kerygma* ('proclamation') theology" of Bultmann and Barth. He criticizes the dichotomy that exists in their theologies between faith and history and attempts a new synthesis between the two. The meaning of events has to be grounded in the events themselves and it must be capable of being read off the events, considered in the light of their wider historical contexts, by historical method. Pannenberg offers historical proof for the Resurrection, as the most satisfactory hypothesis for explaining the New Testament evidence. Considering that he has proved that God raised Jesus from the dead, he then reads theological meaning out of that event, in the light of its context in the traditions of First Century Judaism, and of further contexts into which the news of the event came to be proclaimed. For this, he employs and develops methods borrowed from the study of the history of tradition, particularly in Old Testament studies. While I could not agree with Pannenberg's wish of verifying faith historically, I appreciated the way in which he draws out the meaning of God's action in raising Jesus from the content of Jesus' ministry and preaching as the historical context of the Resurrection.

For my critique of Pannenberg, I paid attention to Bornkamm's approach in *Jesus of Nazareth*, and to essays of Ernst Käsemann's, in particular, to the one that had triggered off the new wave of interest in the question of the "Jesus of History",

> Ernst Käsemann, "The Problem of the Historical Jesus"
> (1954), in: E. Käsemann, *Essays on New Testament Themes*,
> London, SCM, 1964, pp.15-47.[10]

This, too, was part of a common background that I had with others on the Joint Commission at that time. Eric Osborn had had a considerable involvement with Käsemann, and Davis McCaughey, with Günther Bornkamm, through his year in Heidelberg in 1960 and the Bornkamms' visit to Australia in 1963.

I lectured on Christology again in 1968. But the point at which I find the closest correspondence to the draft for the *Basis of Union* is in the structure of the courses in Systematic Theology in the Lay Institute of Theology. Over three years (1969-70 and 1975), each course set out from one theme of Jesus' preaching:

(a)   the Father who is near and cares,

(b)   the will of God in the commandments, and

(c)   God's coming Kingdom.[11]

Each concept was explored back into the Old Testament. In subsequent lectures, the issues that had been raised were each time worked through and resolved through the story of cross and resurrection. These courses follow the three-fold pattern:

(a) revelation and creation,

(b) reconciliation and forgiveness,

(c) eschatology and new creation,

which is very close to the statement in the draft for the *Basis* of what God has done by raising the crucified Jesus from the dead. I have tried to spell out this approach to Christology in the essay,

"Jesus and God", *Colloquium* 6 (1973), pp.19-35.

Another significant element in this draft for Paragraph 3 is the way in which eschatology is used as the link between Jesus, his death and resurrection, on the one hand, and the Church and its ministry and sacraments, on the other. The meaning of Jesus Christ is not exhausted in ecclesiastical realities, but is to be fully expounded only in terms of universal, eschatological reconciliation and renewal. The Church's function is to serve that. Its nature is to be described in terms of participation in the process and anticipation of the end of it. I had worked out this approach in my 1964 lectures on Eschatology; the Holy Spirit and his work of Justification, Sanctification and Equipping with Gifts; Church, Ministry and Sacraments. This lecture course followed on from the Christology of the previous year and used eschatology as the link between the topics of the second and third articles of the Creed.

The main stimulus and challenge for this had been provided by Rudolf Bultmann's

Theology of the New Testament, voll.1-2, London, SCM, vol.1 1952, vol.2 1955.[12]

and

History and Eschatology, Edinburgh, U.P., 1957 (= *The Gifford Lectures*, 1955).[13]

Bultmann is only able to discuss faith, hope and meaning in terms of human self-understanding. Objective statements about the outside world of present or past may be factually true, but can make no difference to who and how and what I am, and so can have no meaning for me. His interpretation of gospel and faith is therefore constricted by dichotomies not unrelated to the Kantian split between theoretical and practical reason.

The challenge was how to connect cross and world, eschatology and history. I sought to do it by understanding the death and resurrection of Jesus Christ as eschatological and representative events, in which God had been dealing with all humans and all the old creation. Their full meaning was therefore only expressible in categories of hope and expectation. The content and focus of hope, on the other hand, were that we should one day see all creatures and all creation embraced by the force of those representative events, the death and resurrection of Jesus Christ. That was what last judgment and new creation would mean. Living in the present by faith and hope was a matter of daily decisions in which we left behind us the old existence to which Christ had already died on our behalf and began to live by the promise and power of the coming new creation within the persisting forms of the old.

In this, I was aware of following much that is to be found in the later work of Karl Barth. Subsequently, I also found some support in

> Jürgen Moltmann, *Theology of Hope: on the Ground and Implications of a Christian Eschatology*, London, SCM, 1967, repr. 1983.[14]

By centring Christology on God's action in raising Jesus, but finding the meaning of that event in the Jesus raised by God, seen in the light of his controversial ministry and his background in Old Testament tradition, the draft for the *Basis* is also seeking new access to the concept of the Word of God. This concept is introduced in what was to become Paragraph 4 of the *Basis*. The connexion back to Paragraph 3 is not spelled out there, but is none the less real:

> By raising Jesus from the dead, God has "confirmed and completed the witness which Jesus bore to him on earth" (par.3); so Jesus is "the Word of [...] God" (par.4).

> By the resurrection, in which he showed himself as the Father who is to be trusted even in death, God "reasserted his claim over the whole of creation" (par.3); so Jesus is the

Word "of the God [...] who brings into being what otherwise could not exist" (par.4).

By the raising of Jesus, God has "pardoned sinners" (par.3); so Jesus is the Word "of the God [...] who acquits the guilty" (par.4).

By the resurrection in which he inaugurated the life of the new creation announced in Jesus' preaching, God "made in Jesus a representative beginning of a new order of righteousness and love" (par.3); so Jesus is the Word "of the God [...] who gives life to the dead" (par.4).

(These quotations are taken from the final form of the *Basis of Union*.)

In this way, a concept of the Word of God can be developed that does not depend upon a prior, trinitarian doctrine of God.[15] That does not mean that the *Basis* is in any sense a rejection of the doctrine of the Trinity. (Only consider its reception of the ancient creeds and the place it gives to the Reformation confessions!) But it lays a foundation for a new approach to the doctrine of the Trinity through Jesus, who is the Word and revelation of God precisely as the resurrected Crucified One.

In the draft for Paragraph 4 of the present *Basis*, the continuity of the Church is confessed as a function of the continuing presence and activity of Jesus Christ with people in and through the news of his completed work. The last phrase is meant to bring out the once and for all character of Christ's death: "It is finished".[16] The way in which the Church's true continuity is seen here follows the line of my earlier paper of August 1961. It now seems to have been acceptable.

The words, "constitutes and continues, rules, reforms and renews", which survive in the *Basis of Union* as "constitutes, rules and renews" were conceived with the statement of the *Scots Confession* in mind, that God had

> [...] preserued, instructed, multipled, honoured, decored, and from death, called to lyfe, his kirk in all agis [...].[17]

But they are more directly an echo of the fifth Düsseldorf Thesis of 1933:

> The Church lives only from the fact that it is called and carried, comforted and ruled by its Lord every day anew.[18]

The way God is designated in this paragraph as "The God who [...]" is, of course, taken from Romans 4:5,17.

The paragraph beginning, "As forms of the Gospel [...]", tried, in its final sentence, to meet the request from the General Assembly of Australia for

> a statement clearly affirming the place of faith in the proper reception of the Sacraments to be added to the section "Concerning the Sacraments".[19]

It sought to ensure that faith would not be regarded as an independent human factor on which grace would depend for its efficacy. Rather, Christ would be seen to give, through sacraments as well as words, not only gifts, but also the faith and hope in which those gifts are received. For this, I vaguely had in mind part of the eighth Arnoldshain Thesis of 1957:

> Faith receives what is promised it and builds on this promise and not on its own deserts.[20]

There is a clearer echo of the second Thesis,

> In the Supper, Jesus Christ acts himself through what the Church is doing as the Lord present by his word in the Holy Spirit,

in the second sentence of the same Paragraph.

NOTES

1   Heinz Eduard Tödt, *Der Menschensohn in der synoptischen Überlieferung*, Gütersloh, Gerd Mohn, 1959. - The English translation is from the 2nd ed, 1963.

2   See Rudolf Bultmann, *Theologie des Neuen Testaments*, Tübingen, Mohr, [1]1953, [5]1965, S.30-32; - ET: *Theology of the New Testament*, voll.1-2, London, SCM, vol.1 1952, vol.2 1955, vol.1, pp.28-30; - Tödt, *Menschensohn*, S.15f,17f; - ET: pp.17f,20f.

3   Rudolf Bultmann, *Die Geschichte der synoptischen Tradition*, 5. Aufl., Göttingen, Vandenhoeck, 1961 (*FRLANT*, N.F. Heft 12), S.117,163; - ET: *The History of the Synoptic Tradition*, Oxford, Basil Blackwell, 1963, pp.112,151f. - Tödt, *Menschensohn*, S.206f; ET: pp.224-226.

4   Tödt, *Menschensohn*, S.50-56; - ET: pp.55-60.

5   Tödt, *Menschensohn*, S.210f; - ET: p.230.

6   Tödt, *Menschensohn*, S.244f; - ET: pp.268f. - The relevance of Tödt's research for the
    renewed interest in the question of the historical Jesus was early recognized in
    Hermann Diem, *Der irdische Jesus und der Christus des Glaubens*, Tübingen, Mohr,
    1957, S.15-19 (= *SGV*, 215); repr. in Helmut Ristow and Karl Matthiae, edd., *Der
    historische Jesus und der kerygmatische Christus [...]*, Berlin, Evangelische
    Verlagsanstalt, 21962, S.219-232, S.228-231; ET: H. Diem, "The Earthly Jesus and the
    Christ of Faith", in Carl E. Braaten & Roy A. Harrisville, edd., *Kerygma and History: A
    Symposium on the Theology of Rudolf Bultmann*, New York & Nashville, Abingdon,
    1962, pp.197-211, pp.207-209. (Tödt is not named in the original edition of Diem's
    paper nor in the English translation, but he is in Ristow and Matthiae, edd., ²1962.)

7   This book first appeared in German as a paperback, *Jesus von Nazareth*, Stuttgart,
    Kohlhammer, 1956 (*Urban-Bücher*, 19).

8   I had written on the 1st German edition, *Grundzüge der Christologie*, Gütersloh,
    Gerd Mohn, 1964.

9   Published in English as Ferdinand Hahn, *The Titles of Jesus in Christology: Their
    History in Early Christology*, London, Lutterworth, 1969.

10 Ernst Käsemann, "Das Problem des historischen Jesus", in E. Käsemann,
    Exegetische Versuche und Besinnungen, voll.1-2, vol.1, S.187-214.

11 The identification of the main strands in Jesus' teaching and preaching was greatly
    helped by Ernst Conzelmann, *Grundriss der Theologie des Neuen Testaments*, Kaiser,
    Munich, 1967 (= *Einführung in die evangelische Theologie*, Bd 2), S.118f, 143-146;
    ET: *An Outline of the Theology of the New Testament*, London, SCM, pp.99f,124-127.

12 See note 2 above. - Vol. 1 of the English edition seemed to be available before
    the German and I can remember Davis McCaughey referring to it in lectures in
    Melbourne in 1953.

13 Rudolf Bultmann, *Geschichte und Eschatologie*, Tübingen, Mohr, 1958.

14 Jürgen Moltmann, *Theologie der Hoffnung [...]*, Munich, Kaiser, ¹1964, ⁷1968. - I
    did not have a copy of this work before the end of December 1968. When Lawrie
    Staton saw it on my desk, he asked, "'Theology of Hoffnung'? Is that the German
    version of the 'Gospel according to Peanuts'?".

15 I have tried to expound this concept systematically in the introduction to *Witness
    of Faith [...]*, Melbourne, Uniting Church Press, 1984, pp.6-8, cf. also 8-11.

16 John 19:30; cf 17:4. - I recognize here the strong echo of an emphasis
    maintained by my Heidelberg teacher, Professor D. Peter Brunner.

17 *Scots Confession*, art.5. in *Witness of Faith*, p.65 (there modernized).

18 "Eine theologische Erklärung zur Gestalt der Kirche", in Wilhelm Niesel, ed.,
    Bekenntnisschriften und Kirchenordnungen der nach Gottes Wort reformierten Kirche,
    1938, repr. Zurich, Theologische Buchhandlung, 1985, S.327-328, S.327. - ET:
    "The Düsseldorf Theses, May, 1933", in Arthur C. Cochrane, *The Church's Confession
    under Hitler*, 2nd ed., Pittsburgh, Penn., Pickwick, 1976 (= *Pittsburgh Reprint
    Series*, 4), p.229.

19 *BB 1967*, min.48.4(d).

20 "The Arnoldshain Theses" (1957). Original in: Niemeier, G., et al., *Zur Lehre vom
    Heiligen Abendmahl. Bericht über das Abendmahlsgespräch der Evangelischen Kirche
    in Deutschland 1947-1957 und Erläuterungen seines Ergebnisses*, Munich, Kaiser,
    1958, S.15-18; - ET in"Report on the Conversations concerning Holy Communion
    in the German Evangelical Church", *The Ecumenical Review*, 11 (1958-59), pp.188-
    191; - also in "Doctrinal Consensus on Holy Communion", *Scottish Journal of
    Theology* 15 (1962), pp.1-35, pp.1-3.

Appendix C[1]

(Draft)

Accepting, by and large, the forms for the opening sections[2] suggested by working group 3,[3] but the [sc. with] the following questions:-

(i) The "Basis" must document an act of union. Would not the traditional "hereby" before "enter into union under the name of the Uniting Church of Australia" make that more clear?

(ii) Does "that hour at which the Kingdom of our Lord will be *manifest* in all the kingdoms of his world.." not sound too much like a *correction* of the Biblical passage?

(iii) Might it not be preferable for the second section to open like this?:-

"The Uniting Church seeks to live and work within the unity and fellowship of the One Holy Catholc [sic] and Apostolic Church and to confess......the fulness of the catholic faith."

Recalling the ecumenicl [sic] councils, etc... (as new para.).

We then continue as follows:-

The Uniting Church acknowledges that the life and unity of the Holy, Catholic and Apostolic Church do not rest in that Church itself, but in the one Lord Jesus Christ. For in him God has taken action to reconcile us men (and all things ?) to himself and to draw all things together again in him as Head. In love for the world, God gave his Son to take away the world's sin. Bowing to the judgment of God in our place, Jesus made the response of humility, obedience and trust which God had sought from us in vain. In raising him to live and reign by his own side, God has confirmed and completed as a true and faithful revelation of[4] himself the witness Jesus bore to him on earth, he has re-asserted his right over the whole of his old creation, has shown forth his pardoning righteousness for all the sinners whose condemnation Jesus bore and has made a representative new beginning of a whole new order of things in righteousness and love.[5]

The Church therefore acknowledges Jesus Christ not only as its own Lord[6], but as Head over all things and as the beginning of a new creation and a new mankind. It is as he reaches out to draw all parts of the old creation into the new life which he represents for it, that he (ever?anew) calls the Church into being as a partial embodiment of the promised universal reconciliation and renewal and as an earthly instrument through which he may work and bear witness to himself. To the being, the life and the mission which it receives from him there thus belong essential oneness and unity, to which it both may and must seek to give the fullest possible expression.

So the Church acknowledges that it is able to live and endure through the changing ages of history, solely because its Lord comes and bears witness to himself every day anew. For the same Jesus Christ who finished his ministry among us men in his death on our behalf and who was thereafter raised to share in the life and rule of the Father for evermore, continues to address and deal with us in and through the news of his completed work. The proclamation of the Gospel from one day to the next serves as a[7] form of[8] his continued presence and activity. Christ himself, present as preached among us, is the living and life-giving Word of the God who justifies the ungodly, raises the dead and calls into being things which do not exist. Through words of human witness and in the power of the Holy Spirit he reaches out to command men's attention and awaken their faith; he gathers them to form the people of God and unites them with himself as his own body; he constitutes and continues, rules, reforms and renews them as his Church.

As forms of the Gospel and expressions of his action through its word, Christ has instituted in his Church the two acts of Baptism and the Lord's Supper. In his grace he himself acts through what the Church does in obedience to his commandmanet [sic]. As in all that he does, his action is aimed at awakening, purifying and confirming men's faith in himself and the final benefits it conveys can be accepted only in faith and hope.

These two effective signs or sacraments of the Gospel accompany its proclamation by word of mouth. It shall be the normal rule of order in the Uniting Church that they shall not be performed apart from it and that the celebration of them shall be entrusted only to those who by ordination have received authority thereto.

Through Baptism Christ[9] incorporates men into his body through participation in his own baptism accomplished once on behalf of all in his death and burial and made available to all when, risen and ascended, he poured out the Holy Spirit at Pentecost. Baptism into Christ's body initiates men into his life and mission and so unites them in a fellowship of love and service, suffering and joy, under the universal name of the Father of heaven and earth and in the power of the Holy Spirit, promised for all flesh. (OR "promised to be poured out on all flesh.")[10]

Baptism, as the sign and seal of entry into the community of God's unbreakable covenant, is given only once. It shall be administered to those who confess the Christian[11] faith and to children[12] who are presented for Baptism and for whom the Church accepts[13] responsibility (OR: "for Baptism, for whom the Church must accept responsibility.")

(Then sedtion [sic] on Lord's Supper, revised.)

Charged with bearing witness to Jesus Christ in his relevance for every aspect of the world's life and every moment of its history, the Church is continually driven to find new forms in which to pass on the message it has received. In its concern to remain faithful to the substance of the messages [sic] in all the changes of its presentation it has come to discover a special value in the Scriptures of the Old and New Testaments. Their witness to God, the Father, the Son and the Holy Spirit, in his mighty acts in Jesus Christ, has proved to be a means by which Christ, the living Word of God, speaks to his Church each new day, to correct and control its message and to discipline and renew its life.

1   The text of my notes for some paragraphs of the *Basis of Union*, typed up in the vacation 1968-69 and passed on to Davis McCaughey.

2   The word "sections" was obviously inserted at the end of this line after "paragraphs" had been crossed out by x's at the beginning of the following line. We were already using 'paragraph' for the sections of the Basis, but it may have seemed ambiguous in this context.

3   A working group of the Joint Commission at the meeting of 27 - 30 November 1967, functioning in parallel to the one in which Davis and I and had participated, had revised the opening sections of the Proposed Basis of 1963, laying the foundations for Paragraphs 1 and 2 of the *Basis of Union*. The opening comments here refer to the text of this group's report and recommendations. The overall task was, of course, a revision of the Proposed Basis of Union of 1963.

4   The typescript reads "to", which I have corrected to "of" in the margin.

5   In the margin, I have written at this point, "Mention gift of Spirit at end of this para.?".

6   Before "Lord", "head" has been crossed out with x's.

7   In the typescript, "the" has been crossed out by hand and replaced by "a".

8   In the typescript, "for" has been changed by hand to "of".

9   Between the previous paragraph and this one beginning, "Through Baptism Christ", the words "By Baptism men" have been typed as the commencement of a new paragraph, but then crossed out by x's. - Compare this paragraph with the statement on Baptism in the Proposed Basis of 1963 (*Church*, p.79; Christian Unity, p.42).

10 Typed in the margin, "(Cf. Acts 2:38f.)".

11 Before "Christian", "child" has been typed and then crossed out with x's.

12 Originally "to infants who", then a question-mark was inserted between "infants" and "who", then "infants?" was crossed out by x's and "children" typed underneath.

13 Originally, "must accept", then "must" was crossed out by x's and an 's' was squeezed in after "accept".

VIII

Davis McCaughey went on to prepare a re-draft of the Basis of Union by March 1968. It was discussed by the Executive and circulated to members. I found that it contained, appropriately revised and simplified, a good part of my material for what are now the Paragraphs 3, 4 and 6. But I was not quite happy with the wording proposed for Paragraph 6,

> The Uniting Church acknowledges that Christ has commanded his Church to preach the Gospel in words and in the two acts of Baptism and the Lord's Supper. He himself acts in what the Church does in obedience to his commandment: he awakens, purifies and confirms men's faith in himself, and by the gift of the Holy Spirit enables men to receive the benefits so conveyed by faith and hope. These two effective signs or sacraments of the Gospel accompany its proclamation by word of mouth. The Uniting Church undertakes that the two sacraments will be observed with the unfailing use of the scriptural words of institution and of the elements ordained therein.

I therefore sent back a proposed rewording for the second sentence:

> He himself acts in and through what the Church does in obedience to his commandment: It is he who confers upon men the forgiveness, the fellowship, the new life and the freedom of which these actions hold promise and it is he who awakens, purifies and confirms in men the faith and hope in which alone such benefits can be accepted.

In explanation, I suggested

(a) that " He himself acts *in* what the Church does [...]" might appear to be tying the activity of Christ too closely to the actual performance of the Church's rites

(b) that "the gift of the Holy Spirit" might just as appropriately be mentioned in connexion with the fact that Christ " awakens, purifies and confirms men's faith in himself" as in the context of what follows. It might be better to leave the work of the

Spirit, which was already covered in Paragraphs 3, 4 and 7, implicit here, rather than mention it in too restrictive a way.

(c) On the other hand, although the " benefits so conveyed" were defined in appropriately differing ways in Paragraphs 7 and 8, not to identify them any further in Paragraph 6 resulted in a rather empty and repetitious sentence.

My (undated) letter to Davis, forwarding this and the rest of three foolscap pages of suggestions, shows that the material had reached me by surface mail and via a former address, leaving scarcely enough time for my reply before the meeting of the Commission. Davis was however able to feed at least the above suggestion into the discussion, as the final form of the *Basis* shows.

IX

The Commission's drafts before and after the meeting of May 1968 shows that the *Basis* was by then already beginning to assume its final format and much of its final form. Davis McCaughey was always very gracious about material or suggestions that I sent him. The last major thing was four-and-a-half pages of badly typed foolscap in response to his working paper for the meetings of the Commission, September-November 1968, on the "Problem of Church Law in the Basis of Union". I felt that I had been rather aggressive. Davis was his usual charming self in reply.

I then followed the further progress of the *Basis of Union* through the papers of the Joint Commission. It was published as:

> *Basis of Union being the final revision prepared by the Joint Commission on Church Union of the Congregational Churches of Australia, the Methodist Church of Australasia and the Presbyterian Church of Australia*, Melbourne, Aldersgate Press, 1970.

The front cover of the pamphlet had another title:

> *The Proposed Basis of Union for the Congregational Churches of Australia, the Methodist Church of Australia* [!] *and the Presbyterian Church of Australia 1970.*

It bore the emblems of the Congregational Churches of Australia, the Methodist Church of Australasia (although it printed its name as the Methodist Church of Australia), and the Presbyterian Church of ... Victoria!

The Presbyterian General Assembly of Australia met in September 1970 and received both the proposed Basis (1970) and a statement from the Joint Constitution Commission on Principles of Constitutional Structure and Practice proposed for the Uniting Church in Australia[1]. The Assembly agreed to forward these documents to State assemblies and presbyteries, together with certain comments that the Assembly was forwarding to the Joint Commission on Church Union. This material was sent both for the information of State assemblies and presbyteries and also with the request that they encourage study of the documents by ministers and communicant members.[2]

The comments that the Assembly forwarded to the Joint Commission on Church Union were initiated by the Revd Professor Crawford Miller, who moved three additional clauses of substance, two of which were approved, and one procedural one, which was also carried.[3] Crawford Miller had been involved as a consultant in the preparation of the Joint Commission's Second Report and the Proposed Basis of 1963.[4] He and his close friend and associate, Principal Alan Dougan, himself an alternate member of the Joint Commission from 1957 on and a member from 1962 to 1967, were disappointed by the churches' reactions to the Proposed Basis of 1963 and unable fully to accept the subsequent direction taken by the Commission's work. Their decision not to enter the Uniting Church will have been a further factor behind the relatively poor acceptance of the union in the Presbyterian Church in New South Wales. Crawford Miller's motion at the 1970 Assembly was aimed at ensuring that the *Basis of Union* would retain features that he considered central to the Presbyterian tradition.

The procedural clause moved by Crawford Miller and approved by the Assembly requested the Joint Commission

> to revise the proposed Basis of Union in the light of the foregoing affirmations[,][5]

meaning the affirmations expressed in the two substantive clauses that Crawford Miller had succeeded in getting carried. Faced with this request, the Joint Commission met again in November 1970 and revised the 1970 Basis, in an attempt to get it into a form acceptable to the Presbyterians before it came before the national councils of the other churches. The "Preface to the 1971 Edition" explains what has happened and identifies the points where revisions were undertaken.[6]

The first of the substantive clauses approved by the Assembly affirmed

> that agreement explicitly stated in the Basis of Union regarding the terms of subscription by ministers and

office-bearers to the Faith and Order of the proposed Uniting Church, liberty of opinion on matters which do not enter into the substance of the Faith being explicitly provided for, is an essential prior condition of entering the Union.[7]

The 1970 Basis of Union had stated that ministers, elders or leaders, deaconesses, and accredited lay preachers or local preachers of the uniting churches would be accepted into equivalent status in the Uniting Church, provided that they were in good standing and adhered to the *Basis of Union*.[8] It was nowhere spelled out what such adherence was supposed to mean. It had seemed to the Presbyterian Assembly that this would leave the way open for very strict or very lax interpretations of the requirement; and past Presbyterian history would naturally create an expectation that provisions for adherence and subscription to the Church's faith and order would be carefully formulated.[9] We note that the Assembly saw the matter as serious enough for it to say that getting it explicitly provided for was "an essential prior condition of entering the Union".

Presbyterian ministers had, in response to questions asked at both ordinations and inductions, to engage "firmly and constantly to adhere" to

the *Westminster Confession of Faith* read in the light of the Declaratory Statement contained in the Basis of Union adopted by this Church on the 24th day of July, 1901[,]

and to the Presbyterian form of government.[10] On the same occasions, they were also required to sign "the Formula", in which they committed themselves firmly and constantly to adhere to the

Subordinate Standard of this Church [...], the purity of worship practised in this Church, and the Presbyterian government thereof [...].[11]

The "Subordinate Standard" of the Presbyterian Church was defined as "the *Westminster Confession of Faith* read in the light of the Declaratory Statement and amended" by the Church at certain points.[12] The Declaratory Statement[13] offered some clarification and balance with regard to a number of the more demandingly Calvinistic elements in the *Westminster Confession* and declared,

> That liberty of opinion is allowed on matters in the Subordinate Standard not essential to the doctrine therein taught, the Church guarding against the abuse of this liberty to the injury of its unity and peace.[14]

It is interesting to note that the Assembly had the power to revise the "Subordinate Standard of the Church" (i.e., the *Westminster Confession of Faith* read in the light of the Declaratory Statement) and it had the power to change the Formula, but it had no power to amend the Declaratory Statement itself.[15] The Assembly was thus identifying in the proposed Basis of Union (1970) the lack of something that had, since 1901, formed an unalterable element in the Basis of Union of the Presbyterian Church of Australia.

In response to the request from the Assembly, the Joint Commission added to the text of Paragraph 14 of the *Basis*, the paragraph,

> In the above sub-paragraphs the phrase "adhere to the Basis of Union" is understood as willingness to live and work within the faith and unity of the One Holy Catholic and Apostolic Church as that way is described in this Basis. Such adherence allows for difference of opinion in matters which do not enter into the substance of the faith.

The second of the substantive clauses carried by the Assembly affirmed,

> that the proposed Basis of Union fails to adhere with sufficient precision of statement to certain fundamental points of the Faith and Order accepted in this Church [...].[16]

The same clause went on to identify five specific points of concern:

(a) The first point related to the Scriptures:

> There is no explicit statement that Holy Scripture contains all things necessary for salvation, and is "the unique earthly instrument through which the Church

hears the living Word, and the decisive measure by which her life on earth is tested and through which it is renewed".

Here, the Assembly was recurring to statements in the Proposed Basis of Union of 1963,[17] which it regretted no longer finding in the Basis of Union of 1970.

In response, the Joint Commission made the following changes:

(i) Inserting the word 'unique' into the opening sentence of Paragraph 5, so that it reads,

> The Uniting Church acknowledges that the Church has received the books of the Old and New Testaments as unique prophetic and apostolic testimony, in which she hears the Word of God and by which her faith and obedience are nourished and regulated (1971).

(ii) Changing the beginning of the third sentence of Paragraph 5 from

> The Word of God addressed to men is to be heard and known from Scripture [...] (1970)

to

> The Word of God on whom man's salvation depends is to be heard and known from Scripture [...] (1971).

The Commission remarked in the "Preface to the 1971 Edition" that[18]

(i) the insertion of 'unique' would

> [...] make doubly clear the authoritative character of the canon of Holy Scripture;

and that

(ii) the wording "on whom man's salvation depends" does two things:

it helps to tie Paragraph 5 to Paragraph 4, where Christ is referred to as the Word of God. What is preached from Scripture is the personal sovereign Christ [...]. Moreover, the revision makes clear that what is to be found as the centre of Scripture is not random information on a number of subjects, but the Word of God on whom *man's salvation depends*.[19]

(b) The second specific point of Faith and Order raised by the Assembly was the lack of an unambiguous affirmation of the fundamental Reformation doctrine that

the whole work of man's salvation is effected by the sovereign Grace of God alone.

Here, too, the Assembly was identifying a statement of the 1963 Proposed Basis of Union[20] that was no longer explicitly contained in the 1970 Basis.

The Joint Commission met this concern by inserting that very sentence at the end of the second paragraph of Paragraph 3 (except for preferring a small 'g' for 'grace'). In the Preface, it emphasized that it did not wish to be understood as "adding a point which is strange to the rest of the document".

It [sc. the Commission] is, at the request of one of the negotiating churches, summarizing what might be said to be "the basis of *The Basis*".[21]

Nevertheless, my later Perth colleague, the Revd Bill Ellis, used to complain both of the substance of this addition to the *Basis of Union* and of the way in which the Presbyterians had been able to insist on this and other changes to the 1970 Basis. He regarded it as an extreme Calvinist statement unacceptable to many Methodists (with what justification, I am not at all sure).

(c) The third point raised concerned the opening sentences of Paragraphs 7 and 8, where, in the judgment of the Assembly, the use of the indefinite article [...] - "The Uniting Church receives Baptism as *an* act -"; "The Uniting Church receives the Lord's Supper - as *an* act -"; on a strict reading is open to the interpretation that the observance of these sacraments is in principle optional.

The Commission restructured the opening sentences of both of these Paragraphs. In Paragraph 7,

The Uniting Church receives Baptism as an act in which Christ incorporates men into his body (1970)

became

The Uniting Church acknowledges that Christ incorporates men into his body by Baptism (1971).

A parallel change was made to the opening of Paragraph 8. On these changes, the Commission commented:

The revision has the advantage of making absolutely clear that it is Christ who is the chief minister in these sacraments, incorporating, signifying and sealing.[22]

The two final points of Faith and Order identified by the Assembly were closely connected, and related to:

(d) Ministers' freedom to exercise the authority given them by their ordination:

Freedom for ministers to exercise the unique ministerial authority conferred upon them by Christ in ordination, both individually as pastors of congregations, and as lawfully associated in the Councils of the Church is inadequately recognized and safeguarded.

(e) The character and authority of the Ministry:

There is insufficient stress upon the unique character and authority of the office of the Holy Ministry as given by Christ in ordination as the act by which Christ confers participation in this unique ministry through the laying on of hands of his ordained servants.

The ministry referred to here is that of the "Ministers of the Word" who, according to the Basis of Union (1970), were to be called "Ministers" (because the uniting churches had opted for this, rather than the "Presbyters" of the Proposed Basis of Union of 1963).

In response to these concerns,

(i) the Joint Commission expanded the sentence in Paragraph 14, sub-paragraph (a)

> She [sc. the Uniting Church] prays to God that through Christ and in the power of the Holy Spirit he will call and set apart members of the Church to be ministers of the Word, who will preach the Gospel, administer the sacraments, and exercise pastoral care (1970)

into the fuller statement

> Since the Church lives by the power of the Word, she is assured that God, who has never left himself without witness to that Word, will, through Christ and in the power of the Holy Spirit, call and set apart members of the Church to be ministers of the Word. These will preach the Gospel, administer the sacraments, and exercise pastoral care so that all may be equipped for their particular ministries, thus maintaining the apostolic witness to Christ in the Church (1971).

The Joint Commission explained in its Preface that this

> greater elucidation of the character of the ministry of Word and Sacrament was prompted by a desire to stress the faithfulness of God in maintaining a continuous witness to Christ,

since the time of the apostles, calling men to this ministry [...].

Paragraph 13 could still be seen as setting this ministry of the Word "within the corporate priesthood of the whole Church" (and the added statement about equipping all the members of the Church for their particular ministries also served to tie the service of the Word back into the community of the many diverse ministries of the preceding Paragraph). But

> It was felt necessary to stress the distinctive character of the ministry of Word and Sacrament: to the maintenance of this ministry the Uniting Church will be committed.[23]

(ii) The Joint Commission inserted a new paragraph into 14 (a), greatly expanding the reference to Ordination. It was now stated that Ordination was to be carried out by the Presbytery, by prayer and the laying on of hands, in the presence of a worshipping congregation. It was also said that, in the act of ordination, the Church

- praises the ascended Christ for conferring gifts on people,

- recognizes Christ's call of the ordinand to be his minister, and

- prays for the enabling power of the Holy Spirit to equip the ordinand for service.

The Church also, by the participation in the act of ordination of those already ordained,

- bears witness to God's faithfulness, and

- declares the hope by which it lives.

The Joint Commission had previously been hesitant to say anything about how ordination was to be done or what it meant. That was because

[...] in every part of the Christian Church the understanding of ordination is being investigated afresh.

The Joint Commission therefore let the new paragraph on ordination end with a commitment for the Uniting Church, "in company with other Christians",

> to seek for a renewed understanding of the way in which the congregation participates in ordination and of the significance of ordination in the life of the Church.[24]

Through its response to the last two points of concern raised by the Presbyterian Assembly, the Joint Commission had therefore considerably strengthened what was said in the *Basis* about the ordained ministry of the Word, partly reinforcing what it had already said in the the 1970 edition, but also going on to make new statements about Ordination. The Commission had used its freedom in working out its response. For instance, the explicit identification of the Presbytery as the ordaining body had not been requested by the Presbyterian Assembly, but was both an effective way of meeting an aspect of the Assembly's concern and a logical further step in the Commission's development of the *Basis*.

I had been a member of the Assembly in 1970, but then left for a year's study leave. At the Assembly, I was appointed a member of the Joint Commission, but I did not attend any meeting of it as a member, due to my absence from the country.

Subsequent to its meeting in November 1970, the Joint Commission published the *Basis of Union* in its final form,

> *Basis of Union being the 1971 revision by the Joint Commission on Church Union of the Congregational Union of Australia, the Methodist Church of Australasia and the Presbyterian Church of Australia*, Melbourne, Aldersgate Press, 1971.

The cover was now entitled

The Basis of Union for the Congregational Union of Australia, the Methodist Church of Australasia and the Presbyterian Church of Australia, as revised 1971

and it had the emblem of the General Assembly and Presbyterian Church of Australia, along with the correct emblems for the other two churches.

The General Assembly of Australia met again in December 1971, received the proposed *Basis of Union* 1971 and remitted it to State general assemblies and presbyteries under the formal procedure of the Barrier Act,[25] thus initiating what was to prove to be a rather difficult process of Presbyterian approval for the completed *Basis of Union*.

NOTES

1 This document was required under the new basis of union of the Presbyterian Church of Australia (cf. *BB 1970*, min.30, sec.15, p.29) and had been requested by the Assembly. The text of the document may be found, *BB 1970*, pp.100-102.

2 *BB 1970*, min.61.1.

3 *BB 1970*, min.60.

4 *Church*, p.5; Christian Unity, p.4.

5 *BB 1970*, min.61.4.

6 *Basis of Union being the 1971 revision by the Joint Commission on Church Union of the Congregational Union of Australia, the Methodist Church of Australasia and the Presbyterian Church of Australia*, Melbourne, Aldersgate Press, 1971, pp.6-8. - "Of all except one of the revisions, the Commission members felt that they were being asked to make clearer what was to them already clear. If, however, the points were not sufficiently clear to others, then they ought to be made clear, for they are important points; and the Commission is glad to try to do so" (*ibid.*, p.6). - The changes made for the 1971 *Basis of Union* are shown in the critical apparatus in *Witness of Faith*, p.33. The raised figure at the end of line 3 of p.28 should be 3, not 2.

7 *BB 1970*, min.61.2.

8 *Basis of Union (1970)*, par.14 (a), (b), (c), (d).

9 This is illustrated by such a work as James Cooper, *Confessions of Faith and Formulas of Subscription in the Reformed Churches of Great Britain and Ireland especially in the Church of Scotland[,] being a Series of Lectures delivered to Students of Church History [...]*, Glasgow, James Maclehose & Sons, 1907.

10 "Questions at the Ordination or Induction of Ministers: Questions for the Minister-elect", Questions ii. and iv., in Presbyterian Church of Australia, *Constitution and Procedure and Practice [...]*, Melbourne, Board of Religious Education of the General Assembly of Australia, 1950, p.62.

11 The "Formula to be signed by Ministers at their ordination or induction, and by

Probationers on receiving licence" is found *Constitution and Procedure and Practice*, p.24.

12 *Constitution and Procedure and Practice*, p.20.

13 The text of the Declaratory Statement is found *Constitution and Procedure and Practice*, pp.21-23 (= 114.-119. or [i] - [vi]).

14 *Constitution and Procedure and Practice*, pp.22f.

15 *Constitution and Procedure and Practice*, p.23.

16 *BB 1970*, min.61.3.

17 *Church*, pp.77f; - Christian Unity, p.41. - Cf *Faith*, p.34; 1978, p.36. - For the Presbyterian background, see the *Westminster Confession*, I.v-vii.

18 *Basis of Union being the 1971 revision*, pp.6-8.

19 *Basis of Union being the 1971 revision*, p.6.

20 "The Uniting Church affirms as the teaching of Holy Scripture that the whole work of man's salvation is effected by the sovereign grace of God alone" (*Church*, p.78; - Christian Unity, p.42).

21 *Basis of Union being the 1971 revision*, p.6.

22 *Basis of Union being the 1971 revision*, p.7.

23 *Basis of Union being the 1971 revision*, p.7.

24 *Basis of Union being the 1971 revision*, p.7.

25 *BB 1971*, min.28.1.

Excursus

Bases of Union in History

In this excursus, we are going to review a number of documents that have served as the foundations for unions between churches, each of which has been termed a "basis of union". Our specific purpose is to explore the background to the request of the General Assembly of the Presbyterian Church of Australia in 1954 that its Christian Unity Committee collaborate with the corresponding committees of the Congregational and Methodist Churches to prepare a possible basis of union for the three churches, for submission to the Assembly at its next meeting.[1] The questions that we are seeking to answer are: Why did the Assembly respond to renewed proposals for church union in this particular way? What did it expect a basis of union to cover and what functions did it expect it to perform? What experiences and memories did the Presbyterian Church bring to the project of negotiating a union with Methodists and Congregationalists? What things were going to be important or vital to it? The answers to such questions will, of course, help us understand, not only the General Assembly's initial approach to the issue of church union, but ways in which Presbyterians responded to successive drafts for a basis of union through the course of the negotiations.

Most of the examples we shall look at come from unions between different Presbyterian churches with far more in common than the three denominations contemplating union in Australia in the 1950's (although we must never forget how keenly particular differences between them used to be felt). At various points of time, groups had separated from the established Church of Scotland and formed the Reformed Presbyterian Church in Scotland (1690), the Secession Church in Scotland (1733), the Relief Church in Scotland (1761) and the Free Church of Scotland (1843).[2] The Secession Synod subsequently split into "Burgher" and "Anti-Burgher" synods (1747), which each divided, in its turn

(1799, 1806), into "Auld Licht" and "New Licht" segments. Over the years, reunion took place between these churches in Scotland, and also between off-shoots of them in other lands. The outcomes of such unions include:

(a)   The Associate Reformed Synod of North America, 1782

A very early instance of reunion was the formation of the Associate Reformed Synod of North America by the union of the Reformed Presbytery in America, all but two of the ministers of the Associate (Anti-Burgher) Presbytery of Pennsylvania, and two ministers connected with the Burgher Synod in Scotland. This union took place on 30 October 1782, i.e. shortly after the War of Independence. According to McKerrow, the basis of union was the *Westminster Confession* and *Catechisms*, except for the parts on the powers of civil government in religious affairs. Particular articles of union dealt with the united church's relation to the *National Covenant* (1638) and *Solemn League and Covenant* (1643), and the principle of free communion.[3] "Free communion", i.e. the occasional admission to communion of members in good standing from other denominations, was considered to be in accordance with the *Confession of Faith* (cap.XXVI.ii).

To understand what was involved in this union and, indeed, in much of the whole history of divisions and reunion, we need to note some of the historical background. In the 1630's, Charles I had been trying to bring the Scottish church into conformity with the Anglo-Catholicism of William Laud, Archbishop of Canterbury. By the *National Covenant* of 1638,[4] the Scottish parliament, church and people bound themselves, to "continue in the profession and obedience of the [true reformed] religion", to "defend the same, and resist all these contrary errors and corruptions", and also to "stand to the defence of our dread sovereign the King's Majesty" (this last suggesting an intention of nothing more than "loyal opposition" to the policies of the King's ministers). They also expressed the conviction that "the present and succeeding generations in this land are bound to keep the foresaid national oath and subscription inviolable". Of this covenant, Burleigh writes that it was "as truly national as any such document can ever be".[5]

In the subsequent Civil War in England, when the English Parliament sought military assistance against the King, the Scots would only comply on the condition of agreement on a common policy in religious affairs. This took the form of the *Solemn League and Covenant* of 1643,[6] negotiated between commissioners of the Scottish General Assembly and Convention of Estates[7] and of the English Parliament and Westminster Assembly of Divines (which was effectively an advisory committee of Parliament). The *Solemn League* was approved by the General Assembly of the Church of Scotland, by the Parliament of England and by the Convention of the Estates of Scotland.[8] On their authority, it was to be "taken and subscribed by all Ranks" in their kingdoms.

As the primary commitment, all who subscribed to the *Solemn League and Covenant* swore to strive for "the preservation of the reformed religion in the Church of Scotland, in doctrine, worship, discipline, and government" and "the reformation of religion in the kingdoms of England and Ireland, in doctrine, worship, discipline, and government, according to the word of GOD, and the example of the best reformed Churches". They also committed themselves to endeavour "to bring the Churches of God in the three kingdoms to the nearest conjunction and uniformity in religion, confession of faith, form of church-government, directory for worship and catechizing". The documents produced by the Westminster Assembly, with participation by eleven commissioners from the Church of Scotland, were intended as the basis for this uniformity.

Two things assumed here are (i) that, under the Gospel, there is one universal, visible church, of which particular churches (such as those in each of the three kingdoms) are branches,[9] and (ii) that rulers have authority and responsibility for promoting and protecting the true religion. This derived from what was expected from, and praised in, kings in the Old Testament.[10] It also has to be understood against the background of the social and political intertwinings of church and feudal system, church and Holy Roman Empire, in the centuries leading up to the Reformation. How were national churches to be reformed, unless rulers were prepared to assume the role of modern Josiahs? Both of these assumptions reflected, by and large, the position of the mainline reformers. The point of the Covenants was, then, that the reformation and preservation of religion was to be the task of governments that had solemnly bound themselves to uphold the true religion and suppress all false religion.

The *Solemn League and Covenant* was, at one level, a treaty between kingdoms that happened to have a king in common, and problems, with that king. In Scotland, it was also a concordat between the General Assembly and the Estates of Parliament. At another level again, it called for the personal subscription and adherence of individuals in all ranks of society. The consensus that it initially represented was, however, unable to withstand the strains of changing situations. The Scots tended to feel greater loyalty towards the Stuart kings than the English did; and they soon began to fall into opposing parties over the relative importance of strict adherence to the religious commitment of the Covenants and of reaching some understanding with Charles I or Charles II. The victory of the English Army made it the greatest power in the land. It was not in sympathy with the pro-Presbyterian policies of the English Parliament. Defeating the supporters of Charles II, it stayed on as an army of occupation in Scotland.[11]

Scots and English Presbyterians supported the Restoration of the Stuarts in 1660, but were disappointed by the policies of Charles II and James II.[12] Persecution of those in Scotland who held out for the full programme of the Covenants and gathered in conventicles for worship in the open-air led to their offering armed resistance to the Government.[13] The Revolution of 1688 and the accession of William and Mary were followed, in 1690, by the establishment of Presbyterianism in Scotland, but in a way that did not meet all the aims of the Covenanters.[14] The situation was aggravated by the union of the two kingdoms in 1707. For, from that time, the civil power with which the established Church of Scotland had to do was a Parliament meeting in London, in which the Scottish representatives were a minority and which had "prelates" of the Church of England sitting in its upper house.[15] In 1712, that Parliament, without consulting the Church, passed the *Patronage Act*, which restored the rights of land-owners to present persons for settlement in parishes of the Church of Scotland and so created the prospect of conflict over the rights of congregations and the powers of presbyteries.[16]

The Reformed Presbytery in America had been constituted in 1774 by four ministers sent out as missionaries by the Reformed Presbyterian Church in Scotland. Their tradition came from the Covenanters, through the Cameronians who had refused to go with the Church of Scotland in the Revolution Settlement of 1690, on the grounds that too little of the programme of the Covenants was realized in that settlement. The Reformed Presbyterians in Scotland refused to accept the legitimacy of the British government, because they held it to be in breach of covenant, and they did not rule out the possibility of pursuing their religious goals by force of arms. During the War of Independence, those in America supported the revolutionary cause and most came to have a far more positive attitude towards the new government of the United States and to realize how much they had in common with the Associate Church groups.

These other two groups involved in the union stemmed from the Secession of 1733, in which ministers left the established Church of Scotland because its courts acquiesced in the intrusion of ministers into congregations, without the consent of those congregations, and were seen as lax against heresy and in the exercise of discipline. The Seceders sought to uphold the spiritual heritage of the Covenants, but insisted on subjection to the government in earthly affairs. They distanced themselves from passages in the *Westminster Confession* that seemed to provide a basis for intolerance and religious persecution. Burghers and Anti-Burghers had divided from each other over an oath by which burgesses of some towns were required to acknowledge the established religion as the true religion. The Associate Presbytery of Pennsylvania, subordinate to the Associate (Anti-Burgher) Synod of Scotland, was organized in 1754. A further presbytery, of New York, was formed in 1776, but did not find approval from the parent body in Scotland, which was concerned at the prospect of a rapprochement between Anti-Burghers and Burghers in America.[17]

This union of 1782 came about because groups from opposing traditions in Scotland found that, in a new environment and under changed political circumstances, what they had in common was more relevant than what had been holding them apart. The Anti-Burgher Synod in Scotland disapproved of the union and sent more ministers to Pennsylvania to replace those who had entered into it.[18] Some Reformed Presbyterian groups also refused to enter the united church. The continuing Associate and Reformed presbyteries were among the first church groups in the United States to take a clear stand against slave-ownership. In 1858, the Associate Church and the Associate Reformed Church entered into union under the name of the United Presbyterian Church of North America.[19]

(b) The United Secession Church, 1820

In 1820, the two main sections of the fragmented Secession Church, the Associate (Burgher) Synod and the General Associate (Anti-Burgher) Synod joined to form the united synod of a United Secession Church, on a basis of union consisting of a preface and six articles numbered from I to VI.[20] The preface disposed of the issue on which Burghers and Anti-Burghers had split. The articles dealt with (i) the Word of God contained in the Scriptures as the only rule of faith and manners; (ii) the *Westminster Confession* and *Catechisms* as the confession of the church's faith and as showing how it understood the Scriptures, with a proviso disapproving anything in the documents that might support intolerance or persecution; (iii) Presbyterian church government, as founded on, and agreeable to, the Word of God, with the *"Directory"*[21] acknowledged to be a "compilation of excellent rules"; (iv) the continuing validity of the grounds of secession; (v) the obligation to maintain the Reformation heritage and the practice of covenanting (without deriving that obligation from the seventeenth century covenants, and also conceding that the practice of covenanting only became a moral duty when the "circumstances of providence" required it); (vi) provision for a "formula" of questions as a way for office-bearers to commit themselves to all the above.

The Secession Church had commenced, not with a basis of union, but with grounds for seceding from the established church and the principle of separating from those with whom one differed on matters of principle. This is probably why, over three-quarters of a century, it had split into four bodies. For it had to work through a number of important issues and kept discovering that its leadership was less agreed on fundamentals than it had supposed. In its relation to the Covenants and *Westminster Confession* and *Catechisms*, it had to grow out of a nostalgic attachment to a Golden Age of Presbyterianism and to find criteria for distinguishing between what it was still bound to uphold and what it was no longer able to answer for. In particular, it needed to detach itself from the Reformers' view of the role of the Christian ruler in reforming the Church and maintaining it in its purity. Despite its conservative stance, it took a lead in some important reappraisals.

The two synods that came into this union of 1820 were the major, "New Licht", elements in the Burgher and Anti-Burgher synods. The corresponding "Auld Licht" groups had been unable to go all the way in rethinking the churches' relation to the Covenants and to the Westminster teaching on the power of the civil government in religious affairs. The "Auld Licht" Burghers rejoined the established church in 1839, and the "Auld Licht" Anti-Burghers united with the Free Church in 1852. A remnant of the latter group, which continued as the United Original Secession Church, was reunited with the Church of Scotland in 1956.[22]

(c) The United Presbyterian Church, 1847

In 1847, the synods of the United Secession Church and the Relief Church combined to form the United Presbyterian Church on a basis of union consisting of ten numbered articles,[23] dealing with (i) the Word of God and (ii) the *Westminster Confession* and *Catechisms*, all substantially as in 1820; (iii) Presbyterian church government, without mention of a standard text; (iv) the ordinances of worship, which were to be administered as hitherto in either church, with the *Directory of Public Worship* as a "compilation of excellent rules"; (v) the condition for membership in the church; (vi) authorization for ministers and elders to act on their conscientious convictions with regard to free communion; (vii) all communicant members, and only they, to elect office-bearers in congregations; (viii) the church's evangelistic and missionary obligations; (ix) the obligation and privilege of members' supporting and extending the ordinances of the Gospel by voluntary contributions; (x) the continuing validity of seceding; thanksgiving for what God had done through the Secession and Relief churches, penitence for imperfections and sins, and new resolution to be more watchful; a feeling of brotherhood with all faithful followers of Christ and willingness to strive to maintain the unity of his body by co-operating with all its members in everything in which they were agreed.[24]

The Relief Church, too, had begun with a secession from the established church over the intrusion into an unwilling congregation of a minister nominated by a patron. It was never as conservative as the Secession Church and had always been opposed to intolerance. It brought the practice of free communion with it into the union. The resultant United Presbyterian Church put emphasis on the participation of the laity in its life. It came to have a Voluntaryist stance, opposed to established churches in principle. It resembled the English free churches in ethos, depended on self-supporting congregations, undertook little in church extension, but a great deal, in overseas missions.

(d)   The Presbyterian Church of Victoria, 1859

The Presbyterian Church of Victoria was formed on 7 April 1859, as a union of the Synod of Victoria (connected with the Church of Scotland), the Free Church Synod, and the Synods of the United Presbyterian Church of Victoria and the United Presbyterian Church of Australia.[25]

Free Church bodies in Australia had arisen through the Disruption of the Church of Scotland, and consequent formation of the Free

Church of Scotland, in 1843. The unwillingness of the Scottish churches to allow the Australians to remain neutral forced a similar division in the Australian church connected with the Church of Scotland.[26] There thus came to be a third type of Presbyterianism in Australia, alongside the Church of Scotland and United Presbyterian traditions.

Through the "Ten Year's Conflict" leading up to the Disruption, an Evangelical majority in the General Assembly had been seeking to resolve old and new issues facing the Church in Scotland. In 1834, the General Assembly tried, by the Veto Act, to meet the gravest objections to the system of patronage. The act provided that, if a majority of the male heads of families in communion with a congregation registered objection to a minister nominated by a patron, a presbytery was to treat that as sufficient grounds for not proceeding to settle that minister in the parish. In the same year, the General Assembly sought, by the Chapels Act, to regularize the position of chapels and ministerial appointments in new areas not adequately covered by the old parish churches. This was part of an energetic programme of church extension to meet the changing needs of Victorian Scotland. Judgments in civil courts not only disallowed both of these acts, but did so in terms that radically denied the power of the church to enact any independent legislation or exercise any independent jurisdiction in such matters.[27] Faced with these judgments, the General Assembly of 1838 approved a resolution in which it asserted that, independently of the civil courts and without detriment to their authority in temporal affairs, the Church possessed a jurisdiction of its own in spiritual matters, deriving from Jesus Christ, the sole Head of the Church.[28] In 1842, it adopted a "Claim of Right" in which it argued this position out at length.[29] Failing to obtain any response to this from the Government, many ministers and elders left the next Assembly, before it had been constituted, tabling a protest as they went,[30] and proceeded to form the Free Church of Scotland.

The Free Church set out to function as a national church, extending ministry to all situations in which ministry was needed. It provided manses and churches for ministers and congregations that had become homeless when they left the established church. Since all foreign missionaries of the Church of Scotland sided with the Free Church, it had to pick up a full overseas mission programme, as well. The example of the great number who had been prepared to walk out into insecurity on a matter of principle stimulated voluntary giving and donations to a level that allowed significant achievements within a short period of time. Since each side in the Scottish Disruption refused to accept a "milk and water" neutrality on the part of Australian Presbyterians, it was inevitable that some in Australia left the body identified with the Church of Scotland to form a Free Church synod.

The United Presbyterian Synod of Victoria had been organized in 1850. The Synod of Australia was a small group that had broken away from it.[31] There was also a split in the Free Church synod in the course of the union negotiations. These were drawn-out and complex, for it was the first union in the world to bring together bodies representing the three main streams of Scottish Presbyterianism. Of the two groups that had separated from the established church, the U.P.'s were opposed to establishment and to State-aid for religion. The Free Church held to the view that rulers were supposed to support the true faith and the true church, but not Papists, heretics or sectaries. They would accept an established church, but only one that enjoyed complete independence in spiritual matters. In the united General Assembly of the Presbyterian Church of Victoria in April 1859, 20 ministers came from the Synod of Victoria, 27 from the Free Church Synod, four from the U.P. Synod of Victoria, and four from the U.P. Synod of Australia.[32]

The Victorian basis of union[33] consisted of a preface, articles numbered I - III, and the formula to be signed by office-bearers.[34] The articles of the union were concerned with (i) the *Westminster Confession of Faith, Catechisms, Form of Church Government, and Directory of Public Worship* and the *Second Book of Discipline* (1578), as the "Standards and Formularies" of the united church; (ii) a declaration that, given a difference of opinion regarding the teaching of the Standards on the power and duty of the civil government in matters of religion, office-bearers subscribing those documents were not to be held as approving persecuting or intolerant principles or professing anything inconsistent with liberty of conscience and the right of private judgment; (iii) the Synod's separate and independent character as a church and its supreme jurisdiction as a court, and the principle that all ministers and probationers from other Presbyterian churches would be received "on an equal footing" and become subject "to its authority alone".

The second article echoed the preamble to an act of the Free Church of Scotland General Assembly from 1846.[35] It will have been of vital importance to the United Presbyterians entering the union, as well as Free Church people. However, some from the U.P. Synod of Victoria remained out of the union, as did the splinter group from the Free Church, the two bodies over opposite principles connected with State support for churches. The continuing Free Church sent a representative to Scotland, to seek recognition from the mother church, but, in 1861, the latter's general assembly, came out strongly in support of the union in Victoria.[36] With encouragement from the Scottish Free Church, and through the efforts of Dr Oswald Dykes, who was living in Melbourne at that time,[37] the Presbyterian Church of Victoria was, by 1867, able to bring all but one of the Free Church dissentients into its fellowship. The continuing U.P. group found itself able to join the united church in 1870, when the Victorian government ceased giving assistance to the churches.[38]

(e)   The Presbyterian Church of New South Wales, 1864

By certain stages, in New South Wales, union took place between the Synod of Australia (connected with the Church of Scotland), the Synod of Eastern Australia (the Free Church synod), the Synod of New South Wales ("Dr Lang's Synod") and a United Presbyterian congregation, the final consummation taking place on 15 November 1864.[39]

The basis of union[40] consisted of four articles, concerning: (i) the designations of the united church, "The Presbyterian Church of New South Wales", and of its General Assembly; (ii) the Word of

God as contained in the Scriptures, much as in (b) and (c) above; (iii) the "subordinate standards" of the united church, naming the same documents as in the first Victorian article; and (iv) explanation concerning how the united church received each of those documents: (1) Every office-bearer would have to testify personal adherence to the *Confession of Faith*; the Catechisms were sanctioned as "Directories for catechizing"; the other documents were "of the nature of regulations, rather than of tests"; (2) the church was not to be held to be "countenancing intolerant or persecuting principles, or any denial or invasion of the right of private judgment"; (3) the church was spiritually independent and, in its own affairs, not subject to the jurisdiction or interference of the civil power; (4) the united church asserted its independence vis-à-vis other churches and the supreme and final authority of its highest court; (5) the church would receive qualified and eligible ministers and probationers from other churches, subject to their signing the "Formula". The first three of these explanatory clauses clearly reflect the influence of the Free Church.[41]

(f)   The United Free Church of Scotland, 1900

The union in Victoria and similar steps in Nova Scotia (1860), Canada (1861) and New Zealand (1862) were among factors that led the Scottish United Presbyterian and Free Churches to commence union negotiations in 1863.[42] These were not initially successful, but a fresh start was made in 1896 and, in 1900, the two churches joined to form the United Free Church.[43]

Those who formed the Free Church had not sympathized with the Voluntaryist campaign mounted from within the Secession and Relief churches in the 1830's. It was largely their differing views on establishment that frustrated the negotiations between the United Presbyterian and Free Churches in the 1860's.[44] Later, around 1875, against the objections of the more conservative in the Free Church, the two churches joined in the movement for disestablishment. That was, above all, in response to the action of the Government and the established church in bringing about the repeal of the Patronage Act, without any recognition of the position of those in other churches who had made considerable sacrifices for their opposition to patronage. Disestablishment could also be presented as the removal of an obstacle to the reunion of the various Presbyterian churches in Scotland. It was certainly in keeping with the liberal spirit of the times and its opposition to any form of privilege.[45] Politically, disestablishment was not to be achieved, but the campaign brought Free Church people and U.P.'s closer together and smoothed the way for the union of 1900. That was then further helped by a subsequent waning of the cause of disestablishment and changes in attitude towards the established church among members of the United Presbyterian Church.[46]

A union had already taken place in 1876 between the Free Church and the smaller Reformed Presbyterian Church.[47]

The unions in 1876 and 1900 do not seem to have involved any document literally referred to as a "basis of union".[48] The Uniting Act of the Free Church and United Presbyterian Church does, however, speak of the proposals submitted to the courts of the two churches as, at different stages, "providing a satisfactory scheme for an incorporating Union of the two Churches" and setting forth a "plan of Union". The Act lists the range of issues covered in those proposals and concludes with four "Declarations anent Union".[49] The questions to be answered by licentiates and ministers were provided with a preamble,[50] setting them in the light of a number of acts of General Assemblies and Synods, including the Free Church act of 1846 referred to above and two "declaratory acts",[51] passed respectively by the the U.P. Synod in 1879,[52] and by the General Assembly of the Free Church of Scotland, in 1892.[53]

These declaratory acts sought to bring new clarity, and to resolve certain difficulties, with regard to the churches' commitment to the Westminster standard documents and the related commitment that they required of their office-bearers. The evangelical movement[54] in Scotland had made people more sensitive to the way in which a strong emphasis on God's free and sovereign grace seemed to lead to the teaching that Jesus Christ had only died to save the "Elect", i.e. those whom God would awaken to faith on the basis of his own prior choice, and that the call of the Gospel could only be effectual in their case, but not for other fallen human beings. There had therefore been controversies about the scope of the Atonement in the course of the nineteenth century.[55] Some other statements in the *Westminster Confession* were creating problems in people's minds; and the old issue of what it said about powers and responsibilities of governments for preserving the true religion was always there. New methods of biblical scholarship and new currents of thought had exposed some theological teachers to charges of heresy.[56] But most knew that some changes would serve the truth; and they did not want the churches to harden into a defensive rigidity.

With some variations in order and differences in emphasis and detail, the declaratory acts of 1879 and 1892, by which the United Presbyterian and Free Churches sought to resolve such issues, (1) emphasized the universal reference of the love of God, of the atoning sacrifice of Jesus Christ, of the free offer of salvation through the Gospel, and of the striving of the Spirit to bring human beings to repentance. They declared (2) that the doctrine of election was to be understood consistently with the will of God for all to be saved and with each person's responsibility for his or her response to the gospel of grace; (3) that, while the Gospel is (or: the ordinances of the Gospel are) the ordinary means of salvation, one need not believe that any who die in infancy are lost or that God cannot extend salvation to those beyond the reach of such means; (4) that the teaching that the nature of fallen human beings is totally corrupt need not imply that they bear no sign of having been created in God's image or have no responsibility under the Law or under the Gospel, nor that they cannot experience the work of the Holy Spirit or perform any good actions; (5) that the respective churches disapproved of intolerance and persecution and did not intend (or: consider) their office-bearers' subscription of the Westminster documents to entail approval of such things, (6) that "liberty of opinion" was allowed (or: "diversity of opinion", recognized) on points in the "Standards" that did not "enter into the substance of the faith" (or: "into the substance of the Reformed faith therein taught"), with each church guarding against abuse of this liberty. The U.P. act offered, as an instance of something that did not "enter into the substance of the faith", the "'six days' in the Mosaic account of the creation".[57]

(g) The Presbyterian Church of Australia, 1901

The Presbyterian churches in the various Australian colonies came together to form the Presbyterian Church of Australia, in the same year as those colonies united as states of the new Commonwealth of Australia. The churches had already been collaborating on some matters in a federal union since July 1886, through a "Federal Assembly of the Presbyterian Churches of Australia and Tasmania".[58] Both the political union of 1901 and the ecclesiastical were still "federal" in form. The General Assembly of the Presbyterian Church of Australia became supreme with regard to the doctrine, worship and discipline of the church, but not its government. The state general assemblies remained supreme in that regard, and were thus not reduced to being synods of a national church.

The "Scheme of Union" of 1901 consisted of: a preamble, the Basis of Union, and articles of agreement.[59] The Preamble spoke of the six state churches as "holding the same Doctrine, Government, Discipline and Form of Worship" and said that it was "under authority of Christ alone, the Head of the Church, and Head over all things to His Church" that they agreed "to unite on the following basis, and subject to the following articles".

The 1901 basis of union consisted of six sections, dealing with (i) the Word of God contained in the Scriptures, as the "supreme standard" of the united church; (ii) the *Westminster Confession*, read in the light of a declaratory statement, as the "subordinate standard"; (iii) a provision that any revision or abridgment of the subordinate standard or restatement of its doctrine or change of the formula would require the prior consent of a majority of the "local" (i.e. state) assemblies and of three-fifths of the presbyteries, and a majority of three-fifths of the members present for the final vote in the General Assembly; (iv) a provision that if, upon any change made in accordance with Section III, a congregation resolved to continue to adhere to the original basis of union, the General Assembly had the power to allow the congregation to keep its property or to take some other action; (v) a provision that any change to Section III or IV had to be made in the way provided in Section III; and (vi) the formula to be signed by ministers, elders and probationers.

This basis of union gave the Presbyterian Church of Australia the classic Presbyterian doctrinal standard, but did not refer to the Westminster documents for catechizing, church government or worship. Educationally, it no longer seemed appropriate to be regulated by the form and content of the Catechisms;[60] the General Assembly of Australia was not supreme in respect of government, anyway; and movements for liturgical renewal were taking the church beyond the approach of the old *Directory of Public Worship*.[61] The 1901 basis of union applied the term 'standard' to the Word of God, as well as the Confession, while making a distinction between the "supreme" standard and any subordinate one. The subordinate standard was the *Westminster Confession of Faith*, but read in the light of a declaratory statement.

The Declaratory Statement drew on the Declaratory Act of the United Presbyterian Church in Scotland of 1879 and a related act of the Presbyterian Church of Victoria of 1882,[62] also following the Scottish Free Church Act of 1892 at two points. The Victorian act arose out of the "Strong Case",[63] which had its background in misgivings felt by many about the preaching and teaching of the minister of Scots' Church, Melbourne, the Revd Charles Strong. These came to a head over an article he published on the Atonement in the *Victorian Review* of October 1880.[64] Most accounts of the controversy have found it hard to avoid being partisan. It is now possible to feel some sympathy both for Strong and for the Presbytery of Melbourne and Victorian Assembly, for they all faced major questions of continuity and change in theology and biblical interpretation, while lacking an adequate frame of reference for working through to answers they might have agreed on. To the Victorian church, Strong's article did not appear compatible with the doctrine that he had vowed to "assert, maintain and defend". The Presbytery had some difficulty in getting Strong to confer with it, but finally adopted a motion, which it understood Strong to accept as settling the matter. The Presbytery's motion expressed its "severe concern and pain at the negative character of the teaching" in the essay, and also at "the absence from it of all distinct mention of the Divine person of the Lord Jesus Christ as the mediator and reconciler working out the Atonement". It said in conclusion:

> [...] And inasmuch as the Christian faith rests upon, and the Christian consciousness takes hold of, certain objective, supernatural, historic facts, especially the incarnation, the atoning life and death, and the resurrection and ascension of our Lord, the Presbytery earnestly, and in the spirit of brotherly kindness, urge upon Mr Strong that, in his future utterances, he make these essential facts prominent.[65]

The Presbytery wished to insist on the centrality of the person and story of Jesus Christ as the real presence of God in human history, revealing himself and bringing about reconciliation through events in Jesus' story, events that were therefore not simply the products of historical forces, but works of divine grace. It tried to do that by the concept of "objective, supernatural, historic facts", which would probably give some difficulty to most philosophies, and could hardly have meant much, at all, in terms of the Idealism that Strong had learned from John Caird in Glasgow.[66] There can have been no meeting of minds between Strong and the church. It was not he, but some of the more liberally minded among his critics, such as Larry Rentoul and Andrew Harper, who led the Victorian church to greater openness and made it possible, by 1907, for that church to accept another product of Glasgow and the Cairds, David Stow Adam, as Professor of Christian Doctrine in its theological hall.[67]

Strong sought to resign from Scots, because of the effects of the controversy on his health, but agreed to take six months leave and then serve for another year. At a meeting of the congregation on 15 August 1881, one of the elders, J.C. Stewart, who had been the church's law agent since 1869, made a fierce attack on other ministers, who condemned Strong for not adhering to the church's standards, yet did not literally adhere to every jot and tittle themselves. As reported in the press, Stewart not only impugned the honesty of the church's ministry, but also denigrated its treasured Westminster documents (to which, as an elder, he was just as committed as ministers were supposed to be).[68] It was this speech of Stewart's, rather than any action of Strong's himself, that led the General Assembly of Victoria to formulate and adopt the declaratory act of 1882.[69]

The Victorian declaratory act did not have the full scope of the U.P. act, but was particularly directed towards answering the issues raised by Stewart. It paralleled the U.P. act in what it had to say on (1) God's eternal decree and the doctrine of election, (2) the outward and ordinary means of salvation, and God's capacity for extending his grace to those beyond the pale of ordinary means, and (3) liberty of opinion on "points in the Standards [...] not essential to the system of doctrine therein taught", such as the "six days" of creation. It then declared (4) that subscription to the Formula bound a person to no more than the "whole doctrine" contained in the Standards, meaning "the system of doctrine in its unity".[70] The church held all admitted to its ministry "pledged to profess, defend, and teach this system in its integrity", and

> while giving due prominence in their teaching to all the doctrines which it includes, to give a chief place to the central and most vital doctrines thereof, with those objective supernatural facts on which they rest, especially the Incarnation, the Perfect Obedience and Expiatory Death, and the Resurrection and Ascension of our Lord [...].[71]

Like the corresponding acts in Scotland, this Victorian act helped to preserve the unity of the church in a time of change and transition, by relieving minds and consciences on some of the harder statements in the doctrinal standards, by calling to a common focus on the fundamentals of the Gospel, by recognizing the place for, and limits of, freedom of opinion, and so opening the way for new developments in theology and historical understanding, and by replacing older conventions, inherited from three different streams of Presbyterianism, about what office-bearers had committed themselves to with an explicit and authoritative statement of the church's expectations.

By using such a declaratory act to redefine the precise nature of a church's relation to its doctrinal standards, the churches were running some risks with regard to their constitutional status and the trusts on which church property was held. The Victorian Assembly recognized this and sought legal advice, which indicated that a fresh act of Parliament would be necessary, before the church could safely modify the formula signed by office-bearers, to incorporate some reference to the new declaratory act.[72] In fact, the Assembly, in November 1882, approved the act

> as explanatory of the mind of the Church, with respect to the statements in the *Confession of Faith* to which it refers, and the meaning and binding force of the Formula [...],[73]

but it deferred formal adoption, because of the state of negotiations for the union of the churches in the Australian colonies. The Free Church of Scotland did not proceed so cautiously. The price that it paid was not only the breaking away of some opposed to its declaratory act, to form the Free Presbyterian Church, but also the successful litigation by opponents of its union with the United Presbyterians in 1900. For one of the arguments accepted by the Lord Chancellor on the final appeal by the continuing "Wee Free" minority to the House of Lords was that the Free Church General Assembly had acted unconstitutionally in adopting the declaratory act of 1892.[74]

The declaratory statement in the Australian basis of union had, of course, an entirely different status, for it was incorporated in the church's fundamental constitutional document right from the start. As far as its content and scope were concerned, it (1) combined the U.P. wording on the universality of the love of God and the free offer of salvation to all in the Gospel, with the Presbytery of Melbourne's[75] insistence on the central importance of "certain objective supernatural historic facts" in the story of Jesus Christ. It repeated the Victorian adaptations of the U.P. paragraphs on (2) "the doctrine of God's eternal decree(s), including the doctrine of election" and (3) the ordinary means of salvation and God's ability to extend his grace beyond them. On what the *Confession of Faith* teaches about the corrupt nature of the fallen human being, the declaratory statement (4) repeated the corresponding paragraph from the declaratory act of the Free Church of Scotland from 1892, with minor changes in wording. In a simplified version of the Victorian adaptation of the U.P. statement, it (5) declared

> That liberty of opinion is allowed on matters in the subordinate standard not essential to the doctrine therein taught, the church guarding against the abuse of this liberty to the injury of its unity and peace.

In a final paragraph on the *Confession of Faith's* teaching on the civil magistrate and his "authority and duty in the sphere of religion", it (6) followed the U.P. act in owning the Lord Jesus Christ as the only King and Head of the Church, but then followed the Free Church disclaimer regarding "intolerant or persecuting principles" and the exemption of its office-bearers from subscribing anything inconsistent with "the liberty of conscience and the right of private judgment",[76] adding a finishing touch of its own, by quoting the *Confession* to the effect that "God alone is Lord of the conscience".[77]

Section III of the 1901 basis of union provided for a procedure by which changes could be made to some, but only some, parts of the basis. That is something that we have not encountered in earlier bases of union. The procedure was that any proposal for change should be "remitted to the local assemblies and through them to the presbyteries", to seek the consent of a sufficient number of them to the proposal. That was known as "Barrier Act Procedure", after the Church of Scotland's act of that name of 1697.[78] Beyond the way in which that procedure was normally followed for legislation in Presbyterian churches, the basis of union contained two further restrictions: (1) A permissible change to the basis of union required not just simple majorities, but approval by "three-fifths of the presbyteries of the whole church" and three-fifths of the members of the General Assembly present for the final vote. (2) The only changes to the basis of union that would be permissible would be: a revision or abridgement of the subordinate standard or a restatement of its doctrine; a change of the formula; or a change in Section III or IV. The first of these would not have affected the text of the basis of union, but only that of a document referred to in it. The second would have affected the formula within Section VI, but nothing else within that section. The third would have affected the provisions for making the first two kinds of changes and for making arrangements for a congregation that did not concur in any such change.

Thus it was possible to revise or abridge the text of the *Westminster Confession* or to restate its doctrine in modern language, but not possible to alter the declaratory statement, in the light of which the *Confession* was to be read. That may seem anomalous, but is comprehensible, when one considers the age of either document and the church's relation to each. The *Confession* is constructed in the thought-forms, and couched in the language, of seventeenth century Calvinist Orthodoxy and English Puritanism. It is one of the more detailed and explicit doctrinal standards in the history of the Church. It was inevitable that, in future centuries, churches would become uncomfortable with some details of its teaching or its wording. A provision such as that in the 1901 basis of union allowing liberty of opinion primarily meets the needs of individual office-bearers. It does permit a church to treat some aspects of the *Confession* as points on which liberty of opinion is allowable, but it does not authorize that church, as a corporate body, to adopt some other position of its own on any of those points. But Section III of the basis of union did authorize that: The Presbyterian Church could, under Barrier Act procedure and by three-fifth majorities where required, revise its subordinate standard. It did that on two or three occasions. It amended cap.XXIV.iv, to allow a man to marry his deceased wife's sister and a woman to marry her deceased husband's brother, thus avoiding a clash between the church's teaching and discipline and new civil legislation. It also qualified the statement in cap. XXVII.iv, that neither of the sacraments may be "dispensed by any but a minister of the word, lawfully ordained", by adding the words, (saving where the General Assembly has made a special provision to the contrary, that the people of God may not be left without these sealing ordinances).[79]

Without this latter amendment, any move in the General Assembly to enable the sacraments to be celebrated in congregations beyond the regular reach of ordained ministry, by a special procedure for authorizing home mission agents to preside, would have had to be ruled out of order. Later, in the fifteen years leading up to union, the church was engaged in a complete revision of the cap.XXIV of the subordinate standard, "Of Marriage and Divorce". But the union of 1977 meant that this was never finally adopted.

The Declaratory Statement was, on the other hand, not a historic document from some situation of the past, but a direct product of the negotiations leading to the union. It was based on similar documents from the United Presbyterian Church and the Free Church of Scotland, and from the Presbyterian Church of Victoria, in which representatives of those two traditions were already united with others from the established Church of Scotland. Its function was to define the precise sense in which the *Westminster Confession of Faith* would function as the subordinate standard of the united church. It was a finely balanced instrument, which enabled six state churches, each with its own individual mix of different kinds of Presbyterianism and with its own experience, wisdom, prejudices and anxieties, to entrust themselves to the much larger fellowship of a national church. The reassurance that it gave the churches, and their ministers, elders and congregations, on the different points that mattered most to each, depended on the fact that it was an utterly stable element in the basis of their union. But then, on what we have seen of bases of union so far, what is exceptional about the Australian basis of 1901 is not that some parts could not be amended, but that there were specific provisions to allow some to be amended.

George Yule seems to have mistaken the status and character of the declaratory statement, when he writes that

[...] the General Assembly of Australia was given sole jurisdiction of doctrinal standards and adopted the

Westminster Confession with a Declaratory Act. This allowed liberty of conscience in those matters that do not enter into the substance of the faith, and gave the Assembly the right to determine what these matters could be in any given case. In the late nineteenth century the issues this safeguard was aimed at were predestination to damnation, and, as there was no established church in Australia, those clauses of the Confession that bordered on Church/state relations.[80]

The General Assembly did not "adopt" the *Confession* "with a Declaratory Act". The church's basis of union gave it the *Confession* as its subordinate standard and provided that, as such, the *Confession* was to be read in the light of the declaratory statement included in the basis of union. Articles of agreement accompanying the basis gave the General Assembly, not "sole jurisdiction", but supreme legislative, administrative and judicial functions, with regard to doctrine and some other matters. As we have seen, any revision of the subordinate standard would require the approval of three-fifths of the presbyteries and a majority of state assemblies, so that decisions on any major doctrinal changes would be broadly based. A "declaratory act" of the General Assembly's would have been approved, and could have been revised or rescinded, in a similar way, but with a simple majority of the presbyteries. The basis of union allowed no change in the declaratory statement. As regards the content of the declaratory statement, George Yule mentions only the fifth clause, as if that were the whole, and he refers to it as allowing "liberty of conscience in those matters that do not enter into the substance of the faith". The actual wording was, however,

> That liberty of opinion is allowed on matters in the Subordinate Standard not essential to the doctrine therein taught [...].

That is not the same thing, at all. "Liberty of conscience" is mentioned, not in the fifth, but in the sixth clause, which is concerned with the *Confession's* doctrine of the civil authorities and their powers with regards to religion. There, it is not a question of allowing liberty of conscience to office-bearers who subscribe the

Confession, but of their not being thereby committed to "any principle inconsistent with the liberty of conscience", i.e. they are not bound to support "intolerant or persecuting principles". Just as the declaratory statement dealt with the powers of the State in religious affairs in this sixth clause, so its second clause dealt with any qualms about the *Confession's* possibly teaching "predestination to damnation". The issues that George Yule offers as examples were thus precisely not left to be covered by the "liberty of opinion" clause and the Assembly's "right to determine" on which matters such liberty was allowable. Comparison with the United Presbyterian, Free Church and Victorian declaratory acts show us where the concerns addressed in the declaratory statement were coming from and how much the declaratory statement belongs within the general reappraisal of Westminster theology in Presbyterian churches in the nineteenth century. What is the point of drawing attention to the fact that "there was no established church in Australia", when the relevant clause in the Australian declaratory statement simply combines sentences from the Scottish U.P. and Free Church acts and the *Confession of Faith* itself? In my opinion, there was a more general orientation on the *Westminster Confession* in the life of the Presbyterian Church of Australia, and also more of a conservative Westminster wing, than George Yule allows. His disregard for the way in which, in its declaratory statement, the Australian church engaged with the substance of the *Confession* over a range of issues may be due to a general tendency to play down the extent to which Australians paid attention to the *Confession* at all.

The 1901 articles of agreement[81] dealt with the meetings, composition and functions of the General Assembly of Australia, which was to have supreme powers in relation to doctrine, worship and discipline, missions to the heathen, the training of students and admission of candidates to the ministry, and the reception of ministers from other churches (i-iv); a judicial commission to exercise judicial functions on the Assembly's behalf (v); a board of assessors to assist lower courts on request in cases involving life or doctrine (vi); missions to the heathen (vii); a uniform scheme of theological training (viii); reception of ministers from other denominations (ix); reports to the General Assembly from the state assemblies on the work and welfare of the Church (x); powers of state general assemblies (xi); a fund for General Assembly expenses (xii); power to form a beneficiary fund (xiii); provision that the articles of agreement might be altered or added to by Barrier Act procedure, with simple majorities of presbyteries and state assemblies (xiv).

The Presbyterian Church of Australia approved a new basis of union for itself in 1970,[82] by which it would have become a truly national church, with synods in place of the state general assemblies. This entailed getting governments to put through fresh Presbyterian Church acts for all states and territories. But the only part of the new basis that ever came into effect was Part III, which contained specific provisions regarding "Union with Other Churches", in order to ensure that the church had the power to enter into the union it was then negotiating with the Congregational and Methodist Churches at that time. One of those provisions was that

> [...] the proposed basis of union with any such church or churches (which shall include a section setting out basic principles of constitutional structure and practice) shall first be remitted to synods and presbyteries under the Barrier Act procedure and may be approved by the general assembly only when approved by a majority of synods and at least three-fifths of the presbyteries of the whole church and three-fifths of the members present when the final vote of the general assembly is taken.[83]

This was the same procedure as prescribed in the 1901 basis for any change to sections of that basis.

(h) The United Church of Canada, 1925

Moves for this union of Congregational, Methodist and Presbyterian churches in Canada began around the turn of the century; and a basis of union was ready by 1908. But strong opposition in the Presbyterian church and the Great War combined to delay the consummation of the union until 1925.[84] The basis of union[85] consists of unnumbered sections: [i] "General" deals with the name of the Church and its policy of fostering the spirit of unity, with the hope of achieving, "so far as Canada is concerned", a national church; [ii] "Doctrine" sets forth "the substance of the Christian faith, as commonly held among us": A preamble identifies "the foundation laid by the apostles and prophets, Jesus Christ himself being the chief corner-stone", affirms belief in the Scriptures as "the primary source and ultimate standard of Christian faith and life",[86] acknowledges the teaching of the ancient creeds, affirms allegiance to "the evangelical doctrines of the Reformation, as set forth in common in the doctrinal standards" adopted by the respective negotiating churches, and introduces a following statement as "a brief summary of our common faith" and as "in substance agreeable to the teaching of the Holy Scriptures" (it consists of about 1,100 words in 20 articles); [iii] "Polity" accepts members of the negotiating churches as members of the United Church, establishes the "pastoral charge", consisting of one or more congregations, as the "unit of organization", and names as the courts of the Church "higher than those of the pastoral charge" (a) the Presbytery, (b) the Conference[87] and (c) the General Council, with details for all of these levels; [iv] "The Ministry" covers the pastoral office, including term of service, training for the ministry, and a minister's relations to the Church's doctrines; [v] "Administration" deals with missions, publications, colleges and benevolent funds; there is finally an appendix on law.

This union was both spoken of in the Australian churches as an example of what could, and ought to, be done, and also held in Presbyterian circles to illustrate the dangers of going about union in too incautious a manner. We understood that, while a good proportion of the Presbyterian ministry had entered the union, many of the congregations had stayed out and called new ministers from abroad.[88] In the Alliance of Reformed Churches throughout the World holding the Presbyterian Order, Australian Presbyterians encountered two Canadian churches, the Presbyterian and the United, with both of which they found it easy to fraternize, although Canadian Presbyterian acquaintances tended to warn one in private about the inadequate doctrinal foundation of the United

Church. This side of the Canadian basis of union suffered from the fact that, at the time when it was drafted (1904-1908), people felt a need to retain some connexion with the traditional theologies of the negotiating churches, but did not see a possibility of, and the need for, combining those traditional positions with the liberal theology and social gospel interests of the day, in some creative new statement.[89]

In 1968, the Canada Conference of the Evangelical United Brethren Church merged with the United Church. It was a small body that had earlier arisen through a revival of Methodist type in communities with a German background.[90]

(j)   The Church of Scotland, 1929

The United Free Church of Scotland and the Church of Scotland united in 1929 under the name of the Church of Scotland, thus bringing the major elements from the Covenanters, the First and Second Secessions and the Disruption back together with the established church again.[91]

The Secession and Relief churches had arisen because a few ministers felt compelled to separate from a church that allowed the civil law to dictate how congregations were provided with ministers, even against the protests of some congregations. These churches came to assume a Voluntaryist stance, opposed to the state establishment of any church. Patronage was one of the issues behind the Disruption, as well, but it there came together with other issues in the fundamental question of whether an established church still had an inherent right to its own independent jurisdiction in spiritual matters. The courts had made it clear that a church could not be both established and also sovereign in its own affairs. The Church of Scotland split in 1843 because those who stayed with the established church believed that the heritage and mission of the national church were too important to be sacrificed, even for the fuller independence that the General Assembly had been trying to claim, while those who went off to form the Free Church believed that the Church's spiritual freedom was an inalienable part of its true being, and essential to its mission, so that the benefits of establishment had to be sacrificed, until the government was prepared to acknowledge and support the Church in its inherent freedom. Attitudes towards the established church and the establishment principle had modified and varied in both the Free Church and the United Presbyterian in the last quarter of the nineteenth century, except in those groups that would remain as the Free Presbyterian Church (from 1892), the "Wee" Free Church of Scotland (from 1900), and the United Free Church (from 1929).

The Free Church case and crisis that followed the union[92] with the United Presbyterian Church in 1900 demonstrated that even a "free" church is liable to find its imagined independence limited by the civil courts.[93] The decision of the House of Lords treated the Free Church as a voluntary association, the powers of which were strictly limited by the terms of its foundation. Action it had taken to redefine its relation to its doctrinal standards and to enter into union with the U.P.'s had been *ultra vires* and entailed a breach of trust, so that it was threatened with the forfeiture of its property to the "Wee Free" remnant. This judgment also delivered a clear message to the established church about the tight limits on its own jurisdiction, even in spiritual matters.[94] Yet the action of the Government in introducing legislation to safeguard the position of the Free Church going into union, and to ensure an equitable division between the uniting and continuing elements, showed a new readiness, in the political sphere, to respect a church's inherent right to follow its own course, in accordance with its own spiritual discernment. This held promise of new possibilities for both established and non-established churches.[95]

The United Free Church responded to the decision of the House of Lords with an "Act anent Spiritual Independence of the Church", 1906, in which it reasserted the claim

> [...] that the Church of Christ has under him as her only Head independent and exclusive jurisdiction and power of legislating in all matters of doctrine, worship, discipline, and government of the Church, including therein the right from time to time to alter, change, add to, or modify, her constitution and laws, Subordinate

Standards, and Church Formulas, and to determine and declare what these are.[96]

The act asserted that this had always been the position taken by the churches that had combined to form the United Free Church. It committed the church, in the exercise of the right it was claiming, always to recognize the authority of the Word of God contained in the Scriptures as the "supreme unchangeable Standard" and to comply with "the safeguards for deliberate action and legislation in such cases provided by the Church herself" (i.e. Barrier Act procedure). How well the church could have asserted its independence in any future civil case is still open to question.

The Church of Scotland and the United Free Church commenced negotiations in 1909. The two main issues that emerged were the spiritual freedom of the Church and the national recognition of religion.[97] A memorandum from the established church side proposed that there should be a new constitution for a united church of Scotland, which would both maintain continuity with the national church of the Reformation and ensure real independence in doctrine and government, that an act of Parliament should be sought to give effect to the new constitution, that issues of endowments should be resolved by a State commission, in such a way as to retain those endowments for religious purposes, and that the united church should make no claim for exclusive privilege.[98] With these proposals approved by the respective general assemblies, their representatives set about drafting, "Articles Declaratory of the Constitution of the Church of Scotland in Matters Spiritual".[99] These were completed by 1919 and given standing in law by the British Parliament's Church of Scotland Act, 1921.[100] This "Act to declare the lawfulness of certain Articles declaratory of the Constitution of the Church of Scotland in matters spiritual prepared with the authority of the General Assembly of the Church" gave the Church of Scotland that full spiritual independence, denial of which had occasioned the Disruption of 1843. A subsequent Church of Scotland (Property and Endowments) Act, 1925,[101] gave the church full control of its finances, and so freed it from all parliamentary control, while preserving its character as the recognized national church.

Judgments vary about its exact status. Burleigh suggests that the Church of Scotland from 1929 on was neither established nor disestablished. He points out that

> The expression 'The Church as by law established' is not of ecclesiastical provenance. It was a novelty in 1690, and the Church was not happy about it as it seemed to deny to it its true nature. [...] But the ideal of a national Church both representing and fostering the Christian faith of the whole people, an ideal which in spite of all division was common to all Presbyterians, was in a manner realized.[102]

Ferguson, on the other hand, speaks of "'establishment' on uniquely favourable terms", "establishment, however disguised by clever formulas stressing 'recognition'".[103]

The two churches united in 1929 on a basis of union and in accordance with a plan of union. The basis of union of 1929[104] consisted of (A) the Uniting Act passed by each of the two general assemblies. In this act the Church of Scotland and the United Free Church of Scotland, "as branches of the Holy Catholic or Universal Church", (i) expressed the belief that it was the Lord's will that his disciples should be one, and acknowledged that the Catholic Visible Church's[105] witness to the Lord is obscured, and the Lord's own work hindered, by division and separation. They listed the divisions that had occurred in the Church of Scotland from 1690 on and the various partial reunions that had already taken place. They narrated the steps followed from 1909 on to bring them to the present point. Thereupon the two assemblies, giving thanks for God's guidance in the past, and praying for the outpouring of God's Spirit in the present and for the future, enacted and declared that the two churches should henceforth constitute one church and that its name should be "The Church of Scotland".

The two general assemblies further enacted (ii) that the two churches entered into union in view of certain declarations that followed: (1) The agreements between the churches were enacted without prejudice to "the inherent liberty of the united church as a branch of the Church of God" to determine and deal with its own constitution and laws, as set out in the Free Church act of 1906 and the Articles Declaratory of 1926.[106] A further declaration listed (2) "leading documents setting forth the constitution, standards, rules and methods of the united Church", including the act of 1906 and articles of 1926 already referred to in (1) above, the *Westminster Confession*, the declaratory acts of the U.P. (1879) and Free (1892 and 1894) churches and a Church of Scotland act of 1910 on the Formula, the Westminster *Form of Presbyterial Church Government* and *Directory for Public Worship*, and, as a standard of discipline, the 1707 *Form of Process* (these last three documents as interpreted and modified by acts of General Assembly and by consuetude). It was (3) declared that the uniting acts of 1847, 1876 and 1900, see (c) and (f) above, were historic documents "the general principles whereof are held to be conserved in the united church"; further (4) that the *Larger* and *Shorter Catechisms* continued to be held in honour, as, too (5), were the chief documents from the reformation of the 16th century. The union was declared (6) to be taking place "on the footing of maintaining liberty of judgment and action heretofore recognized in either of the Churches uniting". In entering the union, those churches (7) reaffirmed both the obligation "to provide the ordinances of religion to the people of Scotland through a territorial ministry and to labour for the universal diffusion of the Gospel" and also "the duty of her members to contribute, according to their ability, both by their service and their means, for the support of the ordinances of religion in this land and the extension of the Kingdom of Christ throughout the world". This final declaration sought to combine the ethos of a national church, as had been maintained by both the established and the Free churches, with that of an unendowed denomination dependent on the voluntary contributions of its members, as the U.P. Church had been in principle, and the Free Church, in practice.

The two uniting general assemblies enacted (iii) that all previous legislation of either of the two churches, unless modified by the basis and plan of union, should continue in force, so long as not repealed or amended by the united church. In cases of conflicting legislation or material difference in practice, Barrier Act procedure should be followed for any change.

When the two general assemblies had met to consummate the union and had adopted the Uniting Act, they were (iv) to have the powers of a General Assembly of the united church to do or authorize whatever else was needed for inaugurating the united church.

Further parts of the basis of union of 1929 were (B) an appendix containing the the Articles Declaratory of 1926 and United Free Church act of 1906[107] and (C) the Preamble, Questions and Formula for use at ordinations and inductions of ministers.[108]

The plan of union[109] dealt with (1) constitution and powers of the courts of the church, (2) training of the ministry, (3) property and finance, (4) rules and forms of procedure, (5) discipline, (6) constitution and administrative regulations of Assembly committees, and (7) relations with other churches, including the recognition of orders and admission of ministers.

(k)   The Church of South India, 1947.

The Church of South India was formed on 27 September 1947. The churches involved in this union were: (1) the South India United Church, itself a union of Presbyterian and Congregational churches dating from 1908, which had been joined in 1919 by the churches of the Malabar district founded by the Basel Mission, (2) the South India Province of the Methodist Church, and (3) the (Anglican) Church of India, Burma and Ceylon (which was letting some of its dioceses enter the union). Proposals for union had begun to be raised and discussed from 1910 on. A joint committee of the S.I.U.C. and the Anglican Church met first in 1920 and was joined by representatives of the Provincial Synod of the Wesleyan Methodist Church of South India in 1925. The first edition of a scheme of union, including a basis of union, was published in 1929. A final, seventh edition appeared in 1941. By 1946, it had been approved by all three churches.[110]

The basis of union of the Church of South India[111] consists of eighteen sections, concerned with (i) the purpose and nature of the union; (ii) the church and its membership; (iii) the faith of the church, with reference to (1) the Holy Scriptures as containing all things necessary to salvation and as the supreme and decisive standard of faith, (2) the *Apostles'* and *Nicene Creeds* as witnessing to, and safeguarding, that faith, (3) a brief, trinitarian, credal statement; together with appended notes, saying that: The two creeds provide a sufficient basis for union, but the united church does not require individuals to assent to every phrase in them, or exclude "reasonable liberty of interpretation", or assert that they are a complete expression of the faith; it will be competent for the united church to issue supplementary statements of the faith; teachers of the united church may use for instruction any confession of faith used by any of the uniting churches not inconsistent with the church's own standards; (iv) the sacraments of Baptism and the Lord's Supper in the church; (v) the ministry in the church, recognizing both the ministry of all members and the special ministry of those called by God and set apart in the church by ordination; (vi) the need for episcopal, presbyteral and congregational elements in the life of the church; (vii) the congregation as locally representing the one, holy, catholic and apostolic church; (viii) presbyters as called and commissioned by God to dispense his word and sacraments, to declare his forgiveness, to build up the church's members in the faith, and to share in government of the church; (ix) the historic episcopate, in a constitutional form, with the bishop as chief pastor and father in God, allowing different views on the nature and necessity of episcopacy, and providing for episcopal ordination of presbyters and deacons and consecration of bishops, without reflecting on the validity of other orders; (x) the initial membership, to consist of all communicant members, baptized members and catechumens of the uniting churches received into the corresponding status in the united church; (xi) the initial ministry, to consist of all bishops, presbyters, deacons and probationers of the uniting churches who assent to the basis of union, retaining their current status, together with other bishops to be consecrated at the time of inauguration; (xii) public worship, allowing freedom to pastors and congregations to use or not to use historic forms, with nothing then in use forbidden, and changes to be subject to local consent, all subject to provisions to be made regarding ordination and consecration and the essential elements and parts of services such as Baptism, Communion and Marriage; (xiii) the autonomy of the united church vis-à-vis both civil government and any church or society external to itself, with recognition of its special relations with the churches through which it came into existence, of the due weight to be given to pronouncements of ecumenical bodies, and of its readiness to participate in any future ecumenical council; (xiv) relations with other churches, to be maintained and cultivated; (xv) relations of ministers and members of the united church with other churches; (xvi) the development of full unity in ministry and life, stating the intention that eventually every minister permanently serving in the united church will have been episcopally ordained; (xvii) relations to other churches in India; (xviii) obligations taken over from uniting churches for "maintained churches" and chaplains.

This was the first corporate union in which Anglicans came together with Presbyterians and others. As a matter of course, the "Lambeth Quadrilateral"[112] received early attention in the union discussions; and each of its elements is easy to find in the final form of the basis of union: the Holy Scriptures and the ancient creeds (iii), the sacraments of Baptism and the Lord's Supper (iv), and the "historic episcopate" (vi,ix). Distinctive features of the South Indian approach to union are (1) the emphasis given to balancing congregational and presbyteral elements alongside the episcopal (vi-ix), (2) the acceptance of the practice of a constitutional episcopacy, without obliging anyone to accept a particular doctrine of episcopacy (ix,xvi), (3) the acceptance of all the members and all the ministers of the uniting churches, without any supplementary laying on of hands or other rite, in recognition of the way in which God has already owned them all (i,x,xi), (4) the intention of maintaining existing relations and practices of inter-communion and inter-celebration with other churches, including non-episcopal ones (xiv,xv).[113]

The South Indian basis of union is formulated as an agreement between the uniting churches: "The uniting Churches affirm ..." (i), "acknowledge" (ii), "accept" (iii,ix), "believe" (iv,v,vii), "recognize" (vi,xii), "agree" (viii,x,xi,xiii,xvi), "desire and hope" (xiv), "clearly understand" (xv). Only in the final two paragraphs, where it is a question of continuing relations with, or obligations devolving from, one or more of the uniting churches themselves, are commitments made on behalf of the united church. Consistently with this approach, the Constitution of the church of South India contains the following section:

19. *The Basis of Union and the Constitution.* -

The Basis of Union is a document in which before the inauguration of union the uniting Churches stated the general nature and purposes of the proposed union, gave an outline of the principles of faith and of Church order on which they agreed and of the fundamental rules for the organization and life of the Church in which they were prepared to unite, and expressed certain hopes and desires for the future of that united Church.

In this Constitution of the Church of South India the substance of the Basis of Union has been incorporated, and provision as far as possible made for giving effect to the intentions and desires of the uniting Churches. As included in this Constitution, these provisions are subject to alteration as provided in Chapter XIV hereof, since the Church of South India cannot remain legally bound by the action of the uniting Churches before union. But it is hereby declared that in any alteration of this Constitution, and particularly of these Governing Principles, full regard shall be paid to the Basis of Union as a permanent record of the intentions and desires of the Churches by the union of which this Church has been formed.[114]

This basis of union is thus not itself the fundamental constitutional document of the united church; and, in this regard, it differs from other bases of union examined in this study. The argument that the united church "cannot remain legally bound by the action of the uniting Churches before union" would not have been considered valid for other unions. For the ultimate action of the uniting churches would have been to constitute themselves as the united church, on the basis agreed between them. But the Church of South India was constituted by the union of only the South India province of the Methodist Church and of only certain dioceses of the Church of India, Burma and Ceylon with the South India United Church (initially excluding at least the North Tamil Church Council of that last church). Thus two of the uniting churches, at least, retained an identity of their own after the union. The C.S.I. basis of union and constitution contain provisions concerning continuing relations of the united church with those uniting churches and also establish its autonomy vis-à-vis them, as well as other churches. Beyond that, the Church of South India had its origins in the missionary activities of various foreign churches and societies. Its scheme of union, containing the draft basis and draft constitution, were prepared for "presentation to the governing bodies of those churches in India *and elsewhere*"(my italics). The less than absolute status given to the basis of union, as the expression of the hopes, desires and intentions of the parent churches, must be seen as an appropriate way of their "letting go", as this new, indigenous church gained its independence. It was a conscious and considered step, for the basis of union and constitution had, as said, been presented and circulated for consideration together, as parts of the one comprehensive scheme of union, through various successive drafts.

Some ministers and members of the Presbyterian Church of Australia served with the South India United Church and the Church of South India; and many others followed the formation and early history of the latter church with great interest.

In our review of bases of union, we have seen them dealing with questions such as the following:

1. What is the ultimate, inescapable authority for the Church? Is it the Bible? Is it the Word of God "contained in" the Scriptures?

2. What is the extent of this authority? Apart from faith and doctrine, does it regulate life and manners, as well?

3. To what extent does a church bind itself to particular ways of understanding the Scriptures? Are there classic documents that set the standard for interpreting them, and for teaching and preaching?

4. Are there standard texts to regulate other dimensions of the church's life and work, such as worship, instruction in the faith, government and discipline?

5. In what sense does a church allow each such document to have authority within it? Does it distance itself in any way from aspects of a document? Does it modify or qualify the way in which any parts apply in the present?

6. Are there other historic events or periods, principles or stances that are going to help determine the identity and character of the church?

7. Are there other ways in which the church needs to commit itself to its calling and mission?

8. Which office-bearers are expected to give personal commitments about accepting the authority of the Scriptures? Which are expected to subscribe other standard documents? In what terms are they required to do so? What liberty of opinion or interpretation does that leave them?

9. How independent is the church in its own, "spiritual" affairs?

10. What freedom will the church have to redefine its relation to its standards or otherwise to modify its basis of union?

11. What are the terms and conditions of membership in the church?

12. What does the church otherwise expect of its members?

13. What is to be the form of government in the church?

14. What ministries are to be officially maintained by the church? What is to be seen as essential to those ministries?

15. What is to be the relation of the united church to other churches?

16. How does it conceive its relation to the One Holy Catholic Church?

17. On what terms will ministers be accepted from other churches?

It has been distinctive for Scottish, and other Presbyterian, church history that churches that separated from each other over particular issues tended still to have a great deal in common. Both in the First and Second Secessions and in the Disruption, groups left the established Church of Scotland because they believed that it was not being true to itself. They largely retained its standards and forms, while striving to apply its principles with greater zeal and greater freedom. As a consequence, some of the matters listed above did not always need to be dealt with explicitly in a basis of union, because the common Presbyterian heritage could be presupposed. This is well illustrated by the Australian Presbyterian scheme of union of 1901, where the preamble could say that the six state churches held "the same Doctrine, Government, Discipline and Form of Worship", although the basis of union and articles of agreement set no standard for worship and the respective state assemblies remained supreme as to church government. Most of the bases of union did not find it necessary to say anything about the Ministry or the Eldership, although those two offices were fundamental to the life of a Presbyterian church. What did concern such office-bearers was, of course, the question of a church's standards and the terms in which ministers and elders were required to subscribe to those standards, which was very often through a particular set formula. In the basis of the Church of South India (1947), some matters had to be treated more fully or differently and others had to be introduced, because it was then a question of bringing together churches with different traditions and heritages. We may note here that it was only in the South Indian basis that the sacraments were mentioned. Otherwise, they would have been seen as adequately covered in the *Confession of Faith*, *Catechisms*, and *Directory for the Public Worship of God*.

In some instances, a basis of union did not commence with the Scriptures. This may have been true of the Associate Reformed basis of 1782 and is certainly true of the Victorian basis of 1859. These churches' relation to the Scriptures was, of course, defined by cap.I of the *Confession of Faith*. Otherwise, the general practice was to follow the example of the United Secession basis of 1820, with its acknowledgment of the "Word of God contained in the Scriptures as the only rule of faith and manners".

The common doctrinal standard for Presbyterian churches was the *Westminster Confession of Faith*, to which the two Westminster Catechisms were sometimes added. The *Confession* could be said to be the confession of the church's faith and to exhibit the sense in which the church understood the scriptures. This last is a significant point. All kinds of churches and groups may affirm the authority of the Bible, and yet interpret it in ways which no Presbyterian church could accept. By recognizing a doctrinal standard such as the *Confession of Faith*, a basis of union says that the church concerned is united in understanding the Scriptures in that particular way.

Such a position can, of course, be taken to the point where the authority of a church's confession effectively overrides or replaces the authority of the Scriptures; and that has happened in various confessional churches of the past and the present. It therefore becomes important, how the authority of a church's doctrinal standard is defined in that church and whether the church reserves any right to modify that standard. For a period of history, the authority of the Westminster documents and Westminster theology was unquestioned in Presbyterian churches. The beginnings of revision sprang from the tension that the quite conservative Seceders experienced, when caught between the powers the *Confession* allowed civil rulers in religious affairs and the actual policies and practices of "uncovenanted" British governments. So bases of union began to include disclaimers regarding "intolerant and persecuting principles" (United Secession, 1820; United Presbyterian, 1847; Victoria, 1859; N.S.W., 1864; etc.). Churches such as the United Presbyterian and the Free Church later sought to redefine their relation to the *Confession of Faith* by declaratory acts. But the Free Church found, as Secession churches had earlier discovered, that revising or supplementing the formulations of an original consensus may well uncover such differences in emphasis and understanding as to threaten a church's unity. It also found that, if a church had not, at its inception, asserted its own inherent freedom in matters of faith and doctrine, any subsequent attempt to exercise such freedom could put its property in jeopardy under the civil law of trusts. So some later bases of union embodied (Australia, 1901), or referred to (United Free, 1900; Church of Scotland, 1929), declaratory statements qualifying the churches' relation to their historic doctrinal standards. They asserted a church's autonomy in its own, spiritual affairs (Church of Scotland, 1929) or contained specific provisions for the revision of doctrinal standards or other changes to the basis of union (Australia, 1901).

Different churches adopted different approaches to any qualifications that they might place on the authority of the *Confession of Faith*. The Secession churches tended to allow that the *Confession* might contain statements from which they needed to distance themselves. The United Presbyterians followed them in that. Indeed, their declaratory act of 1879 commenced with the following bold preamble:

> Whereas the formula in which the Subordinate Standards of this Church are accepted requires assent to them as an exhibition of the sense in which the Scriptures are understood; Whereas these Standards, being of human composition, are necessarily imperfect, and the Church has already allowed exception to be taken to their teaching or supposed teaching on one important subject; And whereas there are other subjects in regard to which it has been found desirable to set forth more fully and clearly the view which the Synod takes of the teaching of Holy Scripture [...].[115]

Here, a church is claiming a direct relation to the Holy Scriptures, by virtue of which it may become possible and necessary for that church to say some critical things about its own doctrinal standards. The Free Church, on the other hand, tended rather to declare that it did not consider that subscribing to the *Confession* did entail commitment to anything objectionable. On one issue, that of open communion, the U.P. basis (1847) had allowed ministers and kirk sessions that understood a passage in the *Confession* to advocate open communion to follow their consciences on that point. This was a different way of dealing with things again, in that the basis did not say how the *Confession* was to be interpreted, but allowed a particular interpretation that would lead to the reversal of a more general practice of close communion. What was happening in this case was a concession to conscientious convictions prevailing in the Relief Church, in face of hesitation and misgivings from the United Secession side. So, in these various ways, churches removed difficulties concerning particular passages and teachings in the *Confession of Faith*. In a more general way, they also began to allow office-bearers liberty of opinion or interpretation on matters in the *Confession* that did not enter into the substance of the faith or were not essential to the doctrine taught in the *Confession*.

In most cases, whether this was expressed through the basis of union, in the formula, or only in the questions asked at ordinations and inductions, ministers and elders were required to subscribe to the *Confession of Faith* as a confession of their own personal faith. The preamble and questions in the Church of Scotland basis (1929) followed a 1910 act of the Church of Scotland on the formula, in only asking ordinands and ministers to signify that they believed "the fundamental doctrines of the Christian faith contained in the *Confession of Faith* of this Church".

In contrast to the Presbyterian orientation on the very detailed *Westminster Confession*, the Church of South India (1947) judged "the fundamental truths embodied" in the two ancient creeds to provide "a sufficient basis of Union", and that without demanding "the assent of individuals to every phrase" and without excluding "reasonable liberty of interpretation". In adopting the two creeds, and them alone, as the doctrinal standard of the united church, the South Indian basis was conforming to the "Lambeth Quadrilateral". That did not, in one sense, confront Presbyterians with any doctrinal novelty, since all the substance of the ancient creeds may be found in the *Confession of Faith*; and one or other of them is included in the services for Sunday worship and for celebration of the sacraments in modern books of common order. But it does reduce doctrinal commitment to a minimum; and one might wonder for how many false teachings room is still comfortably left in a church that is bound to no more than those two creeds.

Another option has been to draft a new statement of faith to express the doctrinal consensus on the basis of which the union is taking place. That course was followed for the United Church of Canada (1925). Shorter statements of this kind are to be found in the first of the "Articles Declaratory of the Constitution of the Church of Scotland in Matters Spiritual" (1926, and appended to the basis of union, 1929) and as the final part of the third section of the South Indian basis (1941). But, in these later cases, the modern statements do not stand alone, but accompany commitments to historic creeds or confessions.

Not all Presbyterian bases of union referred to all of the other Westminster documents; and, in those that did, there was a variety of ways in which, and degrees to which, they allowed them to be authoritative. The Westminster Catechisms were, in the United Secession basis (1820), joined with the *Westminster Confession* to represent the confession of the church's faith and to express the sense in which the church understood the Scriptures. The United Presbyterian basis (1847) allowed them only the latter function. The Victorian basis of 1859 spoke in a differentiating way of "Standards *and Formularies*"(my italics). The N.S.W. basis of 1864 followed a declaration of the Free Church of Scotland (and the acts of the General Assembly of the Church of Scotland in first approving the Catechisms in July 1648), in designating them as "Directories for catechizing". The Free Church and the N.S.W. basis stated further that the other Westminster documents, beyond the *Confession* and Catechisms, had the status of regulations, rather than of tests of anyone's orthodoxy: office-bearers were not required to subscribe them. The *Directory for the Public Worship of God* was, in the U.P. basis (1847), said to be "a compilation of excellent rules", as it had already been called in the United Secession basis, unless the reference there to "the *Directory*" actually meant the Form of Presbyterial Church Government.

Apart from such standard documents, bases of union own a commitment to the heritage of the Reformation, (United Secession, 1820; Church of Scotland, 1929), the Convenanting period (United Secession, 1820), or the Secession (United Secession, 1820; U.P., 1847). The Church of Scotland basis of 1929 rehearses the whole history of divisions and reunions, acknowledges the importance of different stands and steps taken in that history, and appends earlier bases of union and uniting acts as "historic documents the general principles whereof are held to be preserved in the united church".

Bases of union dealt with churches' commitment to their calling and mission in a number of ways. Initially, the *Confession of Faith*, Catechisms, and *Directory for the Public Worship of God* would be held to cover all that needed to be said in that regard. For the Reformed and Secession churches, commitment to the programme of the Covenants was also fundamental to their understanding both of the church's mission and of its mission field. For they held the whole present population of Great Britain to be bound by oaths sworn by their forebears! This attitude to their contemporaries had faded among the Secession churches, by the time of the United Secession basis of 1820. By 1847, the United Presbyterian basis had reached the point of making explicit statements about the church's obligation to mission, speaking of it as

> the obligation to hold forth, as well as to hold fast, the doctrine and law of Christ, and to make exertions for the universal diffusion of the blessings of his Gospel at home and abroad.[116]

The Church of Scotland basis (1929) recognized both the responsibility of a national church for providing ministry wherever people were and a responsibility for sharing in the mission of the universal church to the nations of the world.

The United Presbyterian basis (1847) included a statement of ecumenical openness, although, in accordance with the outlook of the day, that was expressed in terms of readiness to work together with other Christians in all matters on which there was agreement. Both the Church of Scotland (1929) and the Church of South India (1947) bases recognize an inherent relation between unity and mission.

The terms and conditions of church membership were also, on one level, covered by the *Confession of Faith*: the universal visible church consists "of all those throughout the world that profess the true religion, together with their children" (cap.XXV.ii); "Baptism is a sacrament of the New Testament, ordained by Jesus Christ, [...] for the solemn admission of the party baptized into the visible church" (cap.XXVIII.i). When a union of Presbyterian churches took place, members would transfer into the united church with their congregations, and the kirk sessions would see that the rolls were transferred, too. The practice and discipline surrounding membership might scarcely change; and a basis of union might need to say nothing about the conditions of membership. On the other hand, as a union of churches that had come about by secessions from the established church, and which had grown significantly by the continuing accession of further members who were leaving it, the United Presbyterian Church found it appropriate to say, in its basis of union (1847),

> That the term of membership is a credible profession of the Faith of Christ as held by this Church - a profession made with intelligence, and justified by a corresponding character and deportment.[117]

That is expressed in terms of those of an age to make their own profession of faith. It would not be intended to exclude their children, who would be admitted to baptism and to membership on their parents' profession.

Duties of members, too, might initially be thought to follow directly out of a church's historic standards. Secession churches had actually tried to make participation in the "work" of renewing the Covenants a condition of membership. But that was never enforced and had already been dropped among the "New Licht" Seceders, by the time of the United Secession basis of 1820. The United Presbyterian basis (1847) asserted

> the obligation and the privilege of its members [...] to support and extend, by voluntary contribution, the ordinances of the Gospel.[118]

In 1929, the Church of Scotland basis recognized

> the duty of her members to contribute, according to their ability, both by their service and their means, for the support of the ordinances of religion in this land and the extension of the Kingdom of Christ throughout the world,[119]

thus acknowledging, not only giving by the church's members in support of the ministries of others, but also the service that they themselves would render. The South Indian basis of union (1947) took this further:

> All members of the church have equally access to God. All, according to their measure, share in the heavenly High Priesthood of the risen and ascended Christ, from which alone the Church derives its character as a royal priesthood. All alike are called to continue upon earth the priestly work of Christ by showing forth in life and work the glory of the redeeming power of God in Him.[120]

Here, a priesthood of all believers is emphasized, as the participation of all members of the Church in the priestly ministry of Jesus Christ.

On the whole, ministry, ministries and particulars of church government were largely taken for granted in purely Presbyterian bases of union. The Westminster *Form of Presbyterial Church-Government* and such documents from the Reformation of the sixteenth century such as the *First* and *Second Books of Discipline* were sometimes listed among a church's standards. They provided for the ordering of ministries, as well as for church councils and government. But much will simply have proceeded on the basis of a common understanding of the inherent powers of kirk sessions, of presbyteries, and of a general assembly, and of the current state of "procedure and practice" ("consuetude") in the uniting churches. The Church of South India needed to have more details on ministries included in its basis of union, and far more on government, in its constitution.

The purpose of a basis of union is to provide the foundation on which two or more existing denominations may come together to constitute a new, united church. It needs to give each of the uniting churches assurances on a number of points:

(i) There will be a vision of what it might mean to reflect more faithfully the oneness, the holiness, the catholicity and the apostolicity of the Church of God, under the sole Headship of Jesus Christ, and in the power of the one Spirit. This may be a

149

common vision of all the uniting churches. But they will wish to spell out how they intend to pursue that vision in the union they are contemplating.

(ii) There will be issues, perhaps particularly among those listed from 1. to 17. above, on which the uniting churches have differed in the past, in ways that they have understood to necessitate separation between them. Each of the uniting churches will need to see how these differences have been resolved so as to make union possible.

(iii) There will be points on which differences have existed, without anyone's seriously thinking of them as grounds for remaining separate. Each uniting church will still want to know which differences will be allowed to remain, as elements in an enriching diversity, and which have been settled, in one way or another, in the interests of harmony, efficiency and simplicity.

(iv) Each uniting church will need to know what things can be relied on, or have to be accepted, as givens. What will the united church as a whole and all of its ministers be committed to, as far as the faith and doctrine, worship, government and discipline of the church are concerned?

(v) Each uniting church will need to know what limits and safeguards will be provided regarding possible further requirements in the future. It will want to assure its members and ministers that the united church will not keep on making new demands, except by certain procedures and within definite limits.

(vi) Partly through what is covered under (iv) above, but also more generally, there has to be clarity about the basis and extent of mutual recognition and acceptance in the united church. The basis of union needs to establish agreement between those churches on the minimum requirements for unqualified acceptance of members and ministers.

(vii) Both for the assurance of those coming into the union and for the freedom of action of the united church, there has to be clarity about what is fixed and what is variable, and also about how absolutely fixed the fixed is and by what means the variable may be varied.

(viii) The act of union will be a most suitable occasion for renewed commitment and renewal in faith, life and service. For this to be a unifying experience, it will be necessary to indicate the spirit and scope of these in advance.

When it asked to see a draft basis for the proposed union with Congregationalists and Methodists, the Presbyterian Church of Australia will have been coming out of the history sketched in our review of previous bases of union, with whatever collective wisdom and insights, fears and phobias, it had gathered along the way. It will have felt sensitivity about issues of the kind listed from 1. to 17. above. It will have expected any draft basis of union to offer assurances on the points listed as (i) to (viii) immediately above. One matter that the General Assembly subsequently decided to be essential to have laid down in any basis of union was the principles of church government that would apply in a united church.[121] Another was the terms for subscription of the united church's faith and order by ministers and office-bearers, with adequate provision for liberty of opinion on matters that did not enter into the substance of the faith.[122]

Individual members and ministers of the Presbyterian Church will, to varying degrees, have had some clarity or confusion about the past history, the perennial issues, and the necessary preconditions, of bringing churches together into corporate union.

NOTES

1 See above, p.8.

2 These events are summarized in "The Basis and Plan of Union, 1929" of the Church of Scotland, in James T. Cox, ed., *Practice and Procedure in the Church of Scotland*, 5th ed., ed. J.B. Longmuir (= Cox), Edinburgh & London, Committee on General Administration [of the General Assembly], 1964, pp.362-409, p.362. The dates in the text are taken from that source and show the year of separation from the established church. In most cases, the new group did not constitute itself as a church until some later time. - See also J.H.S. Burleigh, *A Church History of Scotland*, London, O.U.P., 1960, pp.262f,279-285,334-369; - Andrew L. Drummond & James Bulloch, *The Scottish Church 1688-1843*, Edinburgh, St Andrew, 1973, repr. 1981, pp.25f,40-44,59-62,220-265; - William Ferguson, *Scotland: 1689 to the Present*, Edinburgh, Mercat, 1968 repr.1990 (= *The Edinburgh History of Scotland*, vol.4), pp.111f, 121-126, 307-317. - The chart on page 162 may help readers to keep track of the various stages of the story in Scotland.

3   A reference to the basis and articles of union may be found in John McKerrow, *History of the Secession Church,* rev. and enlarged ed., Edinburgh & London, Fullarton, 1848, pp.571f, cf pp.333f. - On this union and the uniting churches, see also G.D. Mathews, et al., "Appendix IV: Report on Presbyterian Churches, Div.3: United States of North America", in J. Thomson, ed., *Report of Proceedings of the First General Presbyterian Council convened at Edinburgh, July 1877 [...],* Edinburgh, Thos & Archibald Constable, 1877, pp.320-332, pp.329f,331; - Sydney E. Ahlstrom, *A Religious History of the American People,* New Haven & London, Yale U.P., 1972 repr. 1979, pp.277-279.

4   "The National Covenant; or, The Confession of Faith [...]", in *The Confession of Faith; the Larger and Shorter Catechisms [...],* Edinburgh, Johnstone, Hunter & Co., 1869 & repr., pp.267-272. - The relevant acts of the General Assembly (30 August 1639) and of the Parliament (11 June 1640) are reproduced, *ibid.,* p.266. - See Burleigh, *A Church History,* pp.217f.

5   Burleigh, *A Church History,* p.218.

6   "The Solemn League and Covenant for Reformation and Defence of Religion, the Honour and Happiness of the King, and the Peace and Safety of the Three Kingdoms of Scotland, England and Ireland" (1643), in *The Confession of Faith,* pp.276-278; - also in Samuel Rawson Gardiner, ed., *The Constitutional Documents of the Puritan Revolution 1625-1660,* 3rd rev.ed., Oxford, Clarendon, 1906 repr. 1927, pp.267-271; - and in Henry Bettenson, ed., *Documents of the Christian Church,* 2nd ed., London, O.U.P., 1963, pp.403-407.

7   The Scottish Parliament consisted of the three estates of nobility, higher clergy, and commissioners representing shires and burghs. There was also a Convention of the Estates, with even less power than the Parliament. The Privy Council summoned a meeting of the Convention to ratify the *Solemn League and Covenant,* because the King would not summon Parliament.

8   The General Assembly's approbation (17 August 1643) and the act of the Convention of the Estates (15 July 1644) are reproduced in *The Confession of Faith,* pp.274f. - The English Parliament swore to the *Solemn League and Covenant* on 25 September 1643. - See Burleigh, *A Church History,* pp.224f.

9   See, e.g., *Scots Confession* (1560), artt.16,18; - *Westminster Confession* (1647), cap.XXV.ii,iv.

10 "[...] there can be no doubt that the rediscovery in the historical books of the Old Testament of 'the godly prince', and the argument therefrom *a fortiori* to the authority of the christian sovereign, was one of the most important and significant themes of the Reformers, alike Lutheran, Calvinist, and Anglican" (Norman Sykes, *Old Priest and New Presbyter,* Cambridge, U.P., 1956, p.3, cf cap.1, "The Godly Prince and the Godly Bishop", pp.1-29). - See, too, Gordon Donaldson, *The Scottish Reformation,* Cambridge, U.P., 1960, cap.6, "The 'Godly Magistracy' and the General Assembly", pp.130-148; - for the Scottish reformers, see the *Scots Confession* (1560), art.24.

11 Burleigh, *A Church History,* pp.227-232.

12 Burleigh, *A Church History,* pp.233-242,251f. - For a good short account of the period covered in the preceding paragraphs, see James S. McEwen, "How the Confession came to be Written", in Alasdair I.C. Heron, ed., *The Westminster Confession in the Church Today: Papers Prepared for the Church of Scotland Panel on Doctrine,* Edinburgh, St Andrew, 1982, pp.6-16.

13 Burleigh, *A Church History,* pp.249-251.

14 Burleigh, *A Church History,* pp.252-255.

15 Burleigh, *A Church History,* pp.271-274.

16   Burleigh, *A Church History,* pp.277-279.

17   McKerrow, *History,* pp.257-259,274f,296-302,314f; - in Thomson, ed., *Report of Proceedings,* p.329.

18   McKerrow, *History,* pp.333-336,357f.

19   Mathews, et al., in Thomson, ed., *Report of Proceedings,* p.329,331.

20   The text of the United Secession basis of union (1820) is to be found in McKerrow, *History,* pp.656f.

21   Did this mean that the Westminster *Form of Presbyterial Church-Government* was a good collection of rules for church polity or that the Westminster *Directory for the Public Worship of God* was a good collection for worship? The context in this article suggests the former, the title used, the latter. The United Presbyterian basis seems to have taken this passage in the latter sense.

22   Burleigh, *A Church History,* pp.324,362; - Ferguson, *Scotland: 1689 to the Present,* p.410.

23   "Articles forming the Basis of Union of the United Secession and Relief Churches to form the United Presbyterian Church", in Cox, pp.413f; - "Appendix B: Basis of Union as Adopted by Secession and Relief Synods in 1847", in J.R. Fleming, *A History of the Church in Scotland 1843-1874,* vols 1-2, Edinburgh, T. & T. Clark, 1927, vol.1, pp.265f. - On the union of these two churches, see Fleming, *A History,* vol.1, pp.81-84; - Burleigh, *A Church History,* p.362f; - Andrew L. Drummond & James Bulloch, *The Church in Victorian Scotland 1843-1874,* Edinburgh, St Andrew, 1975, pp.43-45.

24   There is an interesting parallel between this Article X of the United Presbyterian basis and Paragraphs 1 and 2 of the Uniting Church's *Basis of Union.*

25   D[onald] Macrae Stewart, *Growth in Fifty Years: 1859.1909,* Melbourne, Presbyterian Church of Victoria, n.d., pp.36f; - Robert Hamilton, *A Jubilee History of the Presbyterian Church of Victoria, or, The Rise and Progress of Presbyterianism from the Foundation of the Colony to 1888,* Melbourne, Hutchinson / London, Hodder / Edinburgh, Oliphant, Anderson & Ferrier, 1888, pp.181-186.

26   James Cameron, *Centenary History of the Presbyterian Church in New South Wales,* Sydney, Angus & Robertson, 1905, pp.34-40; - Macrae Stewart, Growth, pp.23-27; - Hamilton, *A Jubilee History,* pp.27-34.- This division took place before 1851, when the colony of Victoria separated from N.S.W., and the Presbytery of Melbourne, from the N.S.W.-based Synod of Australia in Connection with the Church of Scotland.

27   Burleigh, *A Church History,* pp.338-342; - Drummond & Bulloch, *The Scottish Church 1688-1843,* pp.225-228,233-235.

28   On this resolution anent the independent jurisdiction of the Church of Scotland, see Burleigh, *A Church History,* pp.342f; - Drummond & Bulloch, *The Scottish Church 1688-1843,* pp.235f.

29   On the "Claim, Declaration and Protest anent the Encroachment of the Court of Sessions", see Burleigh, *A Church History,* pp.348f; - Drummond & Bulloch, *The Scottish Church 1688-1843,* pp.241-243.

30   The text of the Free Church protest of 1843 is to be found as Appendix A in Fleming, *A History,* vol.1, pp.261- 265.

31   Hamilton, *A Jubilee History,* pp.37f,45f,49,112f.

32   Hamilton, *A Jubilee History,* pp.181f.

33   The text of the basis of union 1859 may be found in Hamilton, *A Jubilee History,* p.172.

34 In Presbyterian churches, in services of licensing or ordination, after a licentiate, minister, elder or deacon has answered the prescribed questions, she or he signs the "formula", i.e. a set form of words encapsulating everything declared in answer to the questions. (The Secession church used the term 'formula' for the set of questions, rather than such an additional text.)

35 See in James Cooper, *Confessions of Faith and Formulas of Subscription in the Reformed Churches of Great Britain and Ireland especially in the Church of Scotland[,] being a Series of Lectures Delivered to Students of Church History in the Opening Days of Session 1906-7 (25th to 30th October, 1906)*, Glasgow, Jas Maclehose, 1907, p.91.

36 Macrae Stewart, *Growth*, pp.37f; - Patrick Carnegie Simpson, *The Life of Principal Rainy*, voll.1-2, London, Hodder, 1909, vol.1, pp.143f; - Kenneth R. Ross, *Church and Creed in Scotland: The Free Church Case 1900-1904 and its Origins*, Edinburgh, Rutherford House, 1988, pp.13f.

37 Oswald Dykes acted as an intermediary and drafted a declaratory act to clarify four points in the 1859 basis of union on which the continuing Free Church had doubts. The act was adopted by both churches in November 1866 as the basis of a union between them (Hamilton, *A Jubilee History*, pp.230f,251f). The declaratory act is printed *ibid.*, pp.251f.

38 Macrae Stewart, *Growth*, pp.37-39; - A.J. Campbell, *Fifty Years of Presbyterianism in Victoria: A Jubilee Sketch*, Melbourne, Hutchinson/ Edinburgh, Oliphant, Anderson and Ferrier/ London, Nisbet, [1889?]. pp.55,57-59; - Hamilton, *A Jubilee History*, pp.208,211-215,217,224,226f,228f,230f,233,237,238, 240,241,243,282,283,286-91. - Robert Hamilton, minister of Napier St, Fitzroy, was himself a member of the U.P. group that remained separate until 1870. He is to be distinguished from the Robert Hamilton who was minister of Learmonth and Springs for the Presbyterian Church of Victoria from 1863.

39 Cameron, *Centenary History*, pp.67-85; - C.A. White, *The Challenge of the Years: A History of the Presbyterian Church of Australia in the State of New South Wales*, Sydney & London, Angus & Robertson, (1951), pp.14-23. - The Presbyterians in Queensland had already separated from N.S.W. to form their own united church in November 1863, "on the basis of the *Westminster Confession of Faith*" (letter from Charles Ogg, "Convener", in Thomson, ed., *Report of Proceedings*, pp.362f, p.362; - cf Cameron, *Centenary History*, p.46). A united presbytery was formed in South Australia in 1865 (Hamilton, *A Jubilee History*, p.247; - in Thomson, ed., *Report of Procedings*, p.342).

40 The text of the basis of union of the Presbyterian Church of New South Wales may be found in Cameron, *Centenary History*, pp.71f. - It is also to be found in a paper prepared by the Church Extension Committee of the N.S.W. church for the General Presbyterian Council of 1877, in Thomson, ed., *Report of Proceedings*, pp.359-362, p.359.

41 (1) is derived from that church's "Act and Declaration anent the Publication of the Subordinate Standards [...]", 1851, with minor verbal variations, the omission of the *Directory for Family Worship*, the inclusion of the *Second Book of Discipline*, and the omission, after the words, "of the nature of regulations, rather than of tests", of the further explanatory phrase, "to be enforced by the Church like her other laws" (Cooper, *Confessions of Faith and Formulas*, p.94). (2) is derived from the preamble to the act of the Free Church General Assembly of 1846 and is related to a parallel passage in the Victorian basis of union of 1859 (see n.35 above). (3) echoes the resolution of the General Assembly anent the independent jurisdiction of the Church of Scotland (see above n.28), and the fundamental position of the "Claim of Right" or "Claim, Declaration and Protest anent the

Encroachment of the Court of Sessions", the Government's disregard of which led to the Disruption (see n.29 above).

42 Ross, *Church and Creed*, p.14, p.15 n.32 (p.306). - For the union in Canada, see Robert T. Handy, *A History of the Church in the United States and Canada*, Oxford, Clarendon, 1976, pp.250f. - Kenneth Ross also shows how the "Australian Union" debate of 1861 (see n.36 above) already involved a polarization over issues that would lead to the split of 1900 (Ross, *ibid.*, p.13f).

43 Burleigh, *A Church History*, pp.363-367; - Fleming, *A History*, vol.2, pp.40-50,58f; - Ferguson, *Scotland: 1689 to the Present*, pp.339f.

44 Fleming, *A History*, vol.1, pp.174-184; - Burleigh, *A Church History*, pp.363f. - "[...] the two churches were united in holding the spiritual independence of the Church, and in believing that civil government is an ordinance of God and that the magistrate ought to be guided in legislation by the Bible. What divided them was that the Free Church could not accept the United Presbyterian insistence that there were no conceivable circumstances in which it was competent for the State to establish and endow a particular church" (Ross, *Church and Creed*, p.22).

45 Fleming, *A History*, vol.1, p.238; vol.2, pp.5,26-34; - Burleigh, *A Church History*, pp.364-366; - Ross, *Church and Creed*, pp.119-128.

46 "The cry for disestablishment, however, died down. After 1886 many of the U.P. laity became Unionist in politics and highly critical of disestablishment, so much so that they formed a Laymen's League, the object of which was 'to declare against Disestablishment and the secularizing of the endowments of the Church'. The league also advocated presbyterian reunion in Scotland" (Ferguson, *Scotland: 1689 to the Present*, p.340).

47 Burleigh, *A Church History*, p.362; - Fleming, *A History*, vol.2, pp.35f. - Another union that also took place in 1876 was in England. It resulted in the formation of the Presbyterian Church of England (Fleming, *A History*, vol.2, p.36).

48 See "Uniting Act, 1876: Act of Union of the Free Church of Scotland and the Reformed Presbyterian Church of Scotland", in Cox, pp.415f; - "Uniting Act" [1900], *ibid.*, pp.417-419.

49 In Cox, pp.417f,419.

50 Cooper, *Confessions of Faith and Formulas*, p.101.

51 A.C. Cheyne, *The Transforming of the Kirk: Victorian Scotland[']s Religious Revolution*, Edinburgh, St Andrew, 1983, pp.83-85, cf 73-83. - The texts of these two declaratory acts are to be found in Cox, pp.411f ("Declaratory Act of the United Presbyterian Synod [Adopted May 1879.]") and pp.412f ("Declaratory Act of the General Assembly of the Free Church, 1892 - Anent the Confession of Faith"); - also in Fleming, *A History*, vol.2, pp.306f,307f; - in Cooper, *Confessions of Faith and Formulas*, pp.96f, 99-101; - and in Heron, ed., *The Westminster Confession*, pp.141-144.

52 Fleming, *A History*, vol.2, pp.18f,22f; - Burleigh, *A Church History*, pp.360f,366,384.

53 Fleming, *A History*, vol.2, pp.22f,59f; - Burleigh, *A Church History*, pp.367-369; - Ross, *Church and Creed*, pp.194-211. - Ross discusses the text of the Free Church declaratory act in relation to the aims of its proponents and the criticisms of its opponents, ibid., pp.200-207. - Note, too, the further Free Church Act of 1894 "Anent Declaratory Act, 1892, on Confession of Faith" in Cox, p.413; and also in Cooper, *Confessions of Faith and Formulas*, pp.97f.

54 Burleigh, *A Church History*, pt IV, cap.3, "The Evangelical Revival", pp.309-333. - Ross, *Church and Creed*, pp.73-81,197-199.

55 See Fleming, *A History*, vol.1, pp.45-47,177f; - Burleigh, *A Church History*, pp.331-333; - Drummond & Bulloch, *The Scottish Church 1688-1843*, pp.36f,180f,193f, 196f,201-203,208-211,219; - Ian Hamilton, *The Erosion of Calvinist Orthodoxy: Seceders and Subscription in Scottish Presbyterianism*, Edinburgh, Rutherford House Books, 1990 (*Rutherford Studies Series One: Historical Theology*), pp.34-84; - Cheyne, *Transforming*, pp.61-66.

56 Burleigh, *A Church History*, pp.359f; - Cheyne, *Transforming*, cap.2, "The Biblical Revolution", pp.37-57; - Carnegie Simpson, *Life of Rainy*, vol.1, pp.306-403; - G.F. Barbour, *The Life of Alexander Whyte*, D.D., 7th ed., London, Hodder, 1925, pp.201-222; - Ross, *Church and Creed*, pp.175-184,264-266.

57 In Cox, p.412. - The issue was not whether a minister or elder had to "believe everything that was in the Bible". The extent to which liberty of opinion was allowed was defined with reference to "points in the Standards". That already protected office-bearers from attacks based on a too simplistic biblicism. The "six days" became a possible issue - and a current one, given the new, critical approach to Old Testament scholarship - because they were mentioned in the *Confession*, cap.I.i, in the *Larger Catechism*, q.15, and in the *Shorter*, q.9.

58 The "Basis of Federation" for the federated churches collaborating through the Federal Assembly is printed as "Appendix K", in Hamilton, *A Jubilee History*, p.xxix. - See Macrae Stewart, *Growth*, p.41; - Cameron, *Centenary History*, pp.191-194.

59 The text of the "Scheme of Union" of 1901 may be found in Presbyterian Church of Australia, *Constitution and Procedure and Practice, rev. and issued by the Code Committee*, Melbourne, Board of Religious Education of the General Assembly, 1950, pp.20-35 (there referred to as the "Deed of Union"); - also in *Basic Documents on Presbyterian Polity with Introductions and Notes*, [Melbourne], Board of Christian Education, Presbyterian Church of Australia, 1961, pp.91-100. - The latter edition does not give the text of all of the Articles of Agreement, but is otherwise a better source for the exact original text of the Scheme of Union (apart from one or two misprints). It contains helpful notes on wording and sources prepared by the late F. Maxwell Bradshaw. - See Macrae Stewart, *Growth*, pp.41-45; - Cameron, *Centenary History*, pp.193-199.

60 George Yule writes that "till the 1930s the *Shorter Catechism* was widely used in Sunday schools and this had quite an effect" (G. Yule, "The Westminster Confession in Australia", in Heron, ed., *The Westminster Confession*, pp.101-103, p.102). Candidates for the ministry still sat an entrance examination in "Bible Knowledge and [Shorter] Catechism" for admission to a theological hall in the 1950's.

61 On liturgical developments in the latter part of the nineteenth century, see Macrae Stewart, *Growth*, pp.77-80; - Cheyne, *Transforming*, cap.4, "The Liturgical Revolution", pp.88-107.

62 The Victorian Declaratory Act of 1882 is printed in R. Hamilton, *A Jubilee History*, pp.415f.

63 On the "Strong Case", see Macrae Stewart, *Growth*, pp.73-75; - A.J. Campbell, *Fifty Years*, pp.105-110; - R. Hamilton, *A Jubilee History*, pp.392,400f,402f,409f, 424-427,430-432,434f,442-445; - Jill Roe, "Challenge and Response: Religious Life in Melbourne, 1876-86", in *The Journal of Religious History*, vol.5, no.2 (December 1968), pp.149-166; - C.R. Badger, *The Revd Charles Strong and the Australian Church*, Melbourne, Abacada, 1971, pp.36-92; - Engel, *Australian Christians in Conflict and Unity*, pp.72-75; - Don Chambers, "Theological Hall", in Stuart MacIntyre, ed., *Ormond College: Centenary Essays*, pp.103-121, pp.104f,108, cf 113-115.

64 Reprinted in Badger, *Charles Strong*, pp.239-248.

65 In Hamilton, *A Jubilee History*, p.403. - A.J. Campbell reads, "objective supernatural historical facts" and "the Presbytery earnestly entreat, and in the spirit of brotherly-kindness urge upon," (*Fifty Years*, p.106).

66 "Atonement [...] has also assumed various philosophical forms in the systems of Kant, Fichte, Schelling, and Hegel. [...] Suffice it to say that the general tendency of the philosophers is to idealize the doctrine, letting the historical facts, which are regarded as but the temporary drapery, fall completely into the background. The idea and ideal, it is affirmed, are the real, and in them alone is to be found the truth and the life" (Charles Strong, "The Atonement", in Badger, *Charles Strong*, pp.239-248, p.246). - Badger wishes to understand Strong's article as "a scholarly account of the historical development of the doctrine, [which] nowhere indicated Strong's own views and nowhere professed to be an explanation of any ecclesiastical standpoint" (*ibid.*, p.41). But, following immediately upon the above quotation from the article, Strong continues, "There are several lessons which may be learned... 1. In the first place, acquaintance with the history of this and of other Christian doctrines should teach us that Christianity is a spirit, not a form. [...] Unity of spirit, not uniformity, is the universal law of life. While, therefore, we seek earnestly to find the truest intellectual forms into which to cast our faith, it ought to be remembered that 'it is the Spirit' alone 'which quickeneth'. [...] Such a view of Christianity can alone lead us into a wider charity which is not indifference, and to a profounder insight into the meaning and essence of all doctrines (*ibid.*, p.246). In this and three other lessons that he also develops (pp.246-248), Strong certainly presents his own views. To understand the controversy surrounding his article, it is necessary to recall that, as a minister of the Presbyterian Church, Strong had vowed to "assert, maintain, and defend" the doctrine of the *Confession of Faith*, including its doctrine of the Atonement, and that his presbytery would not have thought him at liberty to publish views of his own inconsistent with that doctrine.

67 Chambers, "Theological Hall", in MacIntyre, ed., *Ormond College*, pp.108-110,113-115; - Macrae Stewart, *Growth*, pp.75f.

68 For accounts of Stewart's speech at this meeting and the church's reaction, see Hamilton, *A Jubilee History*, pp.409f; - Badger, *Charles Strong*, pp.52-54. - The two accounts present quite different aspects of the speech and judge it quite differently.

69 Charles Strong gave further grave offence to the Presbytery and Assembly in 1883, by taking a public stand against the Sabbatarianism that, for Presbyterians of that day, inevitably followed from the *Confession of Faith*, cap.XXI.vii,viii, and also by inviting an Anglican lay person, Mr Justice Higinbotham, generally supposed to be a Unitarian, to give a lecture in Scots Church. The Presbytery moved to commence a process of discipline, and Strong sought to resign from the parish. Scots Church decided to separate itself from the Presbyterian Church of Victoria, by getting a bill through Parliament. Strong was asked to attend the Assembly in November 1883 and make a statement to clear himself. He declined to do so and left Victoria. The Assembly thereupon declared that he was no longer a minister of the Presbyterian Church of Victoria and dissolved the pastoral tie between him and the Scots parish. The Assembly accepted with regret J.C. Stewart's resignation as Law Agent. It gained the support of the Church of England, the Wesleyan, Primitive Methodist and Bible Christian Churches, and the Executive of the Congregational Union, for its opposition to the Scots Church Property Bill, which was defeated in 1884. The special commission of the Assembly that had been active in the matter expressed its appreciation of the services rendered by Mr R. Harper, M.L.A., who had made a long, informative speech against the bill, and by Mr J.M. Davies, who had been

appointed as the new Law Agent (R. Hamilton, *A Jubilee History*, pp.424-427,430-432,434f,439,441,442-445,451f,453f,460f; - Macrae Stewart, *Growth*, pp.74-77; - Badger, *Charles Strong*, pp.95-98). *Charles Strong* returned to Melbourne late in 1884 and was encouraged to hold Sunday services in the Temperance Hall. Out of this grew the Australian Church (Badger, *Charles Strong*, pp.94f,98-100).

70 On the issue of what the phrase "whole doctrine" might mean at this time, see Ross, *Church and Creed*, pp.195f.

71 In Hamilton, *A Jubilee History*, p.416.

72 Hamilton, *A Jubilee History*, pp.416,456.

73 Hamilton, *A Jubilee History*, p.417.

74 The other judges who found for the appellants held the case already to be decided over the "Establishment Principle" and saw no need to pursue this (theologically far more complex) second issue. - See Ross, *Church and Creed*, pp.73-81; - Fleming, *A History*, vol.2, pp.22,59-70; - Burleigh, *A Church History*, pp.361,368, 369; - Cooper, *Confessions of Faith and Formulas*, pp.97f.

75 Maxwell Bradshaw writes of the first paragraph of the Declaratory Statement that "the remainder [...] is a recast form of the final portion of the Declaratory Act adopted by the General Assembly of Victoria in 1882" (in *Basic Documents on Presbyterian Polity*, p.93, n.6). It is, rather, derived directly from the same source as that part of the 1882 act, viz. the resolution of the Presbytery of Melbourne quoted at n.65 above, and it reproduces far more of it than the 1882 act of the Victorian Assembly did, and with far less modification.

76 The United Presbyterian wording allowed that the *Confession* might teach, or might be supposed to teach, "persecuting and intolerant principles in religion". The Free Church tended never to go as far as that, but only to say that it did not consider that anyone subscribing the *Confession* was committed to any such principles. - See Cooper, *Confessions of Faith and Formulas*, p.93.

77 *Confession of Faith*, XX.ii. - There is a possible influence here from the Secession churches, through the U.P. element in the Australian church. For a declaratory act of the General Associate (Anti-Burgher) Synod of 1796 appealed to this statement in the *Confession* in a similar way (McKerrow, *History*, p.381).

78 Printed in Cox, "Appendix I", p.361; - also in *Basic Documents on Presbyterian Polity*, p.87, with an introduction pp.82-86.

79 Presbyterian Church of Australia, *Constitution and Procedure and Practice*, pp.20f,56, with references to the relevant reports and minutes of the General Assembly on pp.137f. - See Maxwell Bradshaw's criticism of the way in which these amendments to the *Westminster Confession* were there printed as amendments to the basis of union, in *Basic Documents on Presbyterian Polity*, p.92, n.4.

80 George Yule, in Heron, ed., *The Westminster Confession*, p.102.

81 This list has been reconstructed from information in Presbyterian Church of Australia, *Constitution and Procedure and Practice*, pp.24-25,138f. The original articles of agreement were subsequently amended and added to.

82 *BB 1970*, min.30.1, the text of the basis of union is embodied in the minute, pp.26-31; - see the report pp.113-123.

83 *BB 1970*, min.30.1, sec.15 of the basis of union 1970.

84 Handy, *A History of the Churches*, pp.364-372; - Rodney M. Booth, *The Winds of God: The Canadian Church Faces the 1980's*, Geneva, W.C.C., & Winfield, B.C., Wood Lake Books, 1982 (= *Risk Books*, 16), pp.49-51. - See, in general, S.D. Chown, *The Story of Church Union in Canada*, Toronto, Ryerson, (1930).

85 "The Basis of Union as prepared by the Joint Committee of the Presbyterian, Methodist and Congregational Churches, and approved by the Supreme Courts of these Churches", in the United Church of Canada, *Record of Proceedings of the First General Council, meeting in Toronto, Ontario, June 10th-18th, 1925, [...]*, Toronto, 1925, pp.239-254 (= app.1).

86 The following "brief summary of our common faith" makes a stronger statement under art.II *Of Revelation*, "[...] and that in the fulness of time He has perfectly revealed Himself in Jesus Christ, the Word made flesh, who is the brightness of the Father's glory and the express image of his person. We receive the Holy Scriptures of the Old and New Testaments, given by inspiration of God, as containing the only infallible rule of faith and life, a faithful record of God's gracious revelations, and as the sure witness to Christ".

87 An influence of the Canadian basis of union, not on the basis of the Uniting Church, but on its polity, can be recognized by comparing the provision that "It shall be the duty of the Conference: [...] (4) To see that, as far as possible, every pastoral charge within its bounds shall have a pastorate without interruption, and that every effective minister shall have a pastoral charge, and to effect this through a Settlement Committee which it shall appoint annually" ("The Basis of Union" [1925], "Polity", sec.22) with the provision for a Joint Presbyteries Settlements Advisory Committee in each synod of the Uniting Church.

88 "The statistics need considerable interpretation for local congregations varied greatly in size, but they show that the 4,797 Methodist, 3,728 Presbyterian, and 166 Congregational churches entered the union at the outset, while 784 Presbyterian (including some of the largest) and 8 Congregational did not. Perhaps slightly less than two-thirds of the Presbyterians entered the United Church [...]" (Handy, *A History of the Churches*, p.371).

89 "The development of a satisfactory doctrinal statement as the first main part of the Basis did not raise serious difficulties. By the early twentieth century, practical and social concerns seemed much more pressing than theological matters. [...] The aim of the committee was to develop a brief new statement of faith which would bring together the characteristic theological features of each participating communion in a non-controversial way. [...]. The [Twenty] Articles brought together mild Calvinism and mild Arminianism in a rather conservative short consensus [...] reflected main Protestant doctrinal positions in quite traditional language, and did not seriously reflect the liberal and social movements that were then conspicuous in the negotiating churches" (Handy, *A History of the Churches*, pp.366f). - "[...] a Plan of Union which critics observed contained 'a harmony of views but a minimum of credal novelty!' Still it was a masterful weaving together of distinctive Christian traditions and differing forms of ecclesiastical organization" (Booth, *The Winds of God*, pp.49f).

90 John Webster Grant, tr. D. Voorgang, "Kanada", in *Evangelisches Kirchenlexikon. Internationale theologische Enzyklopädie*, ed. Erwin Fahlbusch *et al.*, 3rd ed., voll.1-4 + index-vol., Göttingen, Vandenhoeck, 1984-[1997 ?], Bd 2 (1989), Sp.928-933, Sp.929.

91 Fleming, *A History*, vol.2, pp.126-134; - Burleigh, *A Church History*, pp.403f.

92 See above, n.74; - See, too, Ross, *Church and Creed*, esp. pp.41-103,255-300.

93 Fleming, *A History*, vol.2, pp.33,79; - Burleigh, *A Church History*, pp.368f.

94 Fleming, *A History*, vol.2, pp.74f; - Burleigh, *A Church History*, pp.364-366.

95 Fleming, *A History*, vol.2, pp.79f; - Burleigh, *A Church History*, p.369.

96 Printed in Cox, pp.368f; - also in Fleming, *A History*, vol.2, pp.309f (= Appendix D).

97 Fleming, *A History,* vol.2, pp.85-87. - On the other hand, as Burleigh writes, "the realization of the stupendous task of evangelizing the whole people was one of the most powerful motives for the Union of the Churches" (*A Church History,* p.405).

98 Fleming, *A History,* vol.2, pp.90f; - Burleigh, *A Church History,* pp.400f.

99 These "Articles Declaratory [...]" are printed in Cox, pp.366-368, and as the Schedule to Appendix V. - A, pp.447f; - also in Fleming, *A History,* vol.2, pp.310-312 (= Appendix E); - in Heron, ed., *The Westminster Confession,* pp.145-148; - and in Bettenson, ed., *Documents,* 2nd ed., pp.459-461, there abbreviated and with a slightly misleading introduction. - See Fleming, *A History,* vol.2, p.103; - Burleigh, *A Church History,* pp.402f.

100 Printed in Cox, "Appendix V. - A", p.446, with the "Articles Declaratory [...]" as a schedule, pp.447f; - also in Heron, ed., *The Westminster Confession,* pp.144f. - See the important essay by Francis Lyall, "The Westminster Confession: The Legal Position", in Heron, ed., *The Westminster Confession,* pp.55-71; - see also Fleming, *A History,* vol.2, pp.105-107; - Burleigh, *A Church History,* pp.401f.

101 Printed in Cox, "Appendix VI. - B", pp.459-486, with schedules pp.487-498. - See Fleming, *A History,* vol.2, pp.107-111; - Burleigh, *A Church History,* p.403.

102 Burleigh, *A Church History,* pp.404f. "Into the reunited Church in 1929 were gathered the great majority of Presbyterians, forming rather more than four-fifths of the church-going Protestant population of the country" (*ibid.,* p.405). - See, too, Fleming, *A History,* vol.2, p.111.

103 Ferguson, *Scotland: 1689 to the Present,* p.380. - Ferguson refers to an article by R. King Murray, "The Constitutional Position of the Church of Scotland", in *Public Law,* (1958), pp.155-162.

104 In Cox, pp.362-371. - See Fleming, *A History,* vol.2, pp.114f.

105 Cf the *Westminster Confession of Faith,* cap.XXV.ii.-iv.

106 See n.69 and n.72 above. - The date of 1926 for the "Articles Declaratory [...]" is due to the fact that, the Church of Scotland Act, 1921, which declared the lawfulness of the Articles, was to come into operation "after the Declaratory Articles shall have been adopted by an Act of the General Assembly of the Church of Scotland with the consent of a majority of the Presbyteries of the Church" (in Cox, p.446). The United Free Church followed a similar procedure, but had kirk sessions and congregations vote, as well. The General Assembly of the Church of Scotland, meeting in May 1926, found that 76 of its 84 presbyteries had approved the Articles (Fleming, *A History,* vol.2, pp.112f) and was therefore able finally to adopt them itself.

107 In Cox, pp.366-369.

108 In Cox, pp.369-371.

109 In Cox, pp.371-409.

110 D.M. Devashayam, *The South India Church Union Movement with Appendix containing Reprint of Discussions,* Madras, 1938, pp.1-7; - W.J. Noble, *Christian Union in South India: An Adventure in Fellowship,* London, S.C.M. (for Friends of Reunion), 1936, pp.26-30; - *Proposed Scheme of Union including Draft Basis of Union for adoption by the uniting Churches, Draft Constitution of the united Church, and other documents[,] Prepared by the Joint Committee [...] with amendments accepted by the Joint Committee in February 1936,* 6th rev.ed., Madras, Allahabad, Colombo, Christian Literature Society, 1936, pp.iii-vi; - Bettenson, ed., *Documents,* 2nd ed., p.467; - Hans-Georg Link, ed., *Apostolic Faith Today: A Handbook for Study,* Geneva, World Council of Churches, 1978, (= *Faith and Order Paper,* 124), p.151.

111 The text of the final edition of the C.S.I. basis of union may be found as "Appendix I" in *The Constitution of the Church of South India with amendments up to and approved by the Synod of January 1972 together with the Basis of Union as adopted by the Governing Bodies of the Uniting Churches in India and elsewhere,* Madras, Christian Literature Society, 1972, pp.87-100. - Also, in extract, in Bettenson, ed., *Documents,* 2nd ed., pp.467- 470; - and in Link, ed., *Apostolic Faith Today,* pp.151- 155.

112 For an expression of the so-called "Quadrilateral" of Chicago (1886) and Lambeth (1888), see in the Lambeth Appeal of 1920, VIf, in Bettenson, ed., *Documents,* 2nd ed., pp.462-465, pp.464f; - cf Noble, *Christian Union in South India,* p.28; - Devashayam, *The South India Church Union Movement,* p.3.

113 For a discussion and defence of this approach, see J.E. Lesslie Newbigin, *The Reunion of the Church: a Defence of the South India Scheme,* London, SCM, 1948, 2nd rev.ed. 1960.

114 *The Constitution of the Church of South India with amendments up to and approved by the Synod of January 1972,* cap.II,sec.19, pp.16f.

115 "Declaratory Act of the United Presbyterian Synod" (adopted May 1879), in Cox, pp.411f, p.411.

116 "Articles forming the Basis of Union of the United Secession and Relief Churches to form the United Presbyterian Church", (adopted May 1847), in Cox, pp.413f, p.414.

117 In Cox, pp.413f.

118 In Cox, p.414.

119 In Cox, p.365.

120 Church of South India, Basis of Union, 1947, in *The Constitution of the Church of South India with amendments up to and approved by the Synod of January 1972,* p.90.

121 See above, p.129 and n.83.

122 See above, pp.95f and n.7.

Chart of Unions in Scotland

Years in italics, 1820, 1839, etc. Indicate acts of reunion.

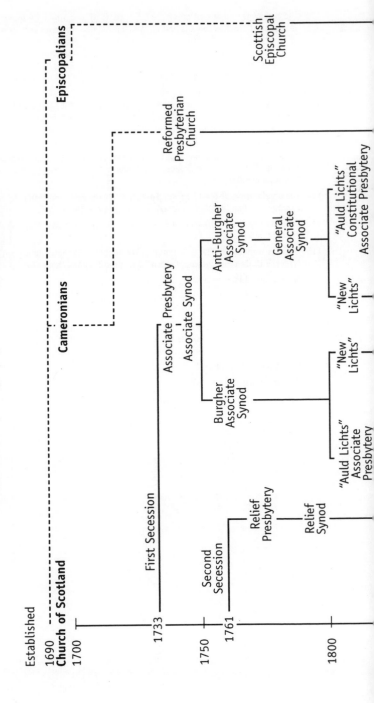

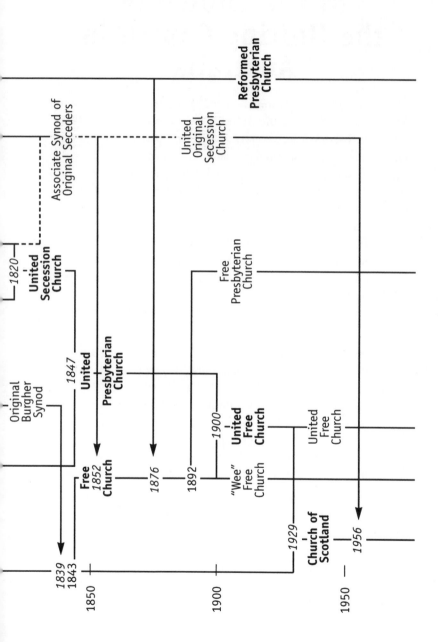

Commitment to the Faith of the Church in the Uniting Church in Australia[1]

While still young and impressionable, I happened once to spend some sixteen months as the Acting Clerk of a Presbytery. Rather unusually, that involved my taking a central part in every service held for the ordination and/or induction of a minister during this time. For the clerk in whose place I was acting was of the firm opinion that a moderator may do very well for reading the set prayers, and also for announcing the psalms and hymns (once the texts and tunes for such services had been fixed by the Presbytery once and for all), but that he could scarcely be entrusted with the putting of the questions appointed and the solemn act of the signing of the Formula, nor with the preamble to this part of the service. For these, only the Clerk could come in question. So it fell to my lot on some five or six occasions to ask, as the second of nine, the question:

> Do you own and accept the *Westminster Confession of Faith*, read in the light of the Declaratory Statement contained in the Basis of Union adopted by this Church on the 24th day of July, 1901, as an exhibition of the sense in which you understand the Holy Scriptures, and as a confession of your faith; and do you engage firmly and constantly to adhere thereto, and to the utmost of your power to maintain, and defend the same?[2]

Without having any illusions about the literary merits of this text, I always welcomed it as a challenge to my powers of reading aloud in public with some measure of coherence and comprehensibility, and I remember it best of all the nine questions. For this, if for no more worthy reason, I have ever been conscious of the way in which our Presbyterian Church follows up the commitment of its ministers to the Word of God contained in the Scriptures of the Old and New

Testaments with a commitment to a confession of faith as exhibiting the way in which those ministers understand the Scriptures and as a confession of their own faith. Tonight, I am proposing that we go on to ask in what ways the *Basis of Union* for the Congregational, Methodist and Presbyterian Churches would commit the ministry and perhaps, too, the membership of the new Uniting Church to a particular understanding of the witness of the Scriptures and of the faith of the Church.

This is, of course, an important question not only for Presbyterians, but also for Congregationalists and Methodists, as they face the final decisions on whether or not they will vote for the union and whether or not they themselves will enter into it. As I understand the situation, Methodist ministers are now, before their ordination, examined as to their agreement with the views expressed in Wesley's *Forty-Four Sermons* and *Notes on the New Testament*, while Congregationalist ministers are not asked about their assent to any particular statements of the faith. The ministers of all three churches are asked to acknowledge the Scriptures of the Old and New Testaments as being - in some sense or other - the Word of God and normative for faith and life. If they wish to enter the ministry of the proposed new Uniting Church in Australia, they will be required to "adhere to the *Basis of Union*", which phrase

> is understood as willingness to live and work within the faith and unity of the One Holy Catholic and Apostolic Church as that way is described in this *Basis*. Such adherence allows for difference of opinion in matters which do not enter into the substance of the faith (par.14).

It is most unfortunate that this definition of "adherence to the *Basis of Union*", which was added to the final edition of the *Basis* for the sake of greater clarity,[3] is so oddly worded:

> [...] willingness to live and work within the faith and unity of the One Holy Catholic and Apostolic Church as that way is described in this *Basis*.

I can only take that to mean: "in such a way as is described" or "in the way described in this *Basis*". (For I cannot believe that "to live and work within the faith and unity" of the Church is here referred to as "the Way", as in Acts 19:23.) Similar adherence to the *Basis of Union* will be required of such other office-bearers as elders, leaders, deaconesses and lay or local preachers. What is required of them all is a willingness to live and work within the faith and unity of the one Church, holy, catholic and apostolic, in such a way as is described in the Uniting Church's *Basis*. Difference of opinion is allowed in matters that do not enter into the substance of the faith, but not in those that do. So ministers and other office-bearers are being asked to accept and abide by some agreed understanding with regard to the substance of the Church's faith. In what way, then, is this proposed common understanding set forth in the *Basis of Union*? What concrete commitment is required of us?

As soon as we ask this, it becomes necessary to note the relatively different forms this commitment will assume for the different office-bearers. It is, after all, a commitment to "live and work" within the faith of the Church. Its concrete implications will depend upon the nature of an individual person's service. But, once such differentiation has begun, it cannot be confined to recognised office-bearers at all. For the *Basis* speaks of the Church's members' being corporately and individually involved in its mission, and in study and confession of the faith, so that they, too, are called to some kind of commitment with regard to the Church's faith (parr.3,5,7,8,9,12,13).

But, to begin with the broadest scope, it is first of all the Uniting Church itself that, in its *Basis of Union*, will bind itself to live and work within the "faith and unity of the One Holy Catholic and Apostolic Church" (par.2, cf. 1). The primary commitment is thus a corporate one. What is asked of the individual member and office-bearer is his or her participation therein, in whatever form is appropriate to his or her personal level of education and understanding and to his or her peculiar gifts and service within the Church and the world.

This intention of the Uniting Church to live and work within the faith and unity of the Church Catholic reflects neither a romantic infatuation with some earlier Golden Age of the Church's history nor an absolute identification of some particular credal formulation with the faith, or of some particular form of organisation with the unity, of the One Holy Catholic and Apostolic Church. After it has stated the involvement of the Uniting Church in the faith and unity of the Church Catholic, both as a matter of conviction and in terms of those denominational, ecumenical and missionary relations that give expression, however partially, to the Church's unity in faith and mission, the *Basis of Union* presses on, beyond what may be said of the Church both ideally and empirically, to make the acknowledgment,

> that the faith and unity of the Holy Catholic and Apostolic Church are built upon the one Lord Jesus Christ (par.3).

This step back from the opening statements about the Church to even more basic statements about Jesus Christ is characteristic of this *Basis of Union*. It is its central Christological assertions that are supposed to bear the weight of all other assertions about the Church, the Scriptures, and the Church's sacraments, creeds and confessions, membership, ministries and government. And it is intended that, through this primary Christological emphasis, various other issues - such as that of the relationship between the Word of God and the human words in the Bible, such as that of the relationship between the efficacy of the sacraments and the faith in which their benefits are to be received - will be brought into proper perspective, and so admit of a generally acceptable solution. So, in this present case, where it is a matter of giving concrete definition to the "faith of the Holy Catholic and Apostolic Church", the *Basis of Union* seeks initially to by-pass the thorny questions of the relation between Scripture and tradition, and of the place and authority of creeds and confessions, and to focus attention for a start on Jesus Christ, as the object, content, lord and preserver of the Church's faith, meaning to return and face these other questions in due course.

This important third Paragraph of the *Basis*, in which its central Christological assertions are contained, begins by speaking of Jesus Christ as the One preached and confessed by the Church and as the One in whom God's work of reconciliation and redemption has been wrought. It does this with reference to the New Testament titles, Christ, Lord and Son of God, and to New Testament formulae of confession, acclamation and proclamation. Next it speaks of the earthly ministry of Jesus and the meaning of his life and death, and of his resurrection.

From that one, particular event of Christ's death and resurrection, the section finally looks forward to the day when the reconciliation effected, and the renewal inaugurated, there will manifestly embrace the whole of Creation. This present period,

> between the time of Christ's death and resurrection and the final consummation of all things which he will bring[,]

is thus seen as the time

(a) in which people hear the good news about Jesus Christ as a call to faith in God,

(b) in which God's Spirit is given

    (i) so that people may so believe

    (ii) and also

> as a pledge and foretaste of that coming reconciliation and renewal which is the end in view for the whole creation[,]

(c) in which the Church lives as

> an instrument through which Christ may work and bear witness to himself (par.3).

This, then, is the view of the Church and its mission that the *Basis of Union* presupposes, when it speaks of the faith of the Church. The Church lives on through the history of this world, on pilgrimage from the decisive action of God in Christ's death and resurrection toward the ultimate realization in all creation of the destiny that has already been decided for it in that event. This Church is a fellowship of human beings who are already beginning to enjoy, in an anticipatory way, the new life and the renewed relations to God and each other that Jesus is bringing for all people. But, on the road to this final end, the Church is Christ's instrument in his outreach to the people of every nation and of each succeeding generation. Through the Church, he works and bears witness to himself.

So the discussion of the Church's faith and mission in the *Basis of Union* presupposes the closest of associations between the Church's witness and the present activity of Jesus Christ himself. The *Basis* must be seen as making two stresses: Firstly, that Christ now works through the Church's witness to him; secondly, that the Church itself is dependent for its existence and continuance on this active presence of its Lord in its midst.

The close association between the witness of the Church and the activity of Jesus Christ is not just a matter of mutual dependence and cooperation. Christ does indeed work through the ministry of human beings, and his activity thus requires the presence of a group of people that stands in his service. It requires, in fact, the Church, as a continuing, organized fellowship that transmits the news of Christ's death and resurrection from one day to the next and from one generation to the next. It requires, in practice, the development and maintenance of a body of Church teaching in which the substance and meaning of this news about the word and work of God in Christ can be examined, clarified, agreed upon, set forth, handed on, and then, of course, re-examined, debated and interpreted anew. This is all unavoidable, if Jesus Christ really comes and speaks to people today and deals with them, as the *Basis* claims, "in and through the news of his completed work", which also means "through human witness in word and action" (par.4). But the most important thing that the *Basis of Union* has to say on this whole question of the Church's continuing identity and continuing serviceableness for Christ's purposes, is that these themselves depend upon the continuing faithfulness and the continued activity of Christ. He it is who sees to it that the instrument he needs for his present work on earth is there to hand. He is the Lord, who wins and frees, motivates and equips people for his service. He is not at all dependent upon the Church and its preaching and teaching, although he has chosen and chooses to work through them, because it finally depends entirely upon his own good pleasure that the Church is there and bears witness at all.

In the light of this emphasis, we can begin to understand the relatively relaxed and largely functional approach of the *Basis of Union* to the Scriptures, the ancient creeds, certain Reformation confessions and the sermons of John Wesley. The implication is certainly not, that, since Christ will finally take care of everything himself, it will not really matter what people care to preach, teach or believe. To draw that conclusion, whether in order to claim absolute liberty of opinion for oneself or in order to demonstrate the dangerous tendencies of this *Basis of Union*, is in effect the same as to suggest that, if we are justified by grace through faith, we should then continue in sin, that grace may abound. Just as our faith that our sins are freely forgiven does not overthrow, but upholds the Law, so our trust that Christ will maintain a human witness through which he may himself speak and work, does not relieve us of all responsibility for proclaiming the gospel, but rather makes it a manageable and significant responsibility. For it reveals the limits of what Christ's commandment requires of us and, also, how our attempts at obedience are placed under the clearest and most direct promise of his enabling presence. The *Basis of Union* is now going to go on to speak of the Church's laying a "serious duty" upon its members, and of its "committing" its ministers and instructors to particular practices and exercises, in regard to the Scriptures, the Creeds and certain confessional documents. The *Basis* is not seeking to avoid the issue of our responsibility for the content of the Church's proclamation. The importance of its emphasis upon the way in which the faith of the Holy Catholic and Apostolic Church is grounded in Jesus Christ, not just as the object and content of the Church's belief, but as the One who awakens, sustains and renews the Church's knowledge of, and trust in, himself, lies in quite another direction. The point is that the Church is preserved in its faith, its unity and its historical continuity by the continued active presence of Jesus Christ in and through the Gospel preached and the actions done in its midst ... and so not by any earthly, creaturely, human, historical institutions, doctrines, documents or rites as such. The significance of the Scriptures, creeds and confessions, and of the ministry, will therefore be more clearly brought out by statements about their functions in relation to the Church's witness and the present activity of Jesus Christ, than by attempts at a final definition of their nature and qualities.

This can at once be illustrated by what the *Basis* has to say about the Bible:

> The Uniting Church acknowledges that the Church has received the books of the Old and New Testaments as unique prophetic and apostolic testimony, in which she hears the Word of God and by which her faith and obedience are nourished and regulated (par.5).

The Scriptures are here defined as testimony, i.e., they are seen as being in themselves comparable to the witness that people bear to Jesus Christ in the present. To say that the Church hears the Word of God in this testimony is also not to say any more than might be true of present-day witness. For Christ, who is himself "present when he is preached among men" (par.4), is the Word of God. But the categorical way in which the Church acknowledges that it does hear the Word of God in the witness of these particular books marks them out as testimony of a special kind.

This is reinforced by their being termed "unique prophetic and apostolic testimony": The Scriptures reflect and record the witness of prophets and apostles to Jesus Christ in a way that has no parallel in the later witness of the Church. As testimony to Christ they are unmatched and unequalled, for they preserve for us the prior witness of Israel to the Word of God, which was then fulfilled in the existence of Jesus, and the subsequent witness of those eye-witnesses of his resurrection who were commissioned by him to proclaim the news of it. If Jesus now speaks to people and deals with them "in and through the news of his completed work", then it is necessary for the Church's preaching to stick to the substance of what is recorded here. The testimony of those historic witnesses who were involved in the story of Jesus, either before, or actually during, or immediately after, the event, thus comes to represent both a continuing source and an abiding standard for all later witness borne by the Church.[4]

The Church's acknowledgment that, in the testimony contained in these books, it does, without any doubt, hear the Word of God further entitles and requires it to allow these books a special place in respect of its life and work. Hence the assertion that the Church's faith and obedience are nourished and regulated by the unique prophetic and apostolic testimony of the Old and New Testaments. Note how this is said of the testimony of the prophets and the apostles, i.e. of the actual text of the Bible, and not just of some idea of a Word of God behind the Scriptures. But note on the other hand, too, how it is said of these documents read and understood as witness to Jesus Christ, who is, in his historic story and living person, himself the Word of God.

The *Basis* next makes two assertions about the place and function of the Scriptures in relation to the Church's witness and the actual, audible presence of God's Word: The first is made from the point of view of the preaching Church,

> When the Church preaches Jesus Christ, her message is controlled by the Biblical witnesses (par.5).

It may not always be true that the Church is proclaiming a message to the world and, even when it is, it may not always be true that it is proclaiming the news about Christ. But when it is preaching Christ as it has been commanded, then its preaching has effectively been controlled by Biblical texts. This is true, whether it has submitted directly or indirectly, intentionally or unintentionally, to the Bible's influence. When we say this, we are, of course, not forgetting that the effective authority of the Scriptures over the Church's faith, message and life depends on the fact that Christ, the living Word of God, makes himself heard through the human witness of prophets and apostles. But the *Basis* stresses here that this authority is exercised through the Biblical texts and in such a way that the Church's faith is regulated and its message controlled by the Biblical witnesses.

The second statement that the *Basis* makes about the place and function of the Scriptures in the life of the Church is made from the point of view of the listening Church,

> The Word of God on whom man's salvation depends is to be heard and known from Scripture appropriated in the worshipping and witnessing life of the Church (par.5).

It has already been said that the Church hears the Word of God in the books of the Old and New Testaments. This further statement defines the context within which we are to seek the Word of God in the Bible. The context is that of the Church's worship and witness. That does not mean that the Word of God can only be heard in the midst of a Church service. Individuals and groups may read, discuss and mention the Bible in all kinds of situations, and still remain within the worshipping and witnessing life of the Church. But the Word of God is to be heard and known when our use of the Bible stands in real relation to praise and thanksgiving, to prayer for forgiveness, renewal and guidance, and to the proclamation of the Gospel in the present. The Word of God is not so palpably present in the printed pages of the Bible that, where worship and witness are neither intended nor wanted, people may seize upon it and wield it for their own advantage. The prophetic and apostolic testimony of the biblical books bears witness to Christ, the living Word of God, who summons people into new fellowship with God and with each other, and who commands those who have experienced such reconciliation to proclaim the news thereof to further people around them. This living Word is only to be heard and known in the human words of the Biblical authors as their witness confronts us with it as a word now addressed to us and calling on us, in our turn, to witness to it in our present situation. So we do not hear the Word of God in the Bible in answer to whatever questions we may choose to put to it, but as we approach it reverently as authoritative witness to the Word proclaimed to us and to be proclaimed by us.

On the basis of this understanding of the Scriptures, and of the unique role they play within the relation between Christ and his Church's proclamation of him, the Uniting Church will lay upon its members the "serious duty of reading the Scriptures" (par.5). This will doubtlessly be done, not only so that all the Church members may listen intelligently and critically to the sermons preached by ministers, but because of the participation of all members of the Church in the mission of Christ to the world (par.8; cf. parr.7,12,14) and the preaching of the Word (par.14). Membership of the Church involves the duty of being a student of the Scriptures.

The Uniting Church will commit its ministers to preach from the Scriptures and to administer the sacraments of Baptism and the

Lord's Supper as effective signs of the Gospel set forth in the Scriptures (par.5). Ministers will be required to accept this commitment in their ordination vows.[5] The definition of the sacraments as "effective signs of the Gospel" concerns us here only to the extent that it shows that, for the *Basis of Union*, the Church's faith includes trust and belief concerning the efficacy of Baptism and the Lord's Supper as signs of the Gospel.[6] The fundamental commitment of the Church's ministers in respect of the faith of the Church is that they are to preach from the Scriptures of the Old and New Testaments and to administer the two scriptural sacraments. Ministers are to do this, knowing that the Church trusts that, inasmuch as their preaching is in fact controlled by the Biblical witnesses, they will be preaching Christ, the Word of God on whom the salvation of human beings depends, and that he himself will be heard and will work through their proclamation.

This fundamental commitment is clearly an engagement to join in a particular activity, within the context of a common understanding and a common hope, rather than adherence to a particular doctrine. The two clearly distinct, yet inseparable sides of this activity are the proclamation of the Gospel and the interpretation of the Scriptures. The emphasis placed upon these in the *Basis of Union* can be seen from Paragraph 11:

> The Uniting Church acknowledges that God has never left his Church without faithful and scholarly interpreters of Scripture, or without those who have reflected deeply upon, and acted trustingly in obedience to, his living Word. In particular she enters into the inheritance of literary, historical and scientific enquiry which has characterised recent years, and thanks God for the knowledge of his ways with men which are open to an informed faith. She lives within a world-wide fellowship of Churches in which she will learn to sharpen her understanding of the will and purposes of God by contact with contemporary thought. Within that fellowship she also stands in relation to contemporary societies in ways which will help her to understand her own nature and mission. She thanks God for the continuing witness and

service of evangelist, of scholar, of prophet and of martyr. She prays that she may be ready when occasion demands to confess her Lord in fresh words and deeds.

This paragraph speaks, of course, not only of the Church's faith and mission, but also of its life and obedience. It reminds us that Christ is to be confessed, not just by the ordained ministry, but by the whole membership of the Church, and not just in word, but also in deed. But it also shows how the confession of the Church's faith and the maintenance of its proclamation involve a continuous process of the interpretation of the Scriptures and of corporate and personal discipleship to Christ, the living Word. It also reminds us that unity of faith can never be secured once and for all. While this last remains Christ's gracious gift to his Church, each new generation can only seek to enter into it, and enjoy it, for its own day, as it strives to understand, in its own new situation, insights handed down by those who have gone before. The free and responsible obedience and the intelligent and intelligible witness, for which the Word of God calls, are only possible where Christians dare to interpret, within the new setting of their own day, both the testimony of the Scriptures and those past interpretations at which the Church has already arrived in its doctrines. Commitment to the faith of the One Holy Catholic and Apostolic Church must, apart from all else, involve commitment to participation in this process of the handing on of the Gospel and the interpretation of the Scriptures.

But this is not all that the *Basis of Union* has to say about commitment to the faith of the Church: Within that process of tradition and interpretation, as it has already taken place over the last nineteen and a half centuries, the *Basis* recognizes certain high points; and it states that the Uniting Church will enter into certain commitments for itself, its ministers and its "instructors" in respect of them. This happens for a start with two ancient creeds:

> The Uniting Church enters into unity with the Church throughout the ages by her use of the confessions known as the *Apostles' Creed* and the *Nicene Creed*. She receives

these as authoritative statements of the Catholic Faith, framed in the language of their day and used by Christians in many days, to declare and to guard the right understanding of that faith (par.9).

So that, in binding itself to live and work within the faith and unity of the One Holy Catholic and Apostolic Church, the Uniting Church will be committing itself to regard and use these two creeds as authoritative interpretations of that faith and as a means of giving expression to that unity. It will thereby be acknowledging that the Church as a whole has a right and an obligation to clarify and to safeguard the right understanding of the faith by credal formulations, and that, in taking such action, the Church binds itself anew to what it believes.

But that clearly cannot be taken to mean that these particular creeds in their given, historic forms are to be accorded an absolute, ultimate authority, exempt from that process of interpretation in which the authority of the Word in the Scriptures is ever to be sought and acknowledged. The *Basis* has already looked forward in Paragraph 2 to a time "when the faith will be further elucidated, and the Church's unity expressed, in similar Councils" to the ecumenical councils of the Fourth Century that produced the *Nicene Creed*. Authoritative declarations of the right understanding of the faith in the past do not remove the need for fresh authoritative decisions in the future, for history moves on, horizons of understanding are constantly changing, and the living truth of the Gospel cannot be uncovered once and for all, and then handed on, as if it were a fossil. The Paragraph of the *Basis* on the Creeds implies the distinction between the language of the day in which they were framed and the languages and thought-forms of those many subsequent days in which Christians have used and still use them. No historic text can be treated as if it were a timeless formula. But the necessity of interpretation does not mean that an ancient statement cannot be authoritative. Those who strive to interpret may be just the ones who are seeking to recognize and accept the authority of what was once decided there in the past.

So the Uniting Church will commit

> her ministers and instructors to careful study of these
> creeds and to the discipline of interpreting their teaching
> in a later age (par.9)[,]

in the belief that it will be precisely in this way that the Creeds will effectively prove themselves to be authoritative statements of the faith. It is interesting that not only ministers are faced with this commitment, but also the Church's "instructors", by which we are surely to understand both those engaged in Theological Education and those engaged in Christian Education. The significance of this can be appreciated, when it is remembered how much our modern Christian Education has grown out of Sunday School and Bible Class movements developing quite consciously and deliberately outside the Church and at some remove from its creed. This commitment should mean a closing of the gap that still undeniably exists between the teaching of Theology and Christian Education.

The Uniting Church will further "commend" to ministers and congregations the use of these two creeds "for instruction in the faith, and their use in worship as acts of allegiance to the Holy Trinity". Before their ordination, ministers will be asked whether they "receive for use in instruction and worship the *Apostles'* and the *Nicene Creeds*".[7]

After thus highlighting these creeds, the *Basis* goes on to various documents of the 16th, 17th and 18th Centuries, that have been regarded as expressive of the faith of one or other of the three churches entering into the Union. The *Scots Confession of Faith* (1560), the *Heidelberg Catechism* (1563) and the *Westminster Confession of Faith* (1647) have all been acknowledged in the Church of Scotland, and the last is the present confession of the Presbyterian Church of Australia. The *Savoy Declaration* (1658) represents a Congregationalist revision of the *Westminster Confession*. A collection of forty-four of John Wesley's sermons (1746-1760; ed. in 8 vols. 1787-88) has been used as a standard of doctrine of the Methodist Church. The *Basis of Union* first states that the Uniting Church will continue

> to learn of the teaching of the Holy Scriptures in the obedience and freedom of faith, and in the power of the promised gift of the Holy Spirit, from the witness of reformation fathers as expressed in various ways

in the first four documents named (par.10). What the Uniting Church is going to hear in these confessions is thus once again witness, and now the witness of "reformation fathers". What it will continue to learn of from their witness is "the teaching of the Holy Scriptures". These Reformation confessions are thus seen as having a historically important place within the process of the interpretation of the Scriptures. Just as one or other of the previous churches has received guidance in the interpretation of the Scriptures from one or other of these documents in the past, so now the Uniting Church will not seek to interpret the Scriptures without continuing to learn about what they teach from the witness of these confessions.

Since this use of the confessions will take place within the continuing work of interpretation, it will occur in the "obedience and freedom of faith" that are the abiding hall-marks of all seeking for the Word of God in the Scriptures: Inasmuch as these confessions confront the Church with the force of the Biblical witness to Christ, the Church is bound to concur in their stand; inasmuch as they reflect the insights and the unavoidable limitations of particular people in particular worlds of thought and particular historical situations, the Church must dare to move beyond their specific affirmations and rejections and, still guided by their witness, to attempt a faithful interpretation of the teaching of the Holy Scriptures for its own time.

It is no wonder that the *Basis* emphasises here that the Church will learn from the confessions in this way "in the power of the promised gift of the Holy Spirit", dangerous though it is to stress the Spirit's work at particular points, as if all the Church's life and speech and thought were not equally dependent thereon. We must, of course, not simply presume on the gift of the Spirit. Christ's promise does not entitle us to go on as if we must be infallibly right in everything we choose to think and indubitably better informed than our spiritual ancestors. But it should give us the courage humbly to enquire after the truth and clearly to affirm that of which we are convinced.

After the *Basis* has spoken of the significance of these Reformation confessions in this way, it states that the Uniting Church will "listen to the preaching of John Wesley in his *Forty-Four Sermons*" - "in like manner". Whatever has been said above in interpretation of the statement about the confessions will thus apply here with equal force.

The Uniting Church will specifically commit

> her ministers and instructors to study these statements, so that the congregation of Christ's people may again and again be reminded of the grace which justifies them through faith, of the centrality of the person and work of Christ the justifier, and of the need for a constant appeal to Holy Scripture (par.10).

The commitment applies, again, both to the ministers of Word and sacraments and to all engaged in Theological and Christian Education. What they are committed to, is the study of particular documents, from which the Church intends to learn of the teaching of Holy Scripture, so their study will, again, be undertaken within the context of the interpretation of Scripture and the communication of the Gospel. The purpose of this commitment is expressed by the underlining of certain matters that are supposed particularly to emerge as the teaching of Holy Scripture from these confessional documents. It might appear unfortunate that these specific items are singled out. But they represent, on closer examination, the Reformation *sola gratia*, *sola fide*, *solo Christo* and *sola scriptura* ("by grace alone", "by faith alone", "by Christ alone", "by Scripture alone") and must be allowed to be sufficiently basic and central not to be restrictive.

Before their ordination, ministers will be asked whether they will continue to allow their minds to be illumined, their consciences to be quickened, and their prayers to be deepened by study of these confessional documents.[8]

This, then, is the scope of commitment to the faith of the Church in the *Basis of Union* for the Uniting Church in Australia. As we have seen, it applies in the first instance to the Uniting Church as a whole, then most explicitly to those ordained to the ministry of Word and sacrament and to any others charged with giving instruction in the faith. But other office-bearers will be asked to undertake to live and work within the faith and unity of the One Holy Catholic and Apostolic Church and, as we have seen, living and working within the faith of the Church involves participation in a never-ceasing activity of listening to, learning from, and interpreting, past witness to the Word of God in the Scriptures. It will not be possible to make water-tight distinctions between what is asked of ministers of the Word and what is asked of lay members in the Church's councils and committees. But, as we have also already said, all the Church's members are committed to confessing the faith of Christ crucified and to helping to bear his message to the world, and so all will be drawn into study, interpretation and communication of the faith on one level or another.

The most striking and, perhaps, the most debatable thing about the way in which commitment to the faith is described in this *Basis of Union*, is that most of what we have said so far has been concerned with the manner of this commitment and not with what might be termed the "substance of the faith". Why this is so, should by now have become clear. If asked, however, to what the Church and, let us say, its ministry are materially committed, we could only begin by instancing a few specific items: Faith in the Holy Trinity seems to be presupposed (parr.1,9,12); much is said about God's work of reconciliation and redemption through Jesus Christ (par.3) and the centrality of the person and work of Christ is emphasized; the doctrine of justification by grace through faith is singled out (par.10) and the unique authority of the Scriptures recognized (parr.5,10); the place and importance of Baptism and the Lord's Supper are dealt with at length (parr.3,5-8); much is said about the mission, membership, ministries and government of the Church (parr.1-3,7,8,12-17). Then we should have to go on to indicate the compass of the confession of the faith in the ancients creeds and the Reformation confessions. In all of the areas, on all of the points, included here, our spiritual ancestors held the substance of the faith somehow to be at issue. The Uniting Church will receive the Creeds as authoritative statements of the Catholic Faith and will continue to learn of the teaching of the Holy Scriptures from the witness of the Reformation fathers and John Wesley.

But, since these various documents will not always be in full agreement among themselves, and since all are drawn into the process of interpretation, it is here that, for many, the problem will arise. How is one to know what does, and what does not, constitute that substance of the faith within which even the Uniting Church will not allow difference of opinion? What degree of force is, for instance, the Reformation teaching on the sacraments going to have, alongside what is said about them in the *Basis of Union* itself? I think that it must be admitted that the *Basis* will require of us not so much assent to a clearly defined and reasonably exhaustive body of doctrine, as agreement that we are going to set out from the common understanding of the Church's faith and mission sketched out in the *Basis* itself and strive to grow together in a deepening understanding of the faith. We are to do this, by engaging together in the task of interpreting the witness the Scriptures bear to Jesus Christ for the people of our times, and thereby listening very carefully to certain ways in which our spiritual ancestors have given an authoritative interpretation of that Scriptural witness in the Ancient Church and in the days of the Reformation and the Evangelical Revival.

By the way in which it acknowledges certain credal, confessional and proclamational documents of the past, the *Basis of Union* asks us to agree that, in the course of the interpretation of the Scriptures down through the centuries, moments have arisen when the Church has been enabled, or driven, to come to definitive statements about the substance of the faith. The fact that the *Basis* does not itself seek to give such a general statement, must be taken to reflect the conviction that our Australian churches and Church people are just not capable of producing anything of that kind at the present time, and that, if it were attempted, it would be more likely to divide than to unite us. But it is not intended that the Uniting Church should merely perpetuate our present poverty of insight and lack of agreement. The three existing churches are to enter into union, looking for a continual renewal

> in which God will use their common worship, witness and service to set forth the word of salvation for all mankind

and remaining open to "constant reform" under Christ's Word (par.1). The Uniting Church will look forward to future ecumenical councils in which the faith will be further elucidated (par.2); and she will pray God that,

> through the gift of the Spirit, he will constantly correct that which is erroneous in her life, will bring her into deeper unity with other Churches, and will use her worship, witness and service to his eternal glory through Jesus Christ the Lord (par.18).

The Uniting Church will thus be hoping to progress in her knowledge and understanding of the Church's faith. As she progresses, the Assembly, as the national council, will bear determining responsibility in matters of doctrine, as well as in those of worship, government and discipline. But it will be

> obligatory for it to seek the concurrence of the other councils, and on occasion of the congregations of the Church, on matters of vital importance to the life of the Church (par.15).

The issues and contentions which will indubitably arise in the course of the Church's life and development will have to be taken seriously, inasmuch as they appear to enter into the substance of the faith. They will require study and thought at all levels of the Church and, in particular intensity, among those entrusted with the public proclamation of the Gospel and the teaching of Theology. They will also, at times, require the Church to come to some corporate decision about its understanding of the witness of the Scriptures and the faith of the One Holy Catholic and Apostolic Church. A commitment to the faith of the Church within the Uniting Church in Australia will thus also include both a willingness to take part in the study and thought that will be needed before such decisions can be made, and an openness for the final results of the Church's decision-making. It must include a readiness to seek to learn and decide together what the Gospel really is, and what it means, in the unknown situations we shall face in the years to come

NOTES

1   This paper represents a revision of the Inaugural Lecture for the 1972 Session of the Theological Hall of the Presbyterian Church in Western Australia and the Barclay Theological Hall of the Methodist Conference of Western Australia.

2   "Questions at the Ordination or Induction of Ministers: Questions for the Minister-elect, ii.", in Presbyterian Church of Australia, *Constitution and Procedure and Practice [...]*, Melbourne, Board of Religious Education of the General Assembly of Australia, 1950, p.62.

3   *Basis of Union being the 1971 revision by the Joint Commission on Church Union of the Congregational Union of Australia, the Methodist Church of Australasia and the Presbyterian Church of Australia*, Melbourne, Aldersgate Press, 1971, pp.7f,16; - in *Witness of Faith*, pp.31,33.

4   One important and direct source of the concept of the Scriptures as unique prophetic and apostolic witness to Jesus Christ, the Word of God, lies in the theology of Karl Barth. See "The Christian Understanding of Revelation", in K. Barth, *Against the Stream: Shorter Post-War Writings 1946-52*, London, SCM, 1954, pp.205-240, pp.211-214,216-220; - K. Barth, *Evangelical Theology: An Introduction*, London, Weidenfeld & Nicolson, 1963, pp.20- 25,26-30.

5   *Basis of Union being the 1971 revision [...]*, contains in its Appendix 2, "Concerning the Ordering of the Ministry" (pp.23-25), a section 3 headed "Ordination", which commences, "(a) The Uniting Church lays down questions to be asked at the Ordination of Ministers in the following form:-". The second and third questions are: "(ii) Do you receive the witness to Christ in the Holy Scriptures of the Old and New Testaments; and do you undertake to preach from these?"; "(iii) Do you undertake to administer the sacraments of Baptism and the Lord's Supper so that the Gospel of Jesus Christ may be clearly proclaimed and made effective in the lives of believers?" (p.24). The Inaugural Assembly in June 1977 received the Appendices to the Basis of Union and requested the Commission on Doctrine to consider matters arising from them, for recommendation to the next meeting of the Assembly. It also directed presbyteries "to use for the time being the Ordination questions and liturgical material in Appendix II" (*Minutes of Proceedings of the first [Inaugural] Assembly of the Uniting Church in Australia, Sydney, 22 June 1977*, min.77.27, p.12.) The text of the Appendices is reprinted in the book of Assembly Minutes, pp.29-31, as "Appendix 2" of that book, without the distinguishing numbering for Appendix I ("Concerning the Celebration of the Sacraments", p.29) and Appendix II ("Concerning the Ordering of the Ministry", pp.30f).

6   The following Paragraph 6 makes it clear that the efficacy of both the words and the sacraments of the Gospel flows from the activity of Jesus Christ himself in and through everything that the Church does in obedience to his commandment.

7   *Basis of Union being the 1971 revision [...]*, Appendix 2, Question (iv).

8   *Basis of Union being the 1971 revision [...]*, Appendix 2, Question (vi).

Adhering to
the *Basis of Union*[1]

Introduction

On 22 June 1977, the Congregational Union of Australia, the Methodist Church of Australasia and the Presbyterian Church of Australia entered into union under the name of the Uniting Church in Australia. They did so in accordance with the *Basis of Union*, which had been agreed to by the three uniting churches prior to that date. In Paragraph 14 of the *Basis of Union*, there were provisions for the recognition and acceptance of certain persons as

(a) Ministers of the Word (Ministers),

(b) Elders or Leaders,

(c) Deaconesses, and

(d) Lay Preachers,

of the Uniting Church. The conditions on which that was to be done were that such persons

1. had held an equivalent office in one of the uniting churches at the time of union,

2. were in good standing, and

3. adhered to the *Basis of Union*.

Since the time of union, further persons admitted to these ministries have also been asked to express their adherence to the *Basis of Union* in the acts of their setting apart, commissioning or accrediting. In this study, we shall explore what is meant by "adhering to the *Basis of Union*".

I

The *Basis of Union* was formulated through a lengthy process, during which preparatory material and drafts were submitted on a number of occasions for consideration in the three churches. A document of this kind has the function of giving assurance to churches contemplating union, and to their members and ministers, that fundamental issues will have been resolved to their satisfaction in the new church to result from the union. It has to show that essential things will be safeguarded and that things quite unacceptable will neither be imposed nor permitted. So the preparation of such a document requires discussion and deliberation until all sides are satisfied.

The churches were only able to proceed to union when they had agreed upon the *Basis of Union*. Initially, it was corporate approval by each of the uniting denominations that was needed. Individual members of the churches were still free to form their own judgments about the *Basis* and about the new Uniting Church. If they felt sufficiently opposed to that particular union, they were free to keep out of it altogether. They were also at liberty to continue in membership of their current congregations and to go on into the Uniting Church, retaining any reservations that they might have about particular features of the *Basis* and the union. The churches of the uniting traditions do not ask for detailed and sweeping commitments from their members. The central and fundamental commitment for which they do ask can easily be seen from the questions posed at services of adult baptism and confirmation. Beyond such explicit commitment, members are free to hold their own dissenting convictions about the Church's position and practice in all kinds of areas.

There is still, of course, a question of what members may appropriately do with their dissent. If a person has, despite serious reservations, decided to continue in membership of the Uniting Church, that person is entitled to acceptance and tolerance from the Church, but also has an obligation to extend to the Church a corresponding respect and a corresponding tolerance. If one makes a decision to remain a member of a body that has openly declared its character in a document like the *Basis of Union*, then one cannot, with any fairness, denigrate the body for being what it is, while continuing to enjoy the position of a member of that body. There are ways of acknowledging difference and owning where one stands without attacking those from whom one differs. Dissent and dissension are not the same thing, at all.

Constructive criticism and destructive criticism are also totally different things. Constructive criticism is a form of critical participation in the life and work of the community. It seeks changes through which growth and reconciliation can be achieved. It comes to grips with things where, at least in faith and hope, fruitful change can be envisaged. Destructive criticism is a far more defensive and negative activity, often springing from fear of change and growth. It does not truly engage with reality or real possibilities; and it has a strong streak of denial in it. In other words, the energy of its attack upon some things springs from an unacknowledged determination not to face some other things. Church members who wish to pursue an issue on which they differ from the Church owe it to other members to do so in constructive, rather than destructive, ways.

II

One of the realities to be faced by members of the Church who wish to work for positive changes is the givenness of the *Basis of Union*. It is the foundation on which the three churches agreed to unite and it is the document to which office-bearers have been required to adhere as the concrete focus of their commitment to ministry on the revised assumptions of the new church. It is the *Basis of Union* that gives the Uniting Church its character. In order to be true to itself and true to its members, ministers and other office-bearers, the Uniting Church must continue to be the church standing on this foundation. It would normally be neither realistic nor constructive for someone to begin to demand changes that would effectively mean the removal of some of that foundation or the addition of other elements to it.

For there is no provision in the *Basis of Union* for any changes to the *Basis of Union*. It would, of course, have been possible to include such a provision. There was, indeed, one in the Proposed Basis of Union of 1963, which read

> The Uniting Church has the right to interpret the General Articles and to modify and add to them, but

always in agreement with Holy Scripture, and consistently with the provisions of the first Article concerning Doctrinal Standards, adherence to which, as interpreted by the Church, is essential to its continuity and corporate life. Such modifications to the General Articles shall be made only by a 75 per cent. affirmative vote of those present and voting in the General Assembly, after a 75 per cent. affirmative vote in a majority of Presbyteries.[2]

The General Articles were contained in Section III of the Proposed Basis. Following the first article on Doctrinal Standards, there were five others, on the Sacraments, Church Membership, the Ministry, the Councils of the Church and Orders of Worship. The provision quoted above, misleadingly entitled, "Concerning Revision of Statements of Doctrine", formed the seventh such General Article. As we see, it, in fact, expressly declared adherence to the first Article, as interpreted by the Church, to be essential to the Church's continuity and corporate life. That first article covered the matters dealt with in the present *Basis of Union* at the commencement of Paragraph 2 and in Paragraphs 5, 9 and 10. There were no provisions for modifications to any other Sections of the Proposed Basis.

In preparing the ultimate *Basis of Union*, the Joint Commission decided that it should have a form that ought not to require amendment or addition in the future. It would include only what was needed to lay the foundation for the Uniting Church. More detailed or technical matters were put into appendices, which did not constitute part of the *Basis*, but were referred to the Assembly of the Uniting Church. The *Basis* was formulated in ways that would not be likely to date or to prove too restrictive as time went on. The Joint Commission therefore did not include any provision for amendment to parts or all of the *Basis* in the *Basis* itself; and the three uniting churches approved it in this form.

The Uniting Church could still, of course, revise its *Basis of Union* or provide itself with a new one. The final stage in that process would be getting the parliaments of all states to approve amending legislation to their respective Uniting Church in Australia Acts, replacing the old form of the *Basis* in the schedules to those acts with the new one, and achieving the same for any territory in which there was also a Uniting Church Act. In order to get governments to agree to this action, it would be necessary for the Church to demonstrate strong consensus on the change that was being sought. There would need to be good majorities in favour of the change in a good majority of presbyteries and synods and, probably also, in a good majority of congregations. The question of the rights of any members dissenting from the changes may be raised by the governments at that time or may have to be faced later in the courts.

It is for this reason that it has to be said that it would normally be neither realistic nor constructive for someone to begin to demand changes in the Church that would effectively mean changes to the *Basis of Union*. The possibility of some future initiative towards that end cannot simply be ruled out.

Apart from a full and deliberate process for the amendment or replacement of the *Basis*, including amending legislation in the parliaments, the Uniting Church and its councils must themselves abide by the *Basis of Union*, in accordance with which the Church was formed. To fail to do so, would be to break faith with all who have entered the Church on the understanding that it was founded on that basis, and also to create a completely contradictory situation for office-bearers who are themselves required to adhere to the *Basis of Union*.

There are some constitutional complications that also need to be recognized, but they are best held over till the final section of this study.

III

People entrusted with a ministry in the Church fall somewhere in between the Church as a corporate body and individual members of it. For that reason, their relation to the *Basis of Union* has to be considered as a distinct, though related, issue. When one is entrusted with a ministry, one is authorized to exercise that particular function in the service of others, in the name of Jesus Christ, and under the discipline and order of one's particular denomination. By the authorization that it gives an office-bearer, the Church assumes responsibility for the kind and quality of ministry that that person will provide. In accepting and acting upon the authority given, the office-bearer must also accept the commitment to function within the Church's understanding of that office and of other matters broadly connected with it. This is the point of the requirement for Ministers, Elders, Deacon[esse]s and Lay Preachers to adhere to the *Basis of Union*.

A most important aspect of this is the way in which the *Basis of Union* and the provision for adherence to it clarify what may be expected. Congregationalists, Methodists and Presbyterians worked carefully together over an extended period and then came together as one new body on the *Basis of Union*. The *Basis* established what they were all able to agree on. It also, and this is just as important, established what they were able to agree to be a necessary, sufficient and appropriate level of agreement for entering into union with each other. Each body involved could say, "If we are able to agree to this, then we can expect them to unite with us without reservation. If they are able to agree to this, then they can rightly expect us to unite with them without reservation". Each body could also say, "Now that we have agreed on the essentials, we can see how much room for diversity there is. Now we have agreed that these are the essentials, we can know that noone will later be able to insist that we also have to accept further things in order to be part of the Uniting Church".

For the acceptance and recognition of ministers, it meant that we gave each other an assurance both that we shared a common understanding of what our ministries were fundamentally about and also that this was a sufficient basis for accepting each other fully and without reservation.

This was important at the time of union, but continues to be equally important in the present. A presbytery settling a minister in a parish or a synod settling a minister in a chaplaincy needs to be sure that the ministry that will be provided will accord with the Church's fundamental assumptions about such ministry. The same is true, when elders are elected and commissioned or an accredited lay preacher joins a congregation from interstate and asks to be included on the preaching plan. Those who entrust a particular kind of ministry and a particular sphere of ministry to any person have an obligation to the Church and to the public to ensure that what purports to be Uniting Church ministry will in truth be just that.

Ministers and other office-bearers who accept responsibility for giving ministry of any kind in the name of the Church also need to have assurance about the fundamental expectations attached to it. The requirement that they adhere to the *Basis of Union* lets them know what can rightly be expected of them as people entrusted with this or that office. This could, of course, be twisted into a silly kind of "fundamentalism", by which a minister might, for example, claim that, by doing all that the *Basis* literally required, she or he was proof against any charges of sloth, negligence or incompetence. But assuming good faith and common sense, adherence to the *Basis* does cover what the Church expects of an office-bearer by virtue of his or her holding that office. Being aware of the scope and limits of such expectations clarifies not only one's obligations, but, equally or even more, one's freedom to function in accordance with one's own vision, conscience and gifts.

IV

What does the Uniting Church mean by "adhering to the *Basis of Union*"? This is defined in the *Basis* itself, following the sub-paragraphs 14 (a) - (d) on the acceptance and recognition of Ministers, Elders, Deaconesses and Lay Preachers, in the following words:

> In the above sub-paragraphs the phrase "adhere to the *Basis of Union*" is understood as willingness to live and work within the faith and unity of the One Holy Catholic and Apostolic Church as that way is described in this *Basis*. Such adherence allows for difference of opinion in matters which do not enter into the substance of the faith (par.14).

Let us explore the elements of this definition.

1.   "[...] the phrase 'adhere to the *Basis of Union*' is understood as

willingness to live and work [...]". Adherence to the *Basis* is not primarily intellectual assent, but a determination of the will. The first question is simply, "Are you willing [...]?". There is no room for reservations here. It would not be good enough for someone to answer, "Not entirely, but I want to tag along". That would not be adhering to the *Basis*, in the sense of the *Basis'* own definition of it. What is required is willingness; and if that is not genuinely there, then it is equally harmful for the Church and the office-bearer to play with the idea of there still being some measure of adherence.

2. What adherence means is "willingness *to live and work*", i.e. personally to participate and contribute. It means willingness to be actively involved. Merely working, i.e. performing certain functions, would not be enough. One must be willing to live, which means being personally present and engaged. The *Basis of Union* lays the foundation for a community of faith and hope, love and service. Willingness to live and work within it cannot be reduced to a will to outward compliance and conformity. It must mean that one is ready to participate out of inner conviction and with a clear conscience.[3]

3. We are, of course, not talking about just any willingness or any life and work, but about "willingness to live and work *within the faith and unity of the One Holy Catholic and Apostolic Church*". The three uniting churches came together as the Uniting Church with a quite clear, and quite clearly formulated, vision of "that unity which is both Christ's gift and his will for the Church" (par.1), a unity to which their act of uniting could do no more than bear witness. Trusting in Christ's gift, and seeking to obey his will, the churches felt free and obliged to say that the Uniting Church itself "lives and works within the faith and unity of the One Holy Catholic and Apostolic Church" (par.2). Adhering to the *Basis* means, above all, being willing to participate personally in the life and work of the Uniting Church, within the faith and unity of the One Holy Catholic and Apostolic Church.

4. It is "within the faith *and* unity" of the One Holy Catholic and

Apostolic Church that one is asked to be willing to live and work. Every office-bearer in the Church is expected to live and work within the Church's faith *and* within its unity. Adherence to the *Basis of Union* has both of these dimensions. The way in which one belongs to the Uniting Church and performs one's ministry in it must be embraced by the faith of the One Holy Catholic and Apostolic Church and must also fit harmoniously into its unity.

5.   But this is then qualified in turn by the further clause, *"as that way is described in this Basis"*. Individual office-bearers are not left to discover or decide for themselves what living and working "within the faith and unity of the One Holy Catholic and Apostolic Church" is supposed to mean. The *Basis of Union* provides the orientation needed for determining that.

That happens, on one level, for the Uniting Church as a whole. The *Basis* defines the way in which three traditions have come together to form the Uniting Church (par.1) and indicates ways in which the Uniting Church will express its participation in the Church Universal (par.2). It grounds its understanding of the Church in God's redeeming and reconciling work in Jesus Christ and through the Holy Spirit (par.3). It acknowledges how Jesus Christ, as the living and life-giving Word of God, gathers, continues, nurtures, rules and revives his church, and involves it in his own mission in the world, both through the Scriptures and through words proclaimed, and sacraments celebrated, in accordance with the Scriptures (parr.4-8). It defines the authority and functions of the ancient creeds, of Reformation confessions, and of Wesley's sermons, in the life and work of the Church (parr.9-10) and also acknowledges what it receives, and needs to receive, from many other quarters (par.11). It expresses its understanding of membership, of ministry and of particular ministries, including the ministry of government in the service of the sovereignty of Jesus Christ (parr.12-17). It prays that God will enable it to become what it is seeking to be and to do what it is seeking to do (par.18).

So what the question about adherence to the *Basis* is asking is, "When you think of how the *Basis of Union* describes the way in which the Uniting Church lives and works within the faith and unity of the One Holy Catholic and Apostolic Church, are you willing to participate in that and to play your own part within it?".

6. There is, however, yet another level on which the clause, "as that way is described in this *Basis*", applies. For the *Basis of Union* has some specific things to say about different ministries and, as each office-bearer is asked about her or his willingness to live and work in the way described in the *Basis*, that will have particular regard to her or his office.

This is most obviously true of the Ministers of the Word. The *Basis* says of them, "Such members will be called Ministers [...]" (par.14[a]); and it is they who are meant, when "ministers" are referred to in other Paragraphs. Of them it is said that

> The Uniting Church [...] commits her ministers to preach from these [sc. the Scriptures] and to administer the sacraments of Baptism and the Lord's Supper as effective signs of the Gospel set forth in the Scriptures (par.5).

> The Uniting Church [...] commits her ministers and instructors to careful study of these [sc. the *Apostles'* and *Nicene*] creeds and to the discipline of interpreting their teaching in a later age. She commends to ministers and congregations their use for instruction in the faith, and their use in worship as acts of allegiance to the Holy Trinity (par.9).

> The Uniting Church [...] will commit her ministers and instructors to study these statements [sc. the *Scots Confession*, the *Heidelberg Catechism*, the *Westminster Confession*, the *Savoy Declaration* and John Wesley's *Forty-Four Sermons*], so that the congregation of Christ's people may again and again be reminded of the grace which justifies them through faith, of the

centrality of the person and work of Christ the justifier, and of the need for a constant appeal to Holy Scripture (par.10).

The differentiating terminology in Paragraph 9, with the change from "commits" to "commends" in the two sentences quoted, reinforces what is already the plain sense of the first word. Some statements in the *Basis* lay a real commitment on the Church's Ministers of the Word (and, in two cases, on its "instructors", as well).

Beyond that, something is said about the specific ministries of Ministers, Elders or Leaders, Deacon[esse]s and Lay Preachers in Paragraph 14 (a) - (d), while the role of Elders is amplified in what is said about the Elders' or Leaders' Meeting (par.15 [b]). That whole Paragraph on government and the councils of the Church identifies the structure within which office-bearers will be accountable for their ministries. Living and working within the faith and unity of the Church in the way described in the *Basis* will involve living and working within the order and discipline of this pattern of councils with their mutually balancing and supporting responsibilities.

7. Above, in discussing the statement that adhering to the *Basis of Union* was to be understood as willingness to do certain things, I suggested that that left no room for reservations. Either one is willing to do what is asked or one is not. On the other hand, what the *Basis* asks one to do, viz.

> [...] live and work within the faith and unity of the
> One Holy Catholic and Apostolic Church as that way
> is described in this *Basis*,

is not an awkwardly rigid thing, at all. The *Basis* identifies how the faith and unity of the One Holy Catholic and Apostolic Church are grounded in the one Lord Jesus Christ (par.3). It is Jesus Christ, the living Word of God, who, through human witness and in the power of the Holy Spirit, awakens, purifies and advances people's faith (parr.4,6). The *Basis* defines the status and significance of Scripture and sacraments, creeds and confessional documents, in terms of, and in relation to, this sovereign and personal activity of Jesus Christ (parr.5-10). Later statements about membership, ministry and government of the Church also link back, through those earlier Paragraphs, to the fundamental Christological theme of the *Basis*. The question of adherence is really asking, "Are you willing to trust the dynamic that is outlined in the *Basis* and to apply your gifts in the service of it, within the pattern of relations that the *Basis* also outlines?".

The distinction that we noted above in Paragraph 9, between what the Church "commits" its ministers to and what it "commends" to ministers, illustrates how the language of the *Basis* has been carefully chosen to indicate differing degrees of stringency in what it lays on, or asks of, the Church as a whole and its members and office-bearers. The *Basis* is no more demanding than the three uniting churches agreed that the foundation of their union needed to be; and it amply fulfils the function of "loosing" as well as of "binding", of setting free for life and service as well as of fixing appropriate limits for them.

8. There is one act of "loosing" that is performed in the very definition of what it means to "adhere to the *Basis of Union*" and that is the provision that

> Such adherence allows for difference of opinion in matters which do not enter into the substance of the faith (par.14).

It is still important to emphasize that even this does not give permission for only qualified willingness to live and work within the faith and unity of the Church "as that way is described in this *Basis*". It is rather an essential element in the *Basis'* description of the way in which we are so to live and work. Complete willingness to live and work in the faith and unity of the Church may accept for oneself, and must allow for others, liberty of opinion in matters that do not enter into the substance of the faith.

What the provision that we are now discussing allows for is "difference of opinion". 'Opinion' can be defined as

> [...] persuasion or view that certain facts, ideas &c. are probably true or likely to prove so [...].[4]

or

> [...] a personal view, attitude, or estimation [...].[5]

So what is allowed is difference of belief, of judgment or of persuasion about particular matters, differing views on them. These are allowable, as long as they do not enter into the substance of the faith.

Adherence to the *Basis* is defined as willingness to live and work within the faith and unity of the Church. The limits of the 'difference of opinion' that it allows are, however, defined solely in relation to the Church's faith, and not also in relation to its unity, precisely because opinion is a matter of views and beliefs, and not of actions or behaviour. That does not, of course, mean that difference of opinion is not allowable with regard to the Church's structures and activities. But, in this regard, too, the limit of what is allowable is only reached, when a matter enters into the substance of the Church's faith. It would be a quite different matter, if we were talking about contradictory practices or divergent behaviour. Then limits would need to be indicated to safeguard the unity of the Church's life and work.

It is thus a complete confusion of categories to suggest that the reference in the *Basis of Union* to 'difference of opinion' would allow each Uniting Church minister [...]

> liberty of opinion in the matter of his or her administration of the sacrament of baptism to infants.[6]

We shall discuss subsequently in Section VI whether adherence to the *Basis* could be shown to allow freedom for divergent action in the matter of Baptism on any other arguments. The 'difference of opinion' clause is certainly not concerned with liberty of action. If it were ever declared that it was to be understood in that way, and that the only check on office-bearers' activities was when a matter entered into the substance of the faith, then the requirement to live and work within the unity of the Church would have lost all content. Each office-bearer would be free to "form the opinion" that he or she need not act in accordance with the Church's position on one matter after another. This would be a direct consequence of trying to use a particular provision to resolve a matter that it was never designed to deal with. All that the provision is meant to do is to safeguard the right of office-bearers to hold their own views on any matters that do not enter into the substance of the faith.[7]

Freedom to hold opinions must, of course, include the freedom to express those opinions. The Uniting Church is not going to question an office-bearer's adherence to the *Basis of Union*, simply because the office-bearer expresses opinions that differ from matters in the *Basis* that do not enter into the substance of the faith. But here we do need to recur to what was said above about the differences between dissent and dissension and between positive criticism and negative criticism. If a minister or other office-bearer began to express her or his opinions in divisive and destructive ways, the Church would need to challenge that person. But the issue would then be about how genuinely willing he or she was to live and work within the faith and unity of the Church in the way described in the *Basis*. The office-bearer's behaviour would be under challenge. It would not be an adequate defence to insist that the difference of opinion on which everything centred did not enter into the substance of the faith.

The same would be the case, if an office-bearer were seeking to function within the Church, despite the conviction that its position on certain matters fundamental to its life was quite untenable. It would not then be a question of whether those matters entered into the substance of the faith. The issue would be, rather, whether genuine participation is possible, when one's outward compliance conflicts with one's inner conviction, and whether, under such circumstances, the claim to be willing to live and work within the faith and unity of the church, in the way described in the *Basis*, did not lack all substance.

9. What is meant by the substance of the faith? The Uniting Church has not tried to define that in advance. That is because it acknowledges that

> the faith and unity of the Holy Catholic and Apostolic Church are built upon the one Lord Jesus Christ (par.3).

Faith in the living presence and activity of God in Jesus Christ and through the Holy Spirit certainly has substance to it. The Church has from time to time to be quite firm about what does and what does not belong to the faith. But faith in a person can never be finally captured in words. What the Uniting Church does in its *Basis of Union* is to indicate where it orients itself, and how it proceeds, in the task of saying where the substance of the faith is involved.

So the Uniting Church receives the *Apostles'* and *Nicene Creeds* as

> authoritative statements of the Catholic Faith, framed in the language of their day and used by Christians in many days, to declare and to guard the right understanding of that faith (par.9),

while recognizing that these creeds need to be studied and interpreted in the present. It acknowledges, in the books of the Old and New Testaments,

> [...] unique prophetic and apostolic testimony, in which she [sc. the Church] hears the Word of God and by which her faith and obedience are nourished and regulated (par.5).

It continues to learn of the teaching of these Holy Scriptures from particular confessional, catechetical and proclamational documents belonging to the heritage of the uniting churches (par.10). The Assembly of the Uniting Church has "determining responsibility for matters of doctrine, worship, government and discipline" (par.15 [e]). The Uniting Church also looks forward to future ecumenical councils, in which "the faith will be further elucidated and the Church's unity expressed" (par.2). It is within such a framework that it will be determined from time to time what does, and what does not, "enter into the substance of the faith".

The question of adherence to the *Basis of Union* has been raised in recent times in relation to the issues of the baptism of children, and the ordination of women as Ministers of the Word. The Standing Committee of the 1988 Assembly appeared to many to adopt quite different approaches to these two issues. Let us explore how the above understanding of adherence could apply to each in turn.

V

As far as the ordination of women is concerned, the *Basis of Union* states that

> The Uniting Church, from inception, will seek the guidance of the Holy Spirit to recognize among her members men and women called of God to preach the Gospel, to lead the people in worship, to care for the flock, to share in government and to serve those in need in the world (par.14).

It then goes on to speak of Ministers of the Word, Elders, Deaconesses and Lay Preachers. The functions of ministry listed in the above quotation have to be thought of as distributed between these four ministries, with some being shared by more than one. The quotation quite clearly says that both male and female members of the Church may receive gifts from God for any of the functions listed, with the clear implication that both male and female members may be called and ordained to the ministry of the Word, to "preach the Gospel, administer the sacraments and exercise pastoral care" (par.14 [a]).

Unfortunately, the *Basis* was completed and adopted a short time before there was general sensitivity to a customary use of the masculine in a sense intended to be inclusive, but which was, in fact, already being experienced as exclusive by a growing number of women. So the sub-paragraph on Ministers of the Word can speak of the ascended Christ's conferring gifts upon "men" and refer to the ordinand as "him". That was not meant to exclude women, but to include them. There was absolutely no doubt about that in the drafting of the *Basis* or in the discussion of it prior to union; and it is also clear from the text of the *Basis*, for

1. There were already women ministers to be recognized and accepted as ministers of the Uniting Church under the terms of Paragraph 14 (a) in all three of the uniting churches. It would have needed to be spelled out far more clearly, if there had been an intention not to accept and ordain any more women as ministers after union.

2. The overall emphasis in the context of Paragraphs 13 - 15 is on God's bestowing gifts for ministry on members of the Church, men and women. (This last phrase occurs six times in those Paragraphs.) The clear exception is the ministry of the Deaconess, which was, as its name indicates, for women only. Because, at the time of union, many were seeking a renewal of the diaconal office and ministry, the opening of this ministry to men was held over for such a renewed diaconate (par.14[c]). There is no other, corresponding reservation of a particular ministry for a particular sex.

It has to be accepted that it is in accordance with the *Basis of Union* for the Uniting Church to ordain women as Ministers of the Word and that it would not be in accordance with the *Basis* for the Church to cease to do so. The Church's commitment to women in its ministry has also been expressed quite strongly in other ways than in its *Basis*. But the question that we are facing here is, whether an office-bearer could be held to adhere to the *Basis of Union*, despite a difference of opinion with the Church over the ordination of women, on the argument that this is not a matter that enters into the substance of the faith.

One thing that would have to be tested with such a person would be whether his or her opinion on this issue did or did not compromise his or her willingness to live and work within the faith and unity of the Church. This is the question of how genuinely the office-bearer adheres to the *Basis of Union*. The claim to be still able to adhere to the *Basis* may involve an inner contradiction; and the office-bearer making the claim may need pastoral care and oversight in the matter.

The reasons why the genuiness of the claim to adhere arises so sharply as an issue here are that (1) any minister, elder, deacon[ess] or lay preacher is entrusted with her or his ministry within the living system of the Church community and that (2) the Church itself holds certain strong convictions in relation to its life as that community. Whatever may be her or his opinion on the matter, any Uniting Church office-bearer will be sharing in the life of a church that has women in its ministry. She or he will, at times, be called on to receive ministry from a woman minister or to extend supportive ministry to one. The Church itself believes in gifts for ministry given by God to women and men. In ordaining a woman, the Church gives thanks to God for the gifts that woman has received and it prays for the enabling power of the Holy Spirit to equip her for her ministry. It believes in the unity of the body of Christ, which is built up by the mutual giving and receiving of services, in which God's gifts are employed. A differing opinion about having women as ministers appears, on the face of it, to imply a negative stance towards aspects of the faith and unity of the Church, as the Uniting Church understands them, an attitude that must threaten to impair one's willingness to live and work within them. The Church owes it to the person concerned to explore the apparent contradiction, before accepting his or her assurance of adherence to the *Basis*.

Someone who wished to become or remain a minister of the Word, for instance, while disagreeing with the ordination of women to that ministry, would have to be helped to face such questions as: "Must not your stated opinion render you incapable of providing counselling and support, in the terms and the spirit of the Church's affirmation of its women ministers, to a woman applicant seeking acceptance as a candidate for the Ministry or to a female colleague who experiences rejection in her local ministers' fraternal, ... and so make it nonsense for you to say that you are willing to do so?" - "Can you truly still say that you are willing to play any part the Presbytery may assign to you in the ordination and induction of women ministers?" - "Will you really be willing to accept women ministers in roles of leadership in your parish, presbytery and synod?" - "Given your opinion about women ministers, how fully do you accept women as elders or lay preachers?" - "How comfortable will you be with lay women in roles of significant leadership in the Church?".

This point has had to be laboured, because of the assumption in some circles that the only issue surrounding adherence to the *Basis of Union* is whether there is a difference that enters into the substance of the faith. As we have seen, that is not so. The overall issue is that of a willingness to live and work within the faith and unity of the One Holy Catholic and Apostolic Church in the way described in the *Basis*.

But some of the considerations canvassed above must also lead us to ask whether it is even true to say that the matter of the ministry of women does not enter into the substance of the faith. It was a matter on which some of our Reformation forebears considered it necessary to take a stand; and the stand that they took was the contrary one to that of the Uniting Church. They considered that one or two biblical passages expressly forbade women to exercise a teaching ministry.[8] The Uniting Church considers that the overall tenor of the Scriptures not only allows it, but promises the gifts for such ministry to women and men alike. It has expressed this conviction in its *Basis of Union*, in conscious divergence from this aspect of its own past and from so many other churches in the present. The issue touches the Uniting Church's understanding of the Gospel, of the Scriptures, of God's creation and reconciliation of human beings, of the unity of the Church, and of the gifts of the Spirit. If we were to pursue the issue in any of these directions, we should reach a point where the substance of the faith was beginning to be involved. What this suggests is that it is impossible to make a sweeping judgment that the ordination of women is a matter that either does or does not "enter into the substance of the faith". We need rather to say that, for the Uniting Church, its position on the ordination of women is connected with the substance of the faith and that elements in any serious debate on the matter will begin to enter into that substance. Whether or not a particular difference of opinion impinged on the substance of the faith would still remain to be decided.

In any individual case, those responsible for the care and discipline of an office-bearer, or for the approval of an applicant or candidate, would need to establish whether her or his opinion against the ordination of women did or did not enter into the substance of the faith. If it did, it would not be compatible with adherence to the *Basis of Union*.

There could, on the other hand, conceivably be an opinion against ordaining women that did not enter into the substance of the faith. As we have seen, it, too, would be incompatible with such adherence, if it reduced a person's willingness to live and work within the faith and unity of the One Holy Catholic and Apostolic Church in the way described in the *Basis of Union*.

For a number of years, the Standing Committee of the Assembly had on its agenda the problem of candidates for ordination who do not support the ordination of women. It seems to have had considerable difficulty in resolving the issue.

In March 1990, the Standing Committee received a document, "Why does the Uniting Church in Australia Ordain Women to the Ministry of the Word?"[9] and resolved, among other things, to

3. affirm that the Uniting Church in Australia ordains both women and men to the Ministry of the Word because it believes ordination without discrimination on grounds of gender is a fundamental implication of the gospel of God's love in Christ for all human beings, without distinction. For this understanding the Uniting Church appeals to Scripture as testimony to the living Word, which is Christ;

4. affirm that the Holy Spirit has called and continues to call women as well as men to the Ministry of the Word;

5. acknowledge that in ordaining women as well as men to the Ministry of the Word the Uniting Church in Australia, in company with other churches, has departed from an almost universal practice of the church catholic throughout most of history, but believes that the Uniting Church does so in obedience to the gospel;

6. remind members of the Uniting Church, ministers, candidates for the ordained ministries and, in particular, Presbyteries - which have responsibility for the act of ordination - that adherence to the *Basis of Union* requires acceptance of the ordination of women to the Ministry of the Word;

7. approve the document "Why does the Uniting Church in Australia Ordain Women to the Ministry of the Word?" as expressing the biblical and theological reasoning which leads the Uniting Church to ordain both women and men to the Ministry of the Word.[10]

Clauses 3 - 6 correspond to theses printed in bold type in the document approved under clause 7.[11] They have been slightly reworded, the most important change being in clause 6, where the reminder "that the *Basis of Union* affirms the ordination of women" was altered to the more telling statement

> [...] that adherence to the *Basis of Union* requires acceptance of the ordination of women to the Ministry of the Word.

These decisions of the Standing Committee's were reported in *Western Impact* in terms of the Uniting Church's seeing the ordination of women as "central to faith", "fundamental to the faith which the Church embraces", or "of the substance of the faith".[12] I am told that, after the meeting of the Standing Committee, some of its members spoke of the decision in such terms. That is understandable, for the document approved "as expressing the biblical and theological reasoning" behind the Uniting Church's practice virtually came to that position. But it fell just short of stating it categorically. It said, instead, that

> We would argue that the matter of the ordination of

women would be as close to the 'substance of faith' as for
example, the ordination of black persons[,][13]

and elsewhere suggested that to deny ordination on grounds of race
"would amount to a denial of the Gospel".[14] But it failed to develop
a clear position for the Standing Committee to adopt on whether,
in terms of adherence to the *Basis of Union*, the matter of the
ordination of women enters into the substance of the faith.

There was a predictable reaction to the report in *Western Impact* in
the next issue of that paper,[15] to which the President replied, in the
next issue again, that

> The committee did not confuse the implications of the
> Gospel with the substance of the Gospel [...], nor did it
> deny freedom of conscience on the matter of the equality
> of men and women in all forms of ministry [...].

> The committee was not dealing with the substance of the
> faith. It was concerned in clause 6 with structure and
> forms of ministry, and, with respect thereto, to emphasize
> the fundamental importance of the principle of equality of
> women and men in the life of our church.

> It approved the publication of the document "Why does
> the UCA ordain women [...]", not to promote debate
> within the church but for the information of the church in
> order to encourage more faithful obedience to the
> gospel.[16]

This means that the Standing Committee of the Assembly
determined that "adherence to the *Basis of Union* requires
acceptance of the ordination of women to the Ministry of the
Word", but not on the grounds that the matter entered into the
substance of the faith. The President saw the decision as related (1)
to structure and forms of ministry and, with respect thereto, (2) to
the principle of equality of women and men in the life of the
Church. In terms of our above discussion, it would therefore be fair
to say that ordaining women to the Ministry is supposed to belong
to the faith and unity of the Church, within which we must be
willing to live and work, if we are to adhere to the *Basis*, even if it is

not thought to be a matter that enters into the substance of the faith.

But here we strike a problem in the President's assurance, in response to one correspondent in *Western Impact*, that, by its resolution, the Standing Committee did not

> [...] deny freedom of conscience on the matter of the equality of men and women in all forms of ministry [...].

"Freedom of conscience" is categorically different from the "difference of opinion in matters that do not enter into the substance of the faith" allowed for by adherence to the *Basis of Union*. "Freedom of conscience" implies difference, not only in opinion, (i.e. in judgment or belief, in personal views or estimation), but in action and behaviour. Freedom of conscience on the equality of men and women in ministry means that, if my conscience will not let me treat them as equal, then I have a right to treat them as unequal. But what has then become of "the fundamental importance of the principle of equality of women and men in the life of our church"? One has to wonder, whether the President had not, perhaps, at that point, taken over the language of those to whom he was responding and ended up saying more than he meant or than the Standing Committee meant.

On the other hand, there is still a general lack of clarity about the exact meaning and significance of the resolution. "Adherence to the *Basis of Union* requires acceptance of the ordination of women to the Ministry of the Word." Yes, but now what does "acceptance of the ordination of women" mean? To allow that this is, in fact, what the Uniting Church practices and that this will be the reality of life in the Uniting Church, whatever one thinks of it? To accommodate oneself to this situation, to fit in with it? To agree with the Church's claim that it is in obedience to the Gospel that it ordains women as well as men? It would be helpful, if resolutions as important as this were more carefully formulated.

Both the Standing Committee and the President spoke of the ordination of women as something that the Uniting Church believed it had to do in obedience to the Gospel. The President recognized a distinction between this, as an implication of the Gospel, and the substance of the Gospel. In other correspondence, the terminology varied between "substance of the Gospel" and "substance of the faith". It would, indeed, be hard to keep the two entirely separate, but some people may be working with a broader definition of the faith and a narrower definition of the Gospel, which could open another source of confusion.

A further concept occurred both in the report received by the Standing Committee and in its own resolution, viz. that of

> a fundamental implication of the Gospel of God's love for
> all human beings without distinction.

Anything fundamental, basic, to something else must, in other imagery, be getting very close to the substance of it. In fact, the distinction between "substance" and "implication" may be useful for some purposes, but must not be pressed to the point of separating things that are inherently connected. In the history of the faith, the very substance of the Gospel has, at different times, proved to be at stake in controversies over implications that have only just dawned on some members of the Church, while still bitterly resisted by others.

It is therefore a gross oversimplification for one correspondent in *Impact* to suggest that the ordination of women cannot be "part of 'the substance of the faith'", because otherwise it would already feature in the creeds. Both the *Nicene Creed* and the Reformation confessions witness to certain things as belonging to the substance of the faith, which had not been explicitly identified as such prior to their time.

It is again an oversimplification to argue that the ordination of women cannot belong to the substance of the faith, "when the ordination of men doesn't". It is, rather, true that the calling and setting apart of persons to the ministry of the Gospel both does not, and yet also does, belong to the essence of the Gospel and of corresponding faith. For God has both reconciled the world with himself in Jesus Christ and given the Apostles the ministry of reconciliation. What they preach (i.e. the substance of the Gospel) is, of course, not themselves, but Jesus Christ as Lord, and yet also themselves as their hearers' servants for Jesus' sake (2 Cor.5:18f; 4:5). The ministry of the Gospel is thus both completely subservient to the content of the Gospel and also quite inseparable from it. When we try to isolate the matter of the news from the medium God has established for it, some new medium we have arbitrarily or inadvertently chosen will end up becoming the message. So the ministry of the Gospel can indeed feature in confessions of the Gospel faith, from "Cephas and the Twelve" as the first witnesses of the Resurrection (1 Cor.15:5), through the "ministry, oracles, and ordinances of God", which, according to the *Westminster Confession of Faith*, Christ has given to the catholic visible church,[17] right up to the Uniting Church's own acknowledgment that

> Since the Church lives by the power of the Word, she is assured that God, who has never left himself without witness to that Word, will, through Christ and in the power of the Holy Spirit, call and set apart members of the Church to be ministers of the Word. [...] their setting apart will be known as ordination (*Basis*, par.14 [a]).

The issue is not that the ordination of women to that ministry is being made more important than the ordination of men, but that the exclusion of women from the ministry is perceived to contradict aspects of the very gospel that the ministry is supposed to serve. The assertion that only a male can serve as a minister of Jesus Christ, the living Word, is perceived to be a statement made, not in the service of the Gospel, but in the service of male superiority. The insistence on the male medium is becoming a proclamation about that medium, at the expense of the content of the Gospel. The Gospel is about the grace of God in electing and calling the ineligible and making the inadequate adequate. This grace becomes a dynamic for service in those who receive it; and it is refracted into the many different gifts of grace that the members of the Church receive and that equip them for many different forms of service. It conflicts with Scripture and the Church's experience to deny that women as well as men receive gifts for the ministry of the Word.

It could still be an overstatement simply to claim that the ordination of women belongs to the substance of the faith. But even if that is so, it is none the less true that many stands taken against the ordination of women effectively deny aspects of the Gospel and require the Church to confess the faith again in a way that rebuts those denials and affirms that the gospel of God's free grace calls both men and women into the service of that gospel in the ordained ministry of the Church.

To continue with the story of decisions at Assembly level, two of the clauses in the Standing Committee resolution of March 1990 attracted criticism from a number of people. In March 1991, the Standing Committee therefore rescinded them and replaced them with other formulations. In place of clause 3, the Standing Committee resolved to

> affirm that the Uniting Church ordains both women and men to the Ministry of the Word in the conviction that a fundamental implication of the gospel of God's love in Christ is that there can be no discrimination on grounds of gender. For this understanding the Uniting Church appeals to Scripture as testimony to the living Word, who is Christ.[18]

It is easy to see that the earlier wording, which said that "ordination without discrimination on grounds of gender is a fundamental implication of the gospel [...]", laid itself open to misunderstanding and criticism, by seeming to say that ordination was itself an implication of the Gospel. It is now clear that what the Standing Committee meant is that the Gospel implies that there can be no discrimination on grounds of gender and that this has to apply to ordination, just as much as to anything else. The new clause still employs the concept of a 'fundamental implication of the gospel of God's love'. So the question remains, how anyone could reject such an implication, without that's becoming a matter that entered into the substance of the faith.

Yet the other clause the Standing Committee rescinded was clause 6, which had reminded everyone "and, in particular, Presbyteries [...] that adherence to the *Basis of Union* requires acceptance of the ordination of women to the Ministry of the Word". In its place, the Standing Committee resolved to

advise presbyteries that because

    (a) the Church is committed to recognize among its members men and women called to all forms of ministry within the Church, and, in particular, to ordain both men and women; and because

    (b) the Church requires that a candidate for ordination shall express adherence to the polity and discipline of the Church (Regulation 2.3.1 [a][ii])

a presbytery should not ordain a candidate who

    (i) denies the validity of the ordination or ministry of women as Ministers of the Word; or

    (ii) is unwilling to work with and mutually [sic] support both men and women as colleagues in the ordained ministry; or

    (iii) is unwilling to encourage, equip and support both men and women in all forms of ministry in the Church and to teach the Church's position in this regard.[19]

The Standing Committee thus backed away from the insistence that "adherence to the *Basis of Union* requires acceptance of the ordination of women". This was probably because of uncertainty about how to deal with the objection that, unless the ordination of women entered into the substance of the faith, office-bearers must be allowed liberty of opinion, or even freedom of conscience, with regard to it. The position on which Standing Committee fell back was that (a) the Uniting Church is committed to ordaining women as well as men and that (b) there is a regulation requiring a candidate for ordination to adhere to the Church's polity and discipline. The resolution then went on to apply this by listing the three things (i) - (iii) above as indications that a presbytery ought not to ordain a candidate.

This may be a valid position, on this particular issue. But its strength depends on certain factors not mentioned in the resolution. One is the depth and the nature of the Uniting Church's commitment to recognizing by ordination the call and gifts of both men and women for the ministry of the Word, and also of its commitment to recognizing the gifts that men and women have received for other forms of ministry. Another is the inherent connexion between patterns and functions of ministry and the polity and discipline of the Church. If these points are not presupposed, then the argument that the Standing Committee is attempting requires, as a further step, a declaration by the Assembly that ministers are required to give their personal approval and support either to every commitment into which the Uniting Church enters or to this particular commitment, at least. Such a declaration would impose the commitment on each minister and so make it a matter of the discipline of the Church, to which the minister is supposed to adhere.

The problem about the position as stated in the Standing Committee's resolution is that it might be treated as an invitation to presbyteries to take issue with candidates on other matters to which the Uniting Church has also committed itself. The appeal to Regulation 2.3.1.(a) (ii) seems particularly powerful, because that regulation employs the term 'adhere', without closer definition and without any provision for difference of opinion. But what would the Assembly do, if a presbytery refused to ordain a candidate, on the grounds that the candidate could not identify with the Church's position on some cause of social justice or programme of mission to which the Church was committed? It would probably be technically possible to link the cause or programme with the polity and discipline of the Church, since the commitment would presumably have been made by one or more councils of the Church, in the proper exercise of their powers. But was the regulation ever intended to commit all candidates for ordination, not simply to the principles and system of the Church's polity and discipline, but also to every particular commitment or policy that the Church may undertake or pursue by due means? The Standing Committee appears to have set a precedent that can only encourage the outlook that the policies and preoccupations of the day are more important as tests of eligibility for ordination than the fundamentals on which the Church is founded.

If we look at the three points identified by the Standing Committee as contra-indications, we note that (i) is a straightout denial of the validity of something that the *Basis of Union* lays down for the Church's practice of ordination and ministry. Such a stance must affect a person's willingness to share in this side of the Church's life and work in the way described in the *Basis of Union*. For such willingness has to mean more than being prepared to go through whatever outward motions may be expected of one. The other points, (ii) and (iii), are directly formulated in terms of unwillingness to participate in the life and work of the Church in the way described in the *Basis*, as far as the equal part of men and women in ordained ministry and other forms of ministry is concerned. Anyone covered by (i) can scarcely adhere to the *Basis of Union*. Anyone covered by (ii) or (iii) does not. The Standing Committee should have stuck to its guns and continued to maintain that adherence to the *Basis* required support for the ordination of women. That is a position easy to defend, as soon as one sees that the primary question is that of willingness to live and work within the faith and unity of the One Holy Catholic and Apostolic Church in the way described in the *Basis*, and that the proviso that difference of opinion is allowable, within certain limits, means precisely that, and nothing more.

There are great advantages in staying with the issue of adherence to the *Basis*, rather than developing other tests. The principle of recognizing the gifts of men and women for the ministry of the Word and for other ministries is clearly set forth there, in the document in accordance with which the Uniting Church was formed. The Church's commitment to this principle can therefore be shown to be fundamental to its being and identity, and also to its theology of ministry. Insisting on this principle in this way avoids setting any precedent on which other principles to which the Church may commit itself could also be established as tests. It stays with what the Church has required of its office-bearers since its inauguration. It also stays with a requirement that applies to a range of office-bearers, through the questions asked at their setting apart, commissioning or accreditation. Regulation 2.3.1.(a)(ii) applies only to candidates for ordination. It does not apply to elders, lay preachers, or ministers of the Word already ordained.

But, in any case, the Standing Committee was still running into trouble with the wording of its resolutions and had to consider the matter again a year later, in March 1992. Concern had been expressed at the action of one presbytery in ordaining a candidate whom some did not believe to meet the Church's requirements. This raised the question of whether the tests (i) - (iii) were adequate. The President and General Secretary issued a statement in April 1992, explaining the situation and giving notice that the Standing Committee was revising the wording of the tests in order to eliminate any ambiguity. The statement went on to say that

> Of particular concern to Standing Committee members is the nexus between inner conviction and outward behaviour. The Committee takes the view that it is not possible for a minister to have an inner conviction against the ordination of women without conveying that view in some way, albeit unconsciously, in the practice of his ministry. Therefore the tests to be applied in assessing a candidate's suitability for ordination need to include a personal acceptance of the theological validity of the ordination of women.

> The Assembly is well aware that these issues are not unrelated to a wider question in the Uniting Church - that of how much difference of opinion or freedom of conscience should be permitted in the church, especially amongst those who are ordained. Standing Committee believes that just as the church requires inner convictions about the existence of God or the Holy Trinity, so it is reasonable for the church to require inner convictions about the ordination of women.[20]

The concern expressed here about the "nexus between inner conviction and outward behaviour" approaches the position I advanced above, where I argued that willingness to live and work within the faith and unity of the church has to mean far more than a readiness to act in outward conformity, though in contradiction to one's own convictions. But the Standing Committee has gone beyond that, on this issue, at least, by insisting on acceptance of the ordination of women *out of inner conviction*. In order to require that, the Church first has to determine that the issue enters into the substance of the faith. On any point for which it does not do that, the Church really has to accept that some may be quite willing and able to live and work within the unity of the Church, while holding opinions that differ from the Church's position. Problems would only begin to arise, if any were trying to conform against their own convictions or consciences.

The following paragraph of the statement by the President and General Secretary only confuses the issue further. It links the connexion between conviction and behaviour with the question of "how much difference of opinion or freedom of conscience should be permitted". Without clarifying that question, it then proceeds to make a most unhelpful comparison: "Just as" the Church expects acceptance of the existence of God or of the Trinity to be grounded in inner convictions, so it may rightly require inner convictions "about the ordination of women". Many will feel that this is to compare incomparables. The Standing Committee has since acknowledged that the sentence "is open to misunderstanding".[21] The precise problem in this context is that, while everyone would agree that belief in God and the Trinity enters into the substance of the faith, the Standing Committee is not itself prepared to say that the issue of women's ordination does so. It cannot even mean the "just as" that introduces the comparison! I have suggested above that arguments for and against the ordination of women are likely to involve matters that *do* enter into the substance of the faith. To that extent, there is a degree of validity in the comparison attempted in the statement. But any validity it has only starts to become accessible, as one begins to perceive the connexions; and the Standing Committee does not want to commit itself to there being any direct connexion between the ordination of women and the substance of the faith.

At the Standing Committee meeting of September 1992, the committee resolved to revise Uniting Church policy in respect of the views of candidates on the ordination and ministry of women by replacing the second half of the resolution contained in Standing Committee minute 91.3.3 with the following words:

"a presbytery should not ordain a candidate unless it is satisfied that the candidate -

(i) accepts the theological validity of the ordination of both women and men for ministry in Christ's church as a Minister of the Word/Deacon;

(ii) is willing to work with and support both women and men as colleagues in the ordained ministries; and

(iii) is willing to encourage, equip and support both women and men in all forms of ministry in the Church and to teach the Church's position in this regard."[22]

This wording puts the three tests from March 1991 in a positive form and so lays emphasis on the need for positive convictions and attitudes. But it still follows on from the first part of the original resolution, so that current Uniting Church "policy" is still made to depend on a questionable use of Regulation 2.3.1(a)(ii). The positive form of the tests sets an even clearer precedent for any future insistence that it is not good enough for an office-bearer to share in the life of the Church with a good conscience, whole holding a different opinion on some points. Office-bearers will need to give assurance of having an inner conviction on any matter at all as required.

It must cause concern that the Assembly Standing Committee has only been able to deal with this important issue in such a faltering way. It is a matter on which the Church must be both firm and pastoral; and the Standing Committee's hesitancy in identifying what the Church's stand is has not helped that, at all. The events suggest that, in general, the Assembly needs to ensure that it and its Standing Committee are better resourced with regard to the development and maturing of policy and the formulation of resolutions. In particular, it appears that the crucial thing is for the Uniting Church to achieve clarity and consensus about what is meant by the expectation that office-bearers adhere to the *Basis of Union*.

VI

As far as the baptism of children is concerned, it is expressly provided in the *Basis of Union* that

> The Uniting Church will baptize those who confess the Christian faith, and children who are presented for baptism and for whose instruction and nourishment in the faith the Church takes responsibility (par.7).

The Church recognizes two grounds for Baptism. One is a personal profession of faith. The other is that a child is presented by those responsible for it, parents or others acting in place of parents, in circumstances where the Church judges that it can assume responsibility for the child's instruction and nurture in the faith into which it is to be baptized. One of the prime factors that the Church will take into account in arriving at that judgment will be the part that it can see parents, guardians or sponsors playing in that regard.

Various influences in the years after union led to a questioning of the practice of baptizing children before they could make their own confession of faith. Controversies began to arise in situations where ministers and councils of elders were either discouraging or refusing "infant baptism" or even rebaptizing adults on profession of faith, despite their already having been baptized once as children.

In May 1985, the Fourth Assembly sought to settle the matter. It approved recommendations from the Standing Committee, in terms of which it resolved,

1. To require all Uniting Church Ministers, Elders' Councils and Congregations to preach, teach and administer the sacrament of Baptism in accordance with the Church's adopted position. [...]

3. To require all Presbyteries in assessing candidates' "readiness for ministry" to ensure that each candidate accepts and will

conform to the Church's adopted position relating to Baptism, prior to authorizing ordination. [...]

5. To request Presbyteries to administer the Assembly's requirements for Ministers, Elders and Congregations on Baptism with pastoral sensitivity and compassion. [...][23]

Unfortunately, the text of the recommendation that became the Assembly's resolution failed to spell out what was meant by "the Church's adopted position". (This is not the only occasion on which an Assembly Standing Committee has failed to formulate the consensus and intentions that presumably obtained in its meeting in a way that would communicate them clearly beyond the meeting.) The Standing Committee report to the 1985 Assembly had spoken of two things that the Standing Committee had resolved to "reaffirm" or "re-emphasize" in March 1984. The first decision was to

> reaffirm that the present position of the Uniting Church in Australia relating to the administration of the Sacrament of Baptism, is contained in Appendix C of the Second Assembly as approved by the minute 79.22(7) and is further elucidated in "Questions and Answers Nos. 6 to 14" being Appendix VI of the Minutes of the Third Assembly and its minute 82.53(2).[24]

Was the "Church's adopted position" in the Assembly's resolution identical with the "present position of the Uniting Church in Australia relating to the administration of the Sacrament of Baptism", as contained in a document from the Second Assembly and elucidated by a document from the Third? The possibility that this was so caused a great deal of disquiet among those who felt that they could by no means accept everything that was in those documents.

The second decision that the Standing Committee reported having taken in March 1984 was to

> re-emphasize in particular that:
>
> a) "Baptism is to be administered to those who confess the Christian Faith, and, when there is a founded

hope for their Christian upbringing, to infants presented for Baptism."

b) Baptism is an unrepeatable act.[25]

The first of these two affirmations, a), is from the document referred to in the previous quotation as "Appendix C" to the Minutes of the Second Assembly, which was "An Agreed Statement on Baptism (Uniting Church/Roman Catholic)".[26] It can be seen to be similar to the quotation from the *Basis of Union* with which we began this section.

The debate in the Assembly had certainly focused on these principles, but there was nothing in its resolutions to say that this was all that was meant by the phrase, "the Church's adopted position". Noting that there was some confusion about that term, the Assembly Standing Committee, meeting in September 1985, carried a clarifying resolution and asked the President and Secretary of the Assembly to embody it in a pastoral letter on the matter. Given the powers that belong to the Assembly's Standing Committee under the Constitution, that resolution of the Standing Committee's must be seen as the definitive interpretation of the resolutions of the Fourth Assembly. In other words, whatever the Assembly originally meant, the Standing Committee acted on behalf of the Assembly and with the powers of the Assembly to place a clear meaning on what it had said. There is no reason to think that it is not a true interpretation. But, above all, it is an authoritative interpretation and has to be seen as giving the sense of what the Assembly determined.

"A Pastoral Letter to Members of the Uniting Church in Australia", issued by the President and Secretary of the Assembly at the request of the Standing Committee appeared with the date of 29 October 1985. It contained the declaration by the Standing Committee to the effect that, by the term 'the church's adopted position',

> [...] the Assembly [...] is referring to two principles already affirmed by previous Assemblies, viz.
>
> (i) that "The Uniting Church will baptize those who confess the Christian faith, and children who are

presented for baptism and for whose instruction and nourishment in the faith the Church takes responsibility" (*Basis of Union*, par.7);

(ii) that baptism is unrepeatable.

The President and Secretary went on to explain that

What the Fourth Assembly did was reaffirm, for the good of the church, two important parameters for baptismal *practice*.

Assembly resolution 85.39.1 was proposed by the previous Standing Committee when confronted with the need to deal with contradictory practices within the Uniting Church. Consequently, in March 1984 it drew attention to the "position of the Uniting Church in Australia in relation to the *administration* of the sacrament of baptism ..." emphasizing in particular that

"a) Baptism is to be administered to those who confess the Christian Faith, and, when there is a founded hope for their Christian upbringing, to infants presented for baptism;

b) baptism is an unrepeatable act."

The Assembly's decisions, related to those paragraphs, leave room for continuing dialogue about our understanding of the meaning of baptism, but remove doubt about those who are properly regarded as candidates for baptism, and make clear that any person once baptized as a child or on personal confession of faith may not again be baptized.

This of course continues the common heritage of the Congregational, Methodist and Presbyterian Churches prior to union, and is consistent with our Catholic, Reformed and Evangelical tradition.

Our church considers a certain diversity of faith and expression to be a healthy sign of growing life. Diversity, however, is not to be confused with licence. Each of us is constrained by the discipline of Christ in mutual submission to one another, and in matters of doctrine and worship the specific responsibility for determining that discipline rests with the Assembly. It is expected that these decisions of the Assembly will be respected and fulfilled by all who represent the ministry of the Uniting Church in Australia. [...]

The vast majority of our people have accepted the Assembly's leading on this matter with gratitude and joy. Those whose acceptance has not been without some difficulty deserve our special care and understanding. [...]

Up to this stage, there was doubt in scarcely anyone's mind that the Assembly resolution 85.39.1 made it a requirement for all ministers, elders' councils and congregations of the Uniting Church to preach, teach and administer the sacrament of Baptism "in accordance with the Church's adopted position". The point of addressing the requirement to ministers, councils of elders and congregations was that it is they who are involved in the decision of whom to baptize and in the celebration of a baptism. Both Assembly Minute 85.39.5, requesting presbyteries "to administer the Assembly's requirements for ministers, elders and congregations on Baptism with pastoral sensitivity and compassion", and the final paragraph in the above quotation from the subsequent Pastoral Letter reveal an awareness that, for some, it would not be an easy thing to respect and fulfil the Assembly's decision. But there was a requirement; and the Standing Committee expected it to be met "by all who represent the ministry of the Uniting Church in Australia".

How seriously the requirement was meant for those who were already ordained ministers of the Word was also patent from the matching requirement of Minute 85.39.3 for all presbyteries, in assessing candidates' "readiness for ministry", to ensure "that each candidate accepts and will conform to the Church's adopted position relating to Baptism", prior to authorizing the ordination of those candidates. Noone would in future be ordained to the Ministry who was not willing so to conform.

The initial discomfort in the Church had been over the possibility that the Assembly minute might be requiring ministers to teach everything contained in various documents on Baptism approved by the Second, Third and Fourth Assemblies. The Standing Committee and the Pastoral Letter from President and Secretary established that this was not so. It was not the case that there was supposed to be only "one uniform and exclusive understanding of the meaning of baptism" in the Church. What the Standing Committee in 1984 and the Assembly in 1985 had had to deal with were "contradictory practices". So the Standing Committee had drawn attention to the Church's position "in relation to the *administration* of the sacrament of baptism" and the Assembly had reaffirmed "two important parameters for baptismal *practice*". The Assembly's requirement was to be understood in terms of the two principles re-emphasized by the Standing Committee in 1984 and stated again, in two slightly different wordings, in the Pastoral Letter. Understood in that way, it (1) removed doubt about those who are properly regarded as candidates for baptism, i.e. it reaffirmed that both those who confess the faith and also children presented under favourable circumstances are properly regarded as candidates for baptism, and (2) made clear that any person once baptized may not be baptized again.

Some years later, however, arising out of a particular case, the President was asked to rule on the following questions:

1. Does the Assembly decision 85.39 allow a Minister to refuse to baptize a person on the ground that that person is an infant?

2. Does [sic] the Joint Presbyteries Settlements Advisory Committee and Standing Committee of Synod have power to leave a Minister without settlement on the ground that the Minister refuses to baptize infants?

There was not time for the thorough preparation of a ruling before the meeting of the Fifth Assembly in 1988, so that it was the incoming President who delivered "Presidential Ruling No 11" in September 1988, in which he ruled that

1. Assembly resolution 85.39 does allow a Minister to refuse to baptize a person on the ground that the person is an infant

provided that the Minister fully accepts that the Uniting Church recognizes and practises infant baptism.

2. J[oint] P[resbyteries] S[ettlements] A[dvisory] C[ommittee] and the Standing Committee of Synod do not have the power under Reg.2.4.5(b)(ii) [since 1990 = Reg.2.7.5 (b)(ii)] to leave a Minister without settlement solely on the ground that the Minister refuses to baptize infants.

The Standing Committee of the Assembly subsequently disallowed the ruling on the first question (1. above), stating that it was not in the interests of the Church for there to be any ruling on the matter until the Church had further considered the underlying issues. It appointed a task force to consider those issues in preparation for a major discussion at the 1991 Assembly. When the recommendations of the first task group were not along the lines that the Standing Committee wanted, it appointed another and formulated detailed terms of reference, to ensure that the new task group would do what was wanted.[27]

The Assembly Standing Committee confirmed the ruling on the second question (2. above), stating that this was not to be seen as approval of the position on Baptism held by the minister in question. It was acting on the advice of the Assembly's Legal Reference Committee that, in refusing to list the minister as available for settlement, the Settlements Committee was taking *de facto* disciplinary action, which was not the purpose of Regulation 2.4.5 [now: 2.7.5] (b)(ii).

Since the ruling on the meaning of the Assembly resolution was disallowed, we need not discuss it in great detail. Unfortunately, the President had been provided in some of the documentation with a corrupt text of Minute 85.39.1 and had based much of his argument on the wrong wording. It was a contention of the minister involved that the principal issue was "the liberty of opinion in non-essentials guaranteed in Paragraph 14 of the *Basis of Union*". The President decided that it was unlikely that the Assembly could have intended to deny ministers "any liberty of opinion in the matter of [their] administration of the sacrament of baptism to infants", arguing that

If it were the intention of the Assembly to identify an obligation on every Minister of the Word to administer the sacrament to infants as being of the substance of the faith, then I would have expected a clear declaration to that effect.

We see here the confusion between allowing "difference of opinion" and permitting freedom of action against which I have argued above. It results in the suggestion that the Assembly cannot require anything of a Uniting Church minister, unless it is prepared to declare it a matter that enters into the substance of the faith. This would have the consequence of reducing the Assembly's "determining responsibility in matters of doctrine, worship, government and discipline[28] to a very narrow scope. It would also leave the vow a minister makes at inductions to "accept the discipline of the Uniting Church" subject to the minister's own "opinion" in the matter of whether to function within the Uniting heritage or largely to follow some other tradition.

The Presidential Ruling referred to the Pastoral Letter of the previous President and the Secretary of the Assembly, but drew on it only selectively. It sought to rule on the force of the Assembly's resolution independently of the subsequent resolution of the Standing Committee declaring what the Assembly resolution had been referring to. It proceeded on the assumption that the only matter substantially at issue for the Fourth Assembly and its Standing Committee had been rebaptism, and as if the issue of infant baptism had been only peripherally addressed. In other words, the Ruling did not recognize that the Assembly had been referring to "two principles", as the Standing Committee had declared, nor that it had re-affirmed "two important parameters for baptismal *practice*", as the Pastoral Letter had explained.

While the Standing Committee of the Fifth Assembly disallowed the first part of the President's ruling, it accepted its underlying assumption, viz. that the Fourth Assembly had only been concerned to prevent rebaptism and had not also insisted that ministers, councils of elders and congregations were to regard infants presented in accordance with the *Basis of Union* as rightful subjects of baptism. It did not, therefore, reaffirm the stand taken by the Fourth Assembly and its Standing Committee, but proceeded to open up again the more controversial half of what had been decided in 1985. The terms of reference of the second task group for that purpose, appointed in November 1989, charged it with preparing a discussion paper "for wide distribution in the Church". The paper was both to examine the bases for (a) baptizing infants, as well as adults on profession of faith and (b) baptizing solely on profession of faith, and also to canvass "ways and means whereby the two traditions of baptismal belief and practice, [...] (a) and (b) above, could be accommodated within the Uniting Church". Options to be discussed included allowing ministers to refuse to baptize infants and allowing councils of elders to decide that no infants were to be baptized in their congregations.

Mid-1991, there appeared, in accordance with the task group's instructions,

> *The Water that Unites: A Discussion Paper for the Uniting Church in Australia on Baptismal Practice*, [Sydney], 1991.

The paper follows the line taken by the Standing Committee of the Fifth Assembly, in presenting the action of the Fourth as solely concerned with the unrepeatability of baptism. Its assurance that "there is no intention to alter the church's adopted position on baptism" is given on the presupposition that

> The Uniting Church has not yet authoritatively decided the boundaries between difference of opinion and the obligation to accept and teach and practice that which is required by the *Basis of Union*, Constitution and Assembly, even though an ordained minister may consider some of these requirements to lack adequate scriptural authority.[29]

> The Uniting Church has not considered the possibility or consequences of allowing a council of elders the freedom to approve the baptism only of those who make a personal profession of faith [...].[30]

In fact, the heat of the 1985 debate had come from the awareness on both sides that such questions were exactly what the Assembly was being asked to consider. In the outcome, the Assembly did, as we have seen, decide by a very solid majority,

> To require all Uniting Church Ministers, Elders' Councils and Congregations to preach, teach and administer the sacrament of Baptism in accordance with the Church's adopted position.[31]

The Fourth Assembly had thus already decided, not only that baptism was never to be repeated, but also that ministers, councils of elders and congregations were *all* to be required to treat as appropriate subjects for baptism both those who confessed the Christian faith and children presented for baptism for whose upbringing in the faith the Church was able to take responsibility. Whether or not its individual members were aware of what was happening, the Standing Committee of the Fifth Assembly was indeed, through the discussion paper that it got its task group to produce, trying to change the fundamental position of the Uniting Church on Baptism.

The paper, *The Water that Unites*, was extensively discussed throughout the Church.[32] As reported to the Assembly Standing Committee in September 1993, "an overwhelming majority of presbyteries and synods and a substantial majority of councils of elders" were opposed to making any accommodation for ministers or councils of elders who wanted to refuse baptism to infants.[33] The Standing Committee recurred to earlier decisions of assemblies and their standing committees discussed above. It resolved

1. (a) to declare that all ministers and councils of elders are required to baptize both those unbaptized persons who confess the Christian faith and children who are presented for baptism and for whose instruction and nourishment in the faith the church takes responsibility, and that therefore there is no provision for the accommodation of ministers and councils of elders who will baptize only those who personally confess the Christian faith;

   (b) to require presbyteries to ensure this decision is communicated to all ministers and councils of elders.[34]

Subsequent clauses gave direction to presbyteries on counselling ministers and councils of elders about their duties and required presbyteries to ensure that ministers going into new settlements, candidates for ordination and those applying to be candidates were aware of, and ready to accept, the Church's requirement regarding baptism, as expressed in 1(a) above.[35]

The Seventh Assembly, meeting in 1994, received the Standing Committee's report and itself resolved in the same terms as the committee, except for the omission of a phrase that contemplated a presbytery's counselling a minister about the inappropriateness of his or her remaining a minister of the Uniting Church.[36] This re-established, rather more explicitly, what had been decided on in 1985; and that earlier decision is referred to in the preamble to the Standing Committee and Assembly resolutions, among factors "in the light" of which those resolutions were passed.

These Assembly resolutions ground in the Uniting Church's position on Baptism, as stated by the Assembly, and in what the Assembly requires of all ministers, elders' councils and congregations. They go on to require presbyteries to instruct candidates for ordination, and to inform applicants for the ordained ministries,

> that the church's ordination vows involve an acceptance of the church's position on baptism and an obligation to baptize those who confess the Christian faith and children who are presented for baptism and for whose instruction and nourishment in the faith the church takes responsibility.[37]

That obligation could be held to be implied in the vows about receiving baptism and the eucharist as signs and seals of the Gospel and being resolved to celebrate them with God's people, about adhering to the *Basis* and submitting to the Church's discipline or to any one or any combination of these. Adherence to the *Basis* may be involved, to some extent or other. But the Assembly is not taking its stand on what such adherence entails, but on what the ordination vows entail. Its resolution still leave us to face the question of whether adherence to the *Basis of Union* would or would not already in itself prevent a minister from refusing in principle to baptize children.

In order to consider that issue, we must first review the place of Baptism in the *Basis of Union* and its relation to the ministry of the Word.

The Uniting Church sees Baptism in terms of the continuing activity of the risen Lord Jesus Christ with human beings and with the Church.

> [The Church] is a pilgrim people, always on the way towards a promised goal [...]. On the way Christ feeds her with Word and Sacraments [...] (par.3).

The word and sacraments by which Christ nourishes the Church on its pilgrimage are inherently and intimately related to Jesus Christ himself. For he is the living Word of God, addressed to human beings and dynamically present for them "in and through the news of his completed work", i.e. through words and acts of human witness to him and to his story.

> Christ who is present when he is preached among men is the Word of the God who acquits the guilty, who gives life to the dead and who brings into being what otherwise could not exist. Through human witness in word and action, and in the power of the Holy Spirit, Christ reaches out to command men's attention and awaken their faith; he calls them into the fellowship of his sufferings, to be the disciples of a crucified Lord; in his own strange way he constitutes, rules and renews them as his Church (par.4).

The human witness through which Jesus Christ himself speaks and acts as the Word of God can be any expression of the life and work of his people in the world. It is certainly not confined to what is done by set-apart ministers or to what happens in Church buildings. On the other hand, what the Church does both as a corporate body and through ordained ministers of the Word is only to be understood in terms of (1) the real presence and activity of Jesus Christ in and through human witness in word and action and of (2) Jesus Christ's own institution of central forms of human witness.

The Church therefore also acknowledges that

> [...] Christ has commanded his Church to proclaim the Gospel both in words and in the two visible acts of Baptism and the Lord's Supper. He himself acts in and through everything that the Church does in obedience to his commandment [...] (par.6).

The specific significance of Baptism for the life of the Church consists in the fact that

> [...] Christ incorporates men into his body by Baptism. In this way he enables them to participate in his own baptism, which was accomplished once on behalf of all in his death and burial [...]. Baptism into Christ's body initiates men into his life and mission in the world, so that they are united in one fellowship of love, service, suffering and joy, in one family of the Father of all in heaven and earth, and in the power of the one Spirit (par.7).

This has direct implications for the Uniting Church understanding of Church membership and of ministry.

> [...] membership is open to all who are baptized into the Holy Catholic Church in the name of the Father and of the Son and of the Holy Spirit. The Uniting Church will seek ways in which the baptized may have confirmed to them the promises of God, and be led to deeper commitment to the faith and service into which they have been baptized (par.12).

This last Paragraph also touches on the relation of Baptism to participation in the Holy Communion. The Assembly has since declared that

> in the Uniting Church in Australia it is appropriate and desirable for baptized children, being members of the Church, to participate in the Sacrament of Holy Communion, including reception of the elements.[38]

For the Uniting Church, all the baptized, adults and children alike, are members of the body of Christ. It is Jesus Christ himself who makes them that; and he does so through the baptism that the Church celebrates in obedience to him. The efficacy of Baptism depends on the presence and action of Jesus Christ and the gift of the Holy Spirit. Words spoken, and actions performed, by the Church cannot in themselves bring about what they are aimed at, although they can express Christ's promise about it. But the significance of proclamation by word and sacrament depends on the fact that

> [Christ] himself acts in and through everything that the Church does in obedience to his commandment; it is he who by the gift of the Spirit confers upon men the forgiveness, the fellowship, the new life and the freedom which the proclamation and actions promise; and it is he who awakens, purifies and advances in men the faith and hope in which alone such benefits can be accepted (par.6).

What is promised in the rite of Baptism can only be accepted in faith; and, as incorporation into the body of Christ, Baptism is initiation into the community of faith. But, for the Uniting Church, confession of the faith is not the sole ground for, and thus the precondition of, baptism. For faith is itself the work of Jesus Christ and the Holy Spirit, which may well commence with a child's baptism and continue through its instruction and nurture in the faith, within the life of the community of faith. For the Uniting Church, a child is given the clearest message about God's love for it and the completed work of Jesus Christ on its behalf, when it is included in the membership of God's family in this way. That is simply the best Body-language. The *Basis of Union* therefore states that

> The Uniting Church will baptize [...] children who are presented for baptism and for whose instruction and nourishment in the faith the Church takes responsibility (par.7).

This still leaves it for parents to decide whether to present their children for baptism or not. A Uniting Church family is free to leave its children unbaptized, with the possibility of their seeking believer's baptism for themselves, when of an age to do so. That would, of course, now have the unfortunate consequence of preventing them from being invited to receive Communion along with the baptized children in the congregation.

The importance given to Baptism for membership of the Church is closely connected with the Uniting Church's understanding of the nature of the Church. It is the body of Jesus Christ. This means that it finds its true identity and unity in him: It is *his* body. But it also means that it is a visible community of human beings existing in space and time: It is Christ's *body*. Baptism is an outward rite and a community action: It brings a person into identifiable membership of the earthly community of which we believe that it is the body of Christ. Baptism is a simple act performed on the new member of the community, in obedience to the command of Jesus Christ, in the name of the Father and the Son and the Holy Spirit: It is about what God has done for that person and for all people once and for all, in the death and resurrection of Jesus Christ; it is also about how God does and will make real in the lives of individuals and of the Church what that once and for all event means for them.

As far as the ministry of the Word is concerned, ministers are called and set apart "to preach the Gospel, administer the sacraments and exercise pastoral care" (par.14 [a]). It is because

> The Word of God on whom man's salvation depends is to be heard and known from Scripture appropriated in the worshipping and witnessing life of the Church

that the Uniting Church commits its ministers to preach from the Scriptures and

> to administer the sacraments of Baptism and the Lord's Supper as effective signs of the Gospel set forth in the Scriptures (par.5).

The efficacy of these "effective signs" depends, as we have said above, on the activity of Jesus Christ, and his gift of the Holy Spirit, in and through them (para.6). But the Church both corporately accepts the command to proclaim the Gospel by word and sacrament and also gives it as a specific mandate to those it recognizes to be called and set apart by God for the ministry of the Word, because it believes in Jesus Christ's promise.

Faced with this picture, we have no hesitation in saying that the Assembly has both the right and the duty to insist that adherence to the *Basis of Union* obliges a minister of the Word to preach, teach and administer Baptism in accordance with the understanding of Baptism set forth in the *Basis of Union*, including the baptism of children presented for baptism under the circumstances stated in the *Basis*.

For a start, Baptism is integral to the life, work and unity of the Church; and it is also integral to the ministry of the Word. Contradictory practices in regard to Baptism go to the heart of the Church's membership and its unity. To refuse to baptize children as a matter of principle is to say that they are not acceptable as members of Christ's body and to call into question the membership of all children who have been baptized.

Prior to the decision of the Standing Committee of the Assembly in September 1993, the suggestion was sometimes made that a parish minister might get around any problems of conscience by arranging for a willing colleague to perform all the infant baptisms in his or her place. That completely fails to appreciate how important the pastoral role of the minister of the congregation, in preparing for, and celebrating, a baptism, is for the continuing involvement of the family in the life of the congregation. It also ignores the catastrophic effect on a congregation's perception of Baptism of its own minister's distancing her- or himself from all celebrations of the baptism of a child.

There are, of course, pastoral charges to which a minister can be inducted in which baptisms will not form part of the minister's duties. Resolutions of the Standing Committee (1993) and of the Assembly (1994) could be taken to suggest that it might not be inappropriate for a minister who dissents from the Church's position on Baptism to remain in such a settlement.[39] But the question is still, whether a minister is willing to preach and teach Baptism in accordance with the Church's position, even if never called on to administer it. An objection to baptizing children would seem to imply understandings of the sacraments of the Gospel, and of Christian discipleship and Church membership, seriously at odds with those in the *Basis of Union*. How willing could a person be to provide a ministry of the Word in accordance with the Uniting Church understanding and the *Basis of Union*, if she or he differed with the *Basis* and the Church on these issues? Another of the 1993-1994 resolutions instructs presbyteries not to approve any settlement, until assured that the minister concerned will baptize infants in accordance with the Church's position.[40] The wording does not confine this provision to parish settlements. The Assembly could, at the most, be contemplating leaving a dissenting minister in an existing settlement unchallenged, if there would be no call for infant baptism there. Presbyteries ought not, apparently, approve any new settlement for a minister who would refuse to administer baptism in the ways the Assembly requires.

This is not to say that there will not still be room for difference of opinion on Baptism. The issue is rather how serious such a difference has to be, before it begins to erode one's willingness to live and work within the faith and unity of the Church in the way that the *Basis* describes. As we have argued above, the first consideration in the question of adherence to the *Basis* is whether that willingness is present or not. If it is present, there is still room for difference of opinion in matters that do not enter into the substance of the faith. Where such willingness is not present, there is no question of adherence; and it is irrelevant to ask what differences might still be allowable. For ministers of the Word, a fundamental part of adherence to the *Basis* must be the willingness to peform the fundamental duties of their ministry as set out in the *Basis of Union*. It therefore seems anomalous that the Standing Committee of the Fifth Assembly was prepared to insist that "adherence to the *Basis of Union* requires acceptance of the ordination of women to the Ministry of the Word",[41] but not to declare the same of the baptism of children.

It is impossible to see how a presbytery could settle a minister in a pastoral charge, in face of a declared unwillingness to perform part of the basic functions of his or her office, particularly when a motion of the Assembly explicitly requires all ministers to perform that part of their ministerial duties in accordance with the Church's position.[42] It is one thing to respect a Jehovah's Witness's conscientious stand against transfusions. It is another to agree that he or she is entitled to a job at the Blood Bank.

Confusion about the meaning and intention of the Fourth Assembly's resolution 85.39.1 was caused by the way in which some have wanted to understand and apply the subsequent resolution 85.39.5, requesting "Presbyteries to administer the Assembly's requirements for Ministers, Elders and Congregations on Baptism with pastoral sensitivity and compassion". One might have hoped that this motion would be superfluous. Can presbyteries not be relied on to act with pastoral sensitivity and compassion without being told? But perhaps it was wise to underline the need for them in this case, where presbyteries would have to administer a real requirement, which it could be hard for some ministers or elders to meet. The Pastoral Letter of October 1985 from the President and Secretary of the Assembly both upholds the requirement and emphasizes the need for "special care and understanding" for those for whom it has occasioned some difficulty. But, to some minds, "pastoral concern" means always letting people have what they want, and the Assembly's request that its requirement be administered with sensitivity and compassion meant that it was not actually to be treated as a requirement, if people insisted that they were not going to comply with it. The Presidential Ruling subsequently disallowed by the Standing Committee had drawn support for its conclusion from a document approved by the Synod of New South Wales in 1987, which said, among other things, that

> Ministers of the Word may, for reasons of conviction, and by arrangement with Presbytery and their Elders' Councils, refrain from practices they feel unable to adopt.[43]

Such guidance offered by a synod was subversive of what the Assembly had resolved in May 1985 and what its Standing Committee had resolved in October 1985, and so spread confusion about what their resolutions actually meant.

Never taking a firm stand is, however, not a manifestation of pastoral concern. The Church celebrates Baptism and baptizes children in the service of Jesus Christ, the Chief Shepherd, and so as a central element in its own pastoral ministry. If it truly believes that Jesus Christ himself speaks and acts to add members to his flock, in and through what it does in obedience to his command to baptize, then the Church must insist on the integrity of its own practice. Not to do so is to disclaim the promises it announces, and the good news it proclaims, in the rite of Baptism. It is also to betray those who do faithfully administer infant baptism, those who seek it for their children, and those who have been baptized as children themselves.

When the Church does not take infant baptism seriously itself, it makes more and more people question whether it ought to celebrate it at all. Abiding by its *Basis of Union*, the Church has a right and an obligation to insist that Uniting Church ministers are bound to preach, teach and administer infant baptism in accordance with the *Basis*, as an essential part of living and working within the faith and unity of the One Holy Catholic and Apostolic Church in the way described in the *Basis*.

To test the further question of whether a difference of opinion in the matter of the baptism of children might not after all enter into the substance of the faith, I need to refer to positions that have been advanced in print or discussion in recent years. They appear here as a composite picture and need not be supposed to represent the position of any one person.

I have already reported the view advanced by one minister that the principal issue raised by the Assembly requirement for ministers to preach, teach and administer Baptism in accordance with the Church's position was "the liberty of opinion in non-essentials guaranteed in Paragraph 14 of the *Basis of Union*". In the same document, the minister was also quoted as saying, "I am conscientiously unable to baptize infants". That presents us with an interesting anomaly. Here is a person for whom the Church's practice of infant baptism is a "non-essential", and clearly not a matter that enters into the substance of the faith. But his conscience will not permit him to perform that part of his ministerial duties. For him, there is a major issue here. But, he insists, the Church should be able to regard it as a minor issue or a non-issue.

I can understand the possibility of such a position against the background of the baptismal debate in the Church in the years after the 1985 Assembly. It was triggered largely by the fear that the Assembly resolution 85.39.1 might be intended to force all ministers to preach and teach all of the theology of Baptism to be found in the "Agreed Statement on Baptism" for the Roman Catholic and Uniting Churches approved by the Second Assembly and in the Questions and Answers on Baptism approved by the Third Assembly. Those who objected to the theology of these documents began to quote selected statements from them as proof of their contention that the Uniting Church's formulation of doctrine was beginning to be dominated by a High Church clique. The problem was, however, that the statements to which they were taking exception echoed things said of Baptism in the *Basis of Union* or in the Reformation documents and sermons of John Wesley's acknowledged in Paragraph 10 of the *Basis*.

Faced with this problem, some argued as follows:

1. If the reference to the sacraments as "effective signs of the Gospel" (par.5) is to be understood in the sense of the old term "effectual sign" and is supposed to indicate some efficacy of the sacraments, then it was, in fact, wrong to adhere to the *Basis of Union*. Since one has, however, adhered, then one must remind the Church that, in the *Basis*, it has also pledged itself to "remain open to constant reform" under the Word of Christ, its living Head (par.1); and one must simply wait for the Church to bring its doctrine of the Sacraments into line with the Scriptures, according to which Baptism is only a "sign and seal of faith", through which believers give public expression to their commitment to Jesus as Lord.

2. An outward rite with water may symbolize salvation, sanctification and entry into membership of the Church, but nothing of that can really happen through it. Our salvation depends on our personal decision of faith. The Holy Spirit challenges me from outside through the Word of God, but I have to decide to let the Spirit in. Baptism has nothing to do

with it. As for membership of the Church, it is unbiblical to say that any but believers can be members. Infants cannot belong to the Church.

3. As for the Reformation documents, there was more than one reformation. The Reformers did not go far enough. It was the Anabaptists who got it right. One will not learn much about the teaching of the Holy Scriptures on Baptism from the Reformation confessions listed in the *Basis*.

4. Developments in Methodism after John Wesley have meant that his statements about infant baptism do not represent the position of many later Methodists.

5. Both the Reformation documents and modern Uniting Church documents are mistaken in seeing references to water baptism in many New Testament passages that are simply using the imagery of water and washing to speak of forgiveness and renewal.

6. It is the Church that has changed, not those who are now raising objections. It used to be all right to disagree with the Church's position on Baptism. Now, in the Uniting Church, that is suddenly no longer so.

7. It is still just possible to make a biblical case for infant baptism. Some of us are therefore able to baptize children. Others of us, again, cannot in conscience do so. But we can respect each others' positions and practices and happily remain members and ministers of the one church, even of a church that practises infant baptism.

8. But the Church ought not to make pronouncements on Baptism that we regard as wrong; and it ought not to require us to teach or act contrary to our own convictions.

For those whose position on Baptism runs generally along these lines and who finally come to the conviction that believer's baptism alone has an adequate basis in Scripture, the Church's practice of infant baptism must seem to have no connexion with the Gospel or the substance of the faith. For all whose position runs somewhat along these lines, their agreement in the rejection of the sacramental theology of the Reformers and the *Basis of Union* is far more important than any difference on the non-essential question of whether to baptize infants or not, even if that is a matter of conscience for the few who cannot, and of mixed feelings, for some who do. Their polemic in the debate has therefore been directed, not against the practice of infant baptism, but against attempts to uphold an understanding of Baptism in accordance with the *Basis of Union* and Assembly statements.

Presupposing a position such as we have sketched out above, it is comprehensible how a minister could say, that

(a) he cannot in conscience baptize infants;

(b) he expects the Church to agree that the baptism of infants is a matter that does not enter into the substance of the faith and to allow him to follow his own conscience;

(c) he is happy to serve in a church where infant baptism is the norm and to work in parishes alongside colleagues who baptize infants, indeed, he desires to do so; and

(d) he will not attack the Church's practice of baptizing infants.

But what this is asking the Church to do is to concur in the suggestion that its baptismal practice is a non-essential, which could not possibly be seen as a matter that enters into the substance of the faith. These demands may seem reasonable on the assumptions listed above, but they are quite unacceptable from the point of view of the *Basis of Union* and its theology of Baptism.

Here, too, we need to recognize that the issue of what enters into the substance of the faith must not be approached simplistically. Between the overall position outlined above (1.-8.) and the *Basis of Union*, there is almost certainly a difference in the understanding of what it means to say that something "enters into the substance of the faith".

On one level, the difference is between seeing faith as primarily trust and seeing it as primarily something to believe. When we follow the Reformation in seeing faith as trust in the promise of

God in Jesus Christ, with knowledge and assent as further, secondary elements of faith, then we think it natural for a person's trust to be some distance ahead of his or her knowledge of, and assent to, the truth of God's revelation in Christ. The suggestion that there is more to the substance of the faith than so far perceived need by no means be heard as a threat. But where faith is seen as having to believe certain things, then knowledge of, and assent to, revealed truth comes to have overwhelming importance. From this latter point of view, the suggestion that one more matter "enters into the substance of the faith" is heard as a claim that, "You have to believe this in order to be saved", and, "If you don't believe this, you're not a Christian". I doubt if any in the Uniting Church would want to argue that "believing in infant baptism" is necessary for salvation. But many would want to say that the Church's understanding and practice of infant baptism are closely connected with its faith in salvation by the grace of God.

On another, connected level, it makes a great difference whether the substance of the faith is thought of as comprehended in a few fundamental doctrines or whether the fullness of the catholic faith is seen as a promised goal, to which no body of Christians has, as yet, attained, but on which all are called to orient themselves in hope. From the latter point of view, it is not a condemnation of churches that differ from us to insist that our theology and practice of Baptism involve central elements that enter into the substance of the faith. It just invites and challenges them to look with us at our vision of the fullness of the catholic faith; and it is completely compatible with a corresponding readiness to look at their vision with them

In looking at the place of Baptism in the faith and unity of the One Holy Catholic and Apostolic Church as presented in the *Basis of Union*, we noted the important place that Baptism occupies within the Uniting Church's faith in the continuing activity of Jesus Christ and the Holy Spirit. As good news communicated to human beings in this present age and this present world, the Gospel is not separable from the ministry of the Gospel through word and sacraments. The Church's faith with regard to Baptism is faith in the promise of God in Jesus Christ and in his continuing faithfulness to his promise. The importance that the Uniting Church gives to Baptism is well supported by the creeds and confessional documents acknowledged in the *Basis of Union*. The *Apostles'* and *Nicene Creeds* sprang from confession of the Faith at Baptism in the Western and Eastern churches respectively. They demonstrate one inherent link between Baptism and the substance of the faith. Baptism is baptism into the Faith, and into the community of faith that joins in this confession of the Faith. Rejection of the Uniting Church practice of infant baptism denies that it has the same intrinsic connexion with the substance of the faith as believers' baptism does. It rejects the request of parents who ask of God's church for their child that he or she "be baptized into the faith and family of Jesus Christ",[44] and so withholds from them the ministry of the Gospel.

The Uniting Church receives the two ancient creeds "as authoritative statements of the Catholic Faith", "used [...] to declare and to guard the right understanding of that faith" (*Basis*, par.9). So when, in the words of the *Nicene Creed*,

> We acknowledge one baptism for the forgiveness of sins,

we must suppose that we are there directly concerned with the substance of the faith. The rejection of the Uniting Church practice of infant baptism denies that it is a valid expression of the one baptism, by which we are all baptized into the one body. Rejection of infant baptism forces us to ask whether it is not, in fact, a rejection of the understanding of Baptism as "an effective sign of the Gospel set forth in the Scriptures", in which our practice of infant baptism is grounded. If that is the case, then it denies that any baptism is "baptism for the forgiveness of sins", a means of grace through which Jesus Christ himself, through the gift of the Spirit, bestows the forgiveness promised in the words and act of baptism.

In Reformation theology, the primary signs and notes of the church of Jesus Christ are the true preaching of the Word of God and the right celebration of the sacraments of Jesus Christ.[45] The reason for focusing on these as the marks of the Church, is that they are grounded in the command and promises of God. To determine where the Church is and where to seek the fellowship of God's people, we do well, not to rely on our own judgment about the faith and sincerity of people in this group or that, but to hold to the promises of God and to his faithfulness. Where his Word is truly preached and the sacraments of his Son, our Lord, are rightly administered, we can rely on him to be bringing people to faith and to new life as his community. Rejection of the Uniting Church's practice of infant baptism declares that, in our church, the sacrament of baptism is not rightly administered. That raises questions about our being as a church that demand resolution either by reformation of our practice or by rebuttal of the criticism.

In our judgment, then, the Uniting Church's understanding and practice of Baptism are so intimately connected with the Gospel and the faith that any conscientious objection to our practice of infant baptism must be held to express a difference from the Uniting Church that enters into the substance of the faith, unless careful theological and pastoral conversation should prove that in some case it is strangely not so.

VII

At the end of Section II, I remarked that there were still some constitutional complications to be discussed regarding the thesis that the Uniting Church and its councils must themselves abide by the *Basis of Union*, but that I should hold them over until this final section.

I became aware of the problem in 1976, the year before Union, but did not seem able to do anything about it at the time and did not recognize the full extent of it. Before the Uniting Church could be formed, legislation had to be approved in every state parliament authorizing its formation, so that property trusts could be established and the property of the three uniting churches could be transferred to the new property trusts at the time of union. There were particular reasons why it was simplest to get this legislation through first in Western Australia and in conjunction with complementary legislation for the Presbyterian church that would continue as such after union. Draft legislation had been prepared for all states of the Commonwealth by the Joint Constitution

Commission of the three churches and was being adapted for enactment in Western Australia. The State Government wanted approval of the proposed legislation from each of the uniting churches in Western Australia. I was convener of the Code Committee of the General Assembly of Western Australia, which had the task of advising the Moderator whether to signify our Assembly's approval to the State Government.

As I scrutinized the bill for the Uniting Church in Australia Act, 1976, I found that clause 11 read,

> Notwithstanding anything in this Act or in the *Basis of Union*, it shall be lawful for the Assembly from time to time to resolve that the Church enter into union with other branches of the Christian Church and to determine, declare or interpret matters of doctrine, worship, government and discipline in the Uniting Church.

The Assembly was not to be bound by the *Basis of Union* in any of its decisions on matters of doctrine, worship, government or discipline!.

As I tried to pursue this matter at national level, I was referred to Harold Julian, a lawyer on the Joint Constitution Commission. I rang him and raised my concern with him. In reply, he told me that this provision was necessary, in order to prevent any possibility of the Uniting Church's being caught up in the kind of litigation and delicate property negotiations that the Presbyterian Church was currently involved in between uniting and continuing Presbyterians. Noone would ever be able to argue in court that the Uniting Church Assembly had acted in breach of trust by agreeing to something contrary to the *Basis of Union*, because the Church would not be tied to the *Basis of Union* and its property would be held in trust independently of it. When I suggested that the peculiar difficulties we had faced as Presbyterians, which had tangled historical roots in Britain and Australia, could surely be avoided otherwise than by appearing to weaken the bond between the Uniting Church and its basis of union, Harold Julian told me that the *Basis of Union* was not, in fact, going to have any continuing constitutional significance in the Church after union! It would apply only for "the moment of union". Thereafter, the Church would operate on its constitution. Harold tried to comfort me with the thought that the Assembly could always decide to give the *Basis* a place in the life of the Church, if it wanted to.

The conversation became rather tense. Harold was adamant that I had nothing to say in the matter. The three uniting churches had given the Joint Constitution Commission authority to draw up an interim constitution and to get enabling legislation through all parliaments. Only the Commission could determine the form of the legislation. It had to be the same in all states and no variation from the substance of the draft was acceptable, only adaptation to local circumstances.

There was no doubt at all, in my mind, that the attitude that was here being taken to the *Basis of Union* in the name of the Joint Constitution Commission was contrary to the intention of the three churches. They had, after careful consideration, approved the *Basis of Union*. They had entrusted the Joint Constitution Commission with the task of preparing an interim constitution, of securing the enabling legislation, and of doing whatever else was required for the inauguration of the Uniting Church. But they intended the Church to be founded on the basis that they had approved.

A "basis of union" is fundamental to, and constitutive of, a united church, and therefore the most stable element in it.[46] The obvious exception to this is the 1947 basis of union for the Church of South India, which does have something of the status that Harold Julian was wishing to give the basis of union of the Uniting Church. There were particular reasons why, in South India, the appropriate thing was to allow the basis of union to stand as a historic document expressive of the desires, hopes and intentions of the uniting churches, while the united church functioned on a constitution it had the power to amend. Basis of union and constitution were both part of the scheme of union for the Church of South India and, as such, were prepared as complementary documents, and considered together and adopted together by the uniting churches. The constitution incorporated the substance of the basis of union within itself, partly in the form of "governing principles", which had an overriding effect within the constitution as a whole; and it provided that, in any change to the constitution, and particularly to the governing principles, full regard was to be paid to the basis of union.[47]

The Uniting Church's *Basis* was prepared by the Joint Commission on Church Union between 1957 and 1970, with thorough discussion of successive reports and drafts at all levels of the three uniting churches. The churches had given such careful attention to this material, and requested amendments to it in such detail, because they considered that they were dealing with what would become the abiding foundation of the Uniting Church. The churches finally approved the *Basis of Union* of 1971 and resolved to unite in accordance with it.

The document that they thereby approved is couched in terms that clearly imply its persisting authority for the faith, life and witness of the Uniting Church. It expresses commitments for the church as a whole, its members and its ministers. After the initial act of union in Paragraph 1, it speaks, not, as in the South Indian basis, in the name of the uniting churches, but in the name of the Uniting Church. It defines the Uniting Church's relation to the past of the three uniting traditions, to other churches and to the universal church. It defines the Uniting Church's relation to the Holy Scriptures, to the ancient creeds, to certain documents of the Reformation and the Wesleyan revival, and to their central emphases in respect of faith, grace, justification, Jesus Christ and the Scriptures. It speaks not only of the acceptance of those who had already exercised some specified forms of ministry in one of the uniting churches prior to union, but also of the calling and admission of further persons to such ministries in the future. It describes how the Uniting Church will be governed and how its various councils will behave towards each other. It says how the Uniting Church will deal with its own Church law. The churches resolved to unite, and did unite, in accordance with a document that cannot be read as the description of a moment of transition from three churches into one, but that undeniably defines the foundation for the continuing life of the new church.

The line taken by Harold Julian seemed so indefensible that it was hard to get people to feel seriously about it at that time. I consulted Farquhar Gunn, the chairperson of the Joint Constitution Commission. He confirmed that Harold Julian was the spokesperson for the group that had been entrusted with the task of getting the enabling legislation through. He did not believe that he had the authority to interfere with what they were doing.

Legal advice indicated that it was fallacious to suggest that the full wording of the proposed clause 11 was necessary to render the Church's trust property safe from future litigation over whether the Church was true to its *Basis* or not. It would be quite adequate for the clause to commence,

> Notwithstanding anything in this Act it shall be lawful for the Assembly [...][,]

omitting, "or in the *Basis of Union*". For it was the Act that created the links in law between the Church, its property and the *Basis of Union*. This would avoid giving the appearance that the Act freed the Assembly from all responsibility with regard to the *Basis*, but ensure that any supposed failure to act in accordance with it could not become an issue in the civil courts. But people considered that it was vital to get the legislation for the Uniting and continuing Presbyterian churches through as quickly as possible in Western Australia. That would serve as a pilot for what was needed in the other states and help to speed the resolution of property difficulties between continuing and uniting Presbyterians. Particularly because of threatened litigation, it was most important that there be no public dispute about the standing of the *Basis of Union* in the Uniting Church. Harold Julian's stance could have been used to argue that, in the union procedures, the requirements of the Presbyterian Basis of Union of 1970 had not been met, because the Uniting *Basis of Union* was not, in fact, a "basis of union" in the sense required by Section 15 of the Presbyterian Basis.[48] We were convinced that Harold Julian was wrong. But no one wanted to have that issue argued out in court against continuing Presbyterian lawyers.

I think that it was only an inner group of the Joint Constitution Commission that realized at that time precisely what they were doing. The *Uniting Church in Australia Act, 1976,* empowered the uniting churches to unite in accordance with the *Basis of Union* (Section 6) and empowered the Inaugurating Assembly to adopt a constitution for the Church consistent with the *Basis of Union* (Section 9). It gives the Assembly the power to amend, alter, repeal or replace that inaugural constitution in accordance with the provisions made by the Constitution (Section 10). But it does not spell out a requirement for any amendments, alterations or replacement constitutions to be in accordance with the *Basis*. (Whether the provisions of the Act, taken together, imply such a requirement may need to be clarified.) The Constitution prepared by the Joint Constitution Commission invokes the *Basis of Union* in its preamble, but largely ignores it for the rest. Adherence to the *Basis of Union* is required at the point where office-bearers of the uniting churches are to be recognized as holding corresponding offices in the Uniting Church, but is not prescribed for the admission of further persons to those offices. (It is also not explicitly required of ordinands by the Regulations, but is the subject of one of the ordination vows referred to there.) The Church's regulations, by-laws and rules must be not inconsistent with the Constitution, but are not subject to the *Basis of Union*.

In the Regulations, too, no recognition is given to a continuing role for the *Basis of Union* in the life of the Church. In the matter of the "Presidential Ruling 11" discussed above, it was a major complication that the President may be asked to rule on

> [...] whether the action of any body within the Church conforms to the Constitution, the relevant Regulations, by-laws or rules[,][49]

but not whether it conforms to the *Basis of Union*. This meant that some of the issues involved could not directly be addressed. Similarly, under Regulation 7.8, to which the Legal Reference Committee drew attention for a case where discipline might be called for, the Committee for Discipline cannot consider a complaint that a minister fails to adhere to the *Basis of Union*.

The overall situation in the Uniting Church is thus that the constitutional link with its *Basis of Union* is far more tenuous than most realize. For general working purposes, a group within the Joint Constitution Commission has ensured that the Uniting Church has been established, not on the basis prepared by the Joint Commission on Church Union and approved by the three uniting churches, but on the constitution produced by the Joint Constitution Commission, approved by a larger Joint Constitution Council, and adopted by the Inaugural Assembly. Others involved in the Joint Constitution Commission and the great majority on the Joint Constitution Council did not appreciate what was happening. We had been so caught up in the process of agreeing on a basis of union that the *Basis* in its final form had become the unquestioned presupposition for the next stage of considering constitution and regulations. The knowledge that the *Basis of Union* would be the subject of civil legislation inspired us with a false sense of security regarding its eventual status in the Uniting Church and probably made us less concerned to scrutinize the draft interim constitution regarding the status that it would (or would not) allow the *Basis* to have in the Church for the future. The place of the *Basis of Union* was not supposed to depend on the Constitution! Numerous small anomalies were identified and raised, but the substitution that was being carried out on the grand scale just did not come into focus. For some, it was disappointing that the executive leadership of the Joint Constitution Commission seemed to be thinking on a different plane from the *Basis of Union*, but the idea that they were preparing to consign it to the archives at the point of union was beyond our imagination.

We have seen that the *Basis of Union* presents itself as the permanent foundation of the new church's life. But it most certainly does not present itself as a legal document. In the drafting, there was a conscious attempt to express things in a style congruous with what was being said about them. If the faith and unity of the Church are built on the one Lord Jesus Christ, that has to be acknowledged in language that approaches a confession of faith. If God has reconciled the world with himself through Christ's death and resurrection, the story has to be recited in words that echo those of proclamation and liturgy. The *Basis* states the continuing relevance of the witness of our Reformation forebears for our understanding of the biblical teaching on the justification of the sinner in Jesus Christ by grace and through faith. It is careful to do so in a way that should make it impossible for anyone ever again to pursue through the councils of the Church the question of whether the *Westminster Confession* would allow a council of elders to permit the Church youth to play tennis on the Church courts on a Sunday.[50] This clear distinction in people's minds between the Church's basis of union and its constitution and law probably made it easier for the Constitution to be detached from the *Basis*, and also for the vast majority not to notice that the distinction had been turned into a separation.

There were probably various motives behind what happened. Church administrators and lawyers may have had no great empathy for the sensitive theological considerations behind the formulations of the *Basis*. Out of a particular style of church administration, there came a desire to safeguard certain things not contained in the *Basis*. The Constitution and Regulations did not allow councils of elders to retain the place given them in the *Basis of Union*. A new parish council was introduced, to be a primarily administrative body, superior to the elders' councils (rather on the model of circuit quarterly meetings and local leaders' meetings). The minister was to chair the Parish Council *ex officio;* and this was justified in the Joint Constitution Council by the argument that the chair of the parish administrative body had to be someone that the wider church could discipline. At this and other levels, some decisions made by one body would need ratification by a superior body. In all this, there was an apparent intention that, for the Uniting Church, an administrative pyramid would be more significant than the series of interrelated councils described in Paragraph 15 of the *Basis*. There was probably also a conviction that the Assembly should be free to decide on doctrine, worship, government and discipline in sovereign freedom, unfettered by a document like the *Basis*.

On a more personal level, there appeared to be a degree of estrangement between some of the leaders of the respective joint commissions, which could partly have reflected a polarization between Methodists and Presbyterians or between Sydney and Melbourne (or, indeed, between different parts of Ireland). Davis

McCaughey, one of the joint conveners of the Joint Commission on Church Union, became the President-Elect for the Inaugural Assembly. When he became involved in a dispute between continuing and uniting Presbyterians over the future of a Church school, Winston O'Reilly, the Executive Officer of the Joint Constitution Commission, and Harold Julian proposed that Davis be dropped and another president-elect be chosen, but they did not gain support for that idea. Winston later succeeded Davis as President. At the Third Assembly, in response to the thanks and congratulations expressed to him on his retirement from that office, Winston O'Reilly spoke of having come to the position of President as a completely unexplored and undeveloped field, clearly implying that the inaugural presidency of Davis McCaughey had set no precedents at all for the role of the President in the future. The personal distance that became perceptible at such points probably reflected totally different styles of church leadership. It would have helped to make the Executive Officer of the Joint Constitution Commission quite unwilling to allow the work of the other joint commission to provide the foundation for the new church's life.

If the place of the *Basis of Union* in the Uniting Church today is not nearly as secure as most people think, what becomes of the strong assertions made above in Section II about the need for the Church as a whole and the councils of the Church to abide by the *Basis*? The answer has to be that the position is actually quite ambiguous, but that the assertions are still valid. What needs to happen is for the ambiguity to be removed.

The extent of the ambiguity can be seen from considering (1) how plausible a case could now be made for declaring that the Uniting Church momentarily established itself on the *Basis of Union*, only to go forward in faith, leaving the *Basis* behind as its historic point of departure, and (2) where that would now leave the Church, if it were true, but also (3) how that is just not where we are.

The strongest argument for saying that the *Basis* has no current authority in the Uniting Church can be made by showing how little recognition is given to the *Basis* anywhere in the constitution of the Church or the regulations of the Assembly. These other documents do not treat the *Basis of Union* as the fundamental text on which the Church itself is established. In this regard, the Legal Reference Committee of the Assembly has kept the Church on the course set by the Joint Constitution Commission.

On the other hand, one has to consider what the present position of the Uniting Church would be, if the *Basis* no longer possessed any authority within it. The Uniting Church would have no defined relation to the Holy Scriptures, to the ancient creeds, or to any other authoritative declarations of the faith. It could be shown to have two sacraments, some forms of ministry, and a system of government. But it would lack any certain theological position in one area of its life after another. With no common basis for becoming Uniting, we should all begin to revert to whatever we had known before. Groups would be free to seek to fill the vacuum by getting the Assembly to approve a new definition of what one needed to believe, or to have experienced, in order to be a minister, or even a member, of the Church; and, in this, they would partly be driven by the not unreasonable fear that, failing any such definition, any kind of heresy or nonsense could pass itself off as an allowable position in Uniting Church terms. Of course, the Assembly has already pronounced on some matters and would have the power to pronounce on all others, unrestrained by any agreed frame of reference. Members and ministers would never have a guarantee that changing majorities in the Assembly would not produce radical changes in its character from time to time. There would also be no guaranteed liberty of opinion, because that provision, too, would have been left behind with the *Basis of Union*. The fear that a High Church clique was on the way to setting narrow standards for worship and for the theology of the sacraments would have become a fraction more credible.

This is, of course, not at all where we are, and that not just because it would be a highly undesirable place to be. Whatever the picture that we discern by a careful look at the Constitution and Regulations, the *Basis of Union* does actually carry quite a lot of weight in the Church. It does reflect the vision that led many into the Uniting Church. It does carry for many the promise of reconciliation across old and current divisions. Above all, it does express what the Congregational, Methodist and Presbyterian churches agreed to as the foundation for the new church in which they would unite. It enjoys considerable regard ecumenically as a significant document of Christian unity and Church union. In more practical terms, the resolutions carried by the Fifth Assembly on councils of elders and parish councils[51] show the Church seeking new orientation on the *Basis of Union*, as it attempts to simplify and consolidate its structures. Apart from the historical and inherent authority that the *Basis* possesses in the Uniting Church and beyond, it is of vital significance for the order of the Church, because the Church has, from union on, continued to require its office-bearers to adhere to the *Basis of Union*. It is by such adherence that it obtains their commitment to live and work within the faith and unity of the Church. To benefit from that commitment, the Uniting Church must itself continue to be the Church grounded on the basis to which its office-bearers adhere.

So the ambiguity must be resolved, not by confirming that the *Basis of Union* merely documented a historic step, from which the Uniting Church has continued to stride on out into an ever greater distance, but by an alteration to the Constitution to give belated recognition to the abiding significance of the *Basis* as the definitive expression of the ground of the Uniting Church's life, identity, unity and mission. No complicated revision of the Constitution would be required. The aim would simply be to allow the *Basis* to speak for itself at the centre of the Church's life, with the assurance that, wherever the *Basis of Union* says, "The Uniting Church acknowledges [...]", "The Uniting Church continues to learn [...]", "The Uniting Church will [do such and such]", or makes any similar statement on behalf of the Church, the Uniting Church will hold itself bound by what is said of it there.

Faced with such a proposal, some may be tempted to suggest that we might as well revise and modernize the *Basis*, while we are about it, and make it more satisfactory to this group or that. Any such attempt would be highly perilous. The first thing is to clarify and stabilize the situation. The *Basis of Union* (1971) is the given, historic document to which all in the church have some kind of commitment or other relation. It is the document contained in the schedules to the *Uniting Church Act* in each state. No one can guarantee that any revision or replacement would now unite us as well as that *Basis* did in 1977 and has, *de facto*, continued to do. Attempts to revise or replace it may well prove quite divisive and plunge us into a more confused situation than we now enjoy. Only when we have secured its place as the basis of our union and of our present unity, will we be in a position to consider any serious proposal to review it.

NOTES

1 This study was written late in 1990. Copies were sent to the President and Secretary of the Assembly in February and March 1991, in the hope of making some contribution to the reconsideration of certain issues connected with the ordination of women and Baptism. The study was revised in 1993 and brought up to date early in 1996.

2 *The Church: its Nature, Function and Ordering, Part One being the Second Report of the Joint Commission on Church Union set up by the Congregational Union of Australia, the Methodist Church of Australasia, and the Presbyterian Church of Australia, Part Two being the Proposed Basis of Union for these Churches,* Melbourne, Aldersgate Press, 1964, repr. Melbourne, Uniting Church Press, 1984, pp.87f (Presbyterian Christian Unity ed., p.47).

3 "People who adhere are therefore required, not to accept that the *Basis* is the best possible way of describing, for example the Word, the church or the ministry, but to state that they, as individuals and as recognized servants of Christ, can live, in conscience, within the Uniting Church" (D'Arcy Wood, *Building on a Solid Basis: A Guide to the Basis of Union of the Uniting Church in Australia,* Melbourne, Uniting Church Press, 1986, p.48).

4 Henry Cecil Wyld, ed., *The Universal Dictionary of the English Language,* London, Routledge, 1946, p.802, s.v. 'Opinion'.

5 *The Macquarie Dictionary,* St Leonards, NSW, Macquarie Library, 1981, p.1215, s.v. 'opinion'. - Other elements in the definitions offered by these dictionaries concern: judgment or belief resting on grounds insufficient to produce certainty; an opinion that one gives on something; a counsel's opinion; a judgment on character or merit (a high or low opinion); and a favourable estimate on something. They add nothing to, or do not bear on, the matter under discussion.

6 The Uniting Church in Australia, The Assembly, "Presidential Ruling No.11", Sydney, 29 September 1988, p.8. - This part of the ruling was subsequently disallowed by the Standing Committee of the Assembly. I do not know whether that involved a rejection of this particular suggestion.

7 This understanding of the scope of the provision allowing "difference of opinion" gains further weight from the fact that it was only added to the *Basis of Union* in the very last (1971) revision, in response to a demand from the Presbyterian General Assembly of Australia that "liberty of opinion on matters which do not enter into the substance of the Faith" be explicitly provided for. In the Presbyterian Church's own Basis of Union, there was a similar provision in the Declaratory Statement, but it related specifically to "matters in the Subordinate Standard [i.e. the *Westminster Confession of Faith*] not essential to the doctrine therein taught". See "The Preparation of the Basis of Union",

Section IX, pp.93-96s, and notes 7-14. The use of the concept of the 'substance of the Faith' in this context goes back to the declaratory act of the United Presbyterian Church in Scotland of 1879 (see above in the excursus, pp.118f and nn.52 and 57).

8   "And thairfore it is that we flee ye societie with ye Papisticall Kirk, in participation of thair sacramentis: First because thair ministeris ar na ministeris of Christe Iesus (zea, quhilk is mair horrible) thaye suffer Wemen, quhome the haly Gaist wyll not suffer, to teache in the congregatioun, to Baptise" (*Scots Confession* [1560], art.22, modernized in *Witness of Faith*, p.75). - The statement that the Holy Spirit is not willing to permit women to teach in the congregation is a reference to 1 Tim.2:11f; cf 1 Cor.14:33b-36.

9   Since published as *Why does the Uniting Church in Australia Ordain Women to the Ministry of the Word?*, Sydney, Social Responsibility & Justice Committee for the Assembly Standing Committee, Uniting Church in Australia, 1990. The relevant resolutions of the Standing Committee meeting of 17-18 March 1990 are printed on the back cover.

10   Assembly Standing Committee min.90.32.3-7.

11   *Why does the Uniting Church in Australia Ordain Women*, pp.4-6.

12   *Western Impact,* vol.10, no.4, May 1990, p.2.

13   *Why does the Uniting Church in Australia Ordain Women,* p.5.

14   *Why does the Uniting Church in Australia Ordain Women,* p.3.

15   See the letters by Keith Dowding, Allan Chapple and Margaret Thatcher, in *Western Impact,* vol.10, no.5, June 1990, p.11.

16   *Western Impact,* vol.10, no.6, July 1990, p.7.

17   "Unto this catholic visible church Christ hath given the ministry, oracles, and ordinances of God, for the gathering and perfecting of the saints, in this life, to the end of the world: and doth by his own presence and Spirit according to his promise, make them effectual thereunto" (*The Westminster Confession of Faith,* cap. 25. art.iii, in *Witness of Faith,* p.157).

18   Assembly Standing Committee min.91.3.5.

19   Assembly Standing Committee min.91.3.3. - In its report to the Sixth Assembly in July 1991, the Standing Committee reported the action it had taken, including the relevant resolutions from 1990 as amended in 1991. See *Minutes and Reports of the Sixth Assembly of the Uniting Church in Australia: Brisbane[,] July 14-20,* 1991, Sydney, [1991], pp.63f.

20   Uniting Church in Australia, "Ministerial Candidates and the Ordination of Women: Statement from the Assembly President and General Secretary", April 1992, p.2.

21   Assembly Standing Committee min.92.61.3(d).

22   Assembly Standing Committee min.92.61.5.

23   *Minutes and Reports of the Fourth Assembly of the Uniting Church in Australia: Sydney[,] May 1985,* Melbourne, Uniting Church Press, 1985, min.85.39.1,3,5, p.6.

24   *Minutes and Reports of the Fourth Assembly,* p.42.

25   *Minutes and Reports of the Fourth Assembly,* p.42.

26   *Minutes of Proceedings of the Second Assembly of the Uniting Church in Australia, Sydney, June 1979,* pp.41f; cf min.79.22 (7).

27   The President explained what had happened in terms such as these at a meeting of the Presbytery of Perth, 14 February 1990. The report produced by the second

task group (*The Water that Unites: A Discussion Paper for the Uniting Church in Australia on Baptismal Practice,* [Sydney] 1991) outlines the procedure in sec.2.5, p.4. See, too, *Minutes and Reports of the Sixth Assembly of the Uniting Church in Australia: Brisbane[,] July 14-20, 1991,* Sydney, [1991], Report of the Assembly Standing Committee, secc.4.1; 5, p.62. - The terms of reference for the second task group are printed in *The Water that Unites,* sec.1, p.3.

28   The Uniting Church in Australia, *Constitution and Regulations and the Basis of Union,* Melbourne, Uniting Church Press, 1990, Constitution 38 (a); cf Basis of Union, par.15(e).

29   *The Water that Unites,* sec.6.1, p.11.

30   *The Water that Unites,* sec.7.1, p.12.

31   *Minutes and Reports of the Fourth Assembly,* min.85.39.1, p.6.

32   My own response to the discussion paper was published in *Trinity Occasional Papers,* vol.11, no.2 (March 1993), pp.33-56, under the title, "At the Waters of Strife" , unfortunately with many misprints.

33   Report of the Standing Committee in Uniting Church in Australia, *The Seventh Assembly, 9 - 16 July 1994, Minutes and Reports,* [Uniting Church Assembly Communications Unit], pp.21-35, p.25.

34   *The Seventh Assembly [...] Minutes and Reports,* p.25.

35   *The Seventh Assembly [...] Minutes and Reports,* pp.25f.

36   *The Seventh Assembly [...] Minutes and Reports,* min.94.11.04 (pp.m[inutes]9-11).

37   *The Seventh Assembly [...] Minutes and Reports,* min.94.11.04.4(b),(c) (p.m[inutes]10, cf p.26).

38   *Minutes and Reports of the Fourth Assembly,* min.85.109.2. - In connexion with the resolution concerning children's participation in Holy Communion, notice was given of a further motion that would have allowed ministers and councils of elders to continue the former Presbyterian practice of not admitting children to the Table of the Lord until they had been confirmed. The Assembly rejected the motion. In the debate, it was argued against the motion that families had to be able to find the same practice and discipline regarding the place of children in the life of the Church, if they moved from one congregation to another. Since the Assembly does not issue minutes of its proceedings, but only of its resolutions, there is no public record of this decision.

39   Cf. the Assembly's alteration to the Standing Committee resolution, "(a) that presbyteries, when counselling a minister who declares he or she is unable to accept the church's position and discipline concerning the administration of baptism: [...] (ii) if a minister, after a period of time deemed appropriate by the presbytery, remains unable to accept the church's position and discipline concerning the administration of baptism, counsel the minister concerning the inappropriateness of being in a settlement involving the administration of baptism *and/or the inappropriateness of remaining a minister of the Uniting Church;* [...]" (Uniting Church in Australia, *The Seventh Assembly [...] Minutes and Reports,* min.94.11.04.3 [p.m10]; the words in italics formed part of the resolution of the Standing Committee, see min.3 [pp.25f], but were omitted by the Assembly).

40   Uniting Church in Australia, *The Seventh Assembly [...] Minutes and Reports,* min.94.11.04.4(a) (p.m10); cf min.4(a) (p.26).

41   Admittedly, it later rescinded that resolution regarding the ordination of women. See above at n.19. That is presumably because, in that connexion, too, it did not know how to deal with the objection that, as far as adhering to the *Basis* is

concerned, unless a matter is declared to enter into the substance of the faith, ministers must be allowed to follow their own opinions with regard to it.

42 In 1988, the Standing Committee of the Fifth Assembly upheld the ruling of the President that a Settlements Committee may not deem this a sufficient reason for determining that a minister may be left without settlement under Reg.2.7.5(b)(ii). It was guided in this by advice from the Legal Reference Committee that a Settlements Committee acting in this way would be carrying out *de facto* disciplinary action, which is not the function of that regulation. The Legal Reference Committee advised that any disciplinary action called for should be taken under Reg.7.8. The problem with that was that, for action under the latter regulation, there had first to be a complaint that a minister had "(i) wilfully and persistently neglected the duties of a Minister; [or] (ii) wilfully failed to comply with any provision of the Constitution, of any Regulation, rule or resolution of the Church or any body of the Church" (Reg.7.8.2). What was a Settlements Committee to do, if a minister declared in advance that she or he would neglect an aspect of her or his duties and fail to comply with a requirement of the Assembly? The Legal Reference Committee allowed it no administrative or pastoral discretion in the matter. It had first to help the minister find a settlement and then let someone make a complaint against the minister, when she or he acted as she or he has announced that she or he would. That would, of course, have been incredibly disruptive for the pastoral charge in which the minister had been settled; and it greatly reduced the lee-way that presbyteries and bodies at Synod level have for holding such cases in suspense, while trying to resolve them by pastoral conversation. In this and other ways, as well, some attitudes at Assembly level have seemed to constrict the freedom that councils of the Church used to have for responsible pastoral government at district and regional level. - The advice from the Legal Reference Committee on which the Standing Committee upheld the ruling was significantly different from the President's own argument in the ruling. The President wrote of the discretion that the present Reg.2.7.5 (b)(ii) conferred on a Settlements Committee, "It would be wrong for me to attempt to define exhaustively the scope of the power because one cannot anticipate in advance the circumstances that might warrant its exercise. But it can be said that it must be a substantial reason relevant to the fundamental purposes of the Church and ministry within the Church, a reason that would warrant the serious consequences to a Minister of such a decision". It was because he was ruling that Assembly resolution 85.39 did allow a minister to refuse to baptize an infant solely because it was an infant, that he had to rule that the regulation did not give the Settlements Committee the power to leave a minister without settlement solely because he or she refused to baptize infants. He judged the Settlements Committee to have misunderstood "the intention and ambit of the Assembly resolution and the Church's 'adopted position'". The Standing Committee disallowed his ruling on that first point, but found another reason for upholding his ruling on the second point. Unfortunately, it was one that has set a more restrictive precedent than the President's own reasons for the ruling would have done. - The resolutions of Standing Committee and Assembly in 1993 and 1994 now override that ruling. Presbyteries may only approve a settlement "after assuring themselves that the minister will baptize [...] children who are presented for baptism" under the appropriate circumstances (Uniting Church in Australia, *The Seventh Assembly [...] Minutes and Reports*, min.94.11.04.4[a] [p.m10]; cf.4[a], p.26).

43 The New South Wales Synod approved the document, "Freedom, Discipline and Baptismal Practice in the U.C.A." at its meeting, September-October 1987, "as an additional document for the guidance of our people on pastoral issues in relation to baptism".

254

44 From "Baptism of a Child", in *Uniting in Worship: Leader's Book,* Melbourne, Uniting Church Press, 1988, p.37.

45 See Scots Confession, artt.18,25; *Westminster Confession,* cap.25.iv; - in *Witness of Faith,* pp.72,77,157.

46 See the excursus to "The Preparation of the Basis of Union", above, pp.105-151.

47 See above, pp.139-141.

48 In the new Presbyterian Basis of Union, 1970, Part III was concerned with "Union with Other Churches". It was the only Part to which effect was ever given. Its opening section, Section 15 of the Basis of Union, gives the church the power to enter into union "provided that the proposed basis of union with any such church or churches (which shall include a section setting out basic principles of constitutional structure and practice)" has first been approved by specified majorities of synods and presbyteries and by three-fifths of the members present in the Assembly. This means a basis of union with a similar constitutional status to that of the Presbyterian Basis of Union.

49 Regulation 3.6.14 (a)(ii).

50 Cf "Appeal by Eleven Members of the Victorian Assembly against a Decision of that Court" and min.99, in *Minutes of Proceedings of the General Assembly of the Presbyterian Church of Australia [...] 1959,* pp.34,196f.

51 *Minutes and Reports of the Fifth Assembly of the Uniting Church in Australia: Melbourne, May 1988,* Melbourne, Uniting Church Press, 1988, min.88.17, cf the report of the Standing Committee, item 22, p.45.

DATE DUE

			Printed in USA

HIGHSMITH #45230